Grandma,
Enjoy reminiscing about the delicious food of New Orleans.

Merry Christmas!

Love You
John & Brett

LOST RESTAURANTS
of NEW ORLEANS

LOST RESTAURANTS of NEW ORLEANS

Peggy Scott Laborde and Tom Fitzmorris

PELICAN PUBLISHING COMPANY
Gretna 2012

Copyright © 2011
By Peggy Scott Laborde and Tom Fitzmorris
All rights reserved

First printing, September 2011
Second printing, March 2012

The word "Pelican" and the depiction of a pelican are trademarks of Pelican Publishing Company, Inc., and are registered in the U.S. Patent and Trademark Office.

Library of Congress Cataloging-in-Publication Data

Laborde, Peggy Scott.
  Lost restaurants of New Orleans / Peggy Scott Laborde and Tom Fitzmorris.
     p. cm.
  Includes index.
  ISBN 978-1-58980-997-0 (hardcover : alk. paper) 1. Restaurants—Louisiana—New Orleans—History. 2. Cooking, American—Louisiana style. 3. Cooking—Louisiana—New Orleans. 4. Cookbooks. I. Fitzmorris, Tom, 1951- II. Title.
  TX907.3.L82N448 2011
  647.95763'35—dc23
                                  2011016872

Printed in China
Published by Pelican Publishing Company, Inc.
1000 Burmaster Street, Gretna, Louisiana 70053

Contents

Acknowledgments 9
Introduction 13
A & G Cafeterias 19
Acy's Pool Hall 19
Alonso & Son 20
The Andrew Jackson Restaurant 21
    Recipe: Turkey Poulette 23
Anything Goes 24
Bali Ha'i at the Beach 25
Barrow's Shady Inn 29
Bart's Lighthouse Inn 30
The Bean Pot 31
    Recipe: Green Enchiladas with Crabmeat 33
Bechac's 34
Beef Baron Steak House 35
Berdou's 37
    Recipe: Crabmeat Berdou 38
Bertucci's Restaurant 39
Beverly Dinner Playhouse 40
Bistro Steak Room 41
    Recipe: Eggs Bitoun 43
B. Montalbano Italian Delicatessen 44
Buck Forty-Nine Pancake and Steak House 44
The Bull's Corner 46
Buster Holmes 48
Café Atchafalaya/Dante by the River/Tea 'n' Tiques 52
    Recipe: Crabmeat West Indies 54
Café Pontchartrain (The Silver Whistle) 54
Cafe Sbisa 55
    Recipe: Trout Eugene 58
Caribbean Room 59
    Recipe: Shrimp Saki 61
    Recipe: Mile-High Ice Cream Pie 62
Castillo's 64
Chez Helene 66

Christian's 68
    Recipe: Oysters Roland 72
Chris Steaks 73
Clarence and Lefty's 73
    Recipe: Roast-Beef Poor Boy 74
Compagno's Restaurants 75
Corinne Dunbar's 76
    Recipe: Oysters Dunbar 78
The Cosmopolitan 79
Crozier's/Chateaubriand Steakhouse 79
    Recipe: Veal with Crawfish 83
Delerno's 84
    Recipe: Crawfish Topas 85
Delmonico 86
    Recipe: Creole Eggplant Gratin Delmonico 88
DiPiazza's 89
    Recipe: Eva's Spot Lasagna with Six Cheeses 90
Dragon's Garden 92
    Recipe: Shrimp Toast 93
Eddie's 94
Elmwood Plantation 95
    Recipe: Chicken Grandee 99
El Ranchito 100
The Enraged Chicken 102
España 103
Etienne's Cuisine Francais 104
Flamingos 107
G&E Courtyard Grill 109
    Recipe: Pasta Puttanesca 110
Genghis Khan 111
Gin's Mee Hong 113
Gluck's Restaurant 113
Home Plate Inn 114
Houlihan's Old Place 115
Hummingbird Grill 115
House of Lee 116
Jim's Fried Chicken 117
Jonathan 119
    Recipe: Red Pepper Vichyssoise 122
Kolb's 122
La Cuisine 126
    Recipe: Joe's Hot Shrimp 128
    Recipe: Oysters Deanna 129
Lakeview Seafood 130
    Recipe: Oyster Boat 131
La Louisiane 132

    Recipe: Trout LaFreniere 135
La Riviera 136
Le Chateau 137
Lenfant's 138
LeRuth's 142
    Recipe: Crabmeat St. Francis 149
L'Escale 150
Maison Pierre 152
Marco Polo 153
Martin's Poor Boy Restaurant/Martin Brothers Restaurant 153
Marti's 155
Masson's Restaurant Français 158
    Recipe: Shrimp Robert 161
    Recipe: Almond Torte 162
Maylie's 163
    Recipe: Turtle Soup 168
Meal-A-Minit 168
Michael's Mid-City Grill 169
Moran's Riverside/Bella Luna 169
Morrison's Cafeterias 172
Red Onion 172
    Recipe: Muse's Egglpant with Seafood (Eggplant Vatican) 175
Restaurant de la Tour Eiffel 176
    Recipe: Strawberry Soufflé 178
Restaurant Mandich 179
The Riverbend 181
Rockery Inn 183
Roussel's 183
The Royal Oak Restaurant and Pub 185
    Recipe: Skordalia (Greek Garlic Sauce) 186
Ruggiero's 186
Sam's Place 188
Sclafani's 190
Solari's 191
The Steak Pit 191
Stonebreaker's 193
Tally-Ho 194
Tchoupitoulas Plantation 195
    Recipe: Oysters Tchoupitoulas 196
Toney's Pizza and Spaghetti House 197
    Recipe: Stuffed Macaroni 199
    Recipe: Oysters and Spaghetti Bordelaise 200
Tortorici's Restaurant 200
T. Pittari's 201
    Recipe: Crab Bisque 206
Turci's 207

Recipe: Spaghetti alla Turci	210
Uglesich's	212
Vaucresson Café Creole	214
Versailles	216
Willy Coln's Chalet	219
Recipe: Crawfish Willy Coln	222
Wise Cafeteria	223
The Restaurants of West End Park (1859-2005)	227
Fitzgerald's	229
Pier Orleans	231
The Bounty	231
Maggie & Smitty's Crabnett	232
Pique's Wharf/Willie G's	232
Bruning's	233
Recipe: Whole Flounder Stuffed with Crabmeat	236
Papa Rosselli's	237
Swanson's	237
Fontana's	238
Seymour's	239
Recipe: West End Oyster Stew	239
Some Drugstore Soda Fountains	241
Katz & Besthoff Drug Stores	241
Bradley's Pharmacy	241
Some Pizza Places	243
Domino's Pizza	243
Artista Pizza	243
Sandy's Pizza Place	243
Tower of Pizza	243
Mr. Pizza	243
The Uptown Bistro Boom—The Revolution of 1983	245
Stephen & Martin	245
Indulgence	246
Bouligny	248
Flagons	249
Recipe: Oysters Sazerac	250
World's Fair Fare	252
The World's Fair's Flurry of Fine Dining	255
Henri	255
Recipe: Salmon Soufflé "Auberge de l'Ill"	257
Les Continents	258
Saffron	259
Le Jardin	259
Recipe: All-White Scallops and Grouper	260
Richard Collin, the Underground Gourmet	262
Index	267

Acknowledgments

The foundation for this book was laid by a program produced in 2001 for New Orleans Public Broadcasting Service affiliate WYES-TV called *Lost Restaurants of New Orleans*. Thanks to WYES's Beth Arroyo Utterback and Randall Feldman for their continued interest and support of the production of programs that focus on the history and heritage of our city.

Some of the interviews in the book are from that program. Much gratitude to Dominic Massa for his image research, copyediting, and transcription assistance and for his ongoing encouragement.

Doris Ann Gorman's research efforts for the documentary and gathering of some visual materials for the book are most appreciated.

Special thanks to Priscilla Lawrence, executive director of The Historic New Orleans Collection (HNOC), for making many key images available. The Collection's John Magill compiled the index for this book, no easy feat. Also thanks to Magill and The HNOC's Pamela Arceneaux for their assistance in image research. The HNOC's Mary Lou Eichhorn continues to be helpful on any project.

Always supportive, especially in food-history-related projects, are Poppy Tooker and Maureen Detweiler.

Photographer George Long not only shared photos but also helped spread the word in the New Orleans photography community that we were looking for visual records of lost restaurants. And answering the call for images were Mitchel Osborne, Kevin R. Roberts (KRR Marketing, LLC), Joe Bergeron, Frank Methe, Jackson Hill, and Philip M. Denman. Whenever Peggy had a computer technology question, Larry Roussarie came to her aid.

Sharing items from their collections were Edward Piglia, R. Clive Hardy, Richard Morelock, and Billy Gruber. Craig Kraemer photographed and scanned some of the vintage restaurant images and memorabilia we sprinkled throughout the book. Thanks also to Stephen Tyler, director of the *Lost Restaurants* documentary, who was most helpful with image research for the television program that laid this project's groundwork.

Pelican Publishing Company's continuing interest in publishing books of a local and regional historical nature is encouraging to those of us eager to contribute and to enjoy reading a body of work in print on our city's rich heritage. Many thanks to Dr. Milburn Calhoun, Kathleen Calhoun Nettleton, Nina Kooij, Terry Callaway, Bridget

Newspaper reporter, gourmet, and cook Scoop Kennedy wrote the first opinionated guide to New Orleans restaurants in 1945. He stopped short of being frankly critical—all of his negative opinions were couched deep between the lines. But he was fulsome in his praise of the restaurants he liked. The illustrations by Tilden Landry are marvelous examples of the graphic arts in those days. (From the collection of Peggy Scott Laborde)

McDowell, Scott Campbell, Suzanne Pfefferle, and their fine staff, with whom it remains a continued pleasure to work.

Another treasure trove for New Orleans history research is the New Orleans Public Library's Louisiana Division/City Archives. Irene Wainwright and Wayne Everard were so very supportive.

Tom gives special thanks to Denise Broussard. After losing all his back issues of his publication *The New Orleans Menu* to Hurricane Katrina, he got a note from Denise saying that she had a few and would be happy to give them to him. She actually had every single edition ever published, from 1977 to 1997. Having that resource added tremendously to this book.

Peggy gives special thanks to her parents, Gloria and Warren Scott. Once she, brother Kurt, and sister Nancy were in school, her mother went back to work full-time at D. H. Holmes Department Store on Canal Street. Her mother's work schedule necessitated that the family dine out and hence many experiences of some of the lost restaurants contained in this book. A thank-you to Irving and June Scott, Peggy's aunt and uncle, who enjoyed dining out and took Peggy and her siblings with them.

Finally, yet foremost, thanks to our spouses, Errol Laborde and Mary Ann Fitzmorris, and our families. Their patience and encouragement make anything we do all the more possible.

Peggy Scott Laborde
Tom Fitzmorris

Introduction

Around New Orleans, the question "Where will we eat next?" is always on people's minds. The topic is freighted with facts, opinions, and rumors as to where the eating will be done in the near future. That avid conversation has been going on for a long time here—many decades before the rest of America went restaurant crazy.

Almost as much discussed is the opposite of the question above. It begins, "Remember that place we used to go for . . . ?" It ends with a litany of the great dishes this remembered restaurant served, back in times deemed to have been somehow warmer than they are now. Too bad that place isn't around anymore. Why did it close? Why didn't it come back after the hurricane? Does anybody else cook that way now? What happened to that chef? Remember that crazy waiter that everybody wanted to wait on them?

This is an infectious topic. It made Peggy's original production of *Lost Restaurants of New Orleans* a perennial favorite on WYES-TV. After nearly a decade, it's still running now and then. Every time it broadcasts, people call me during my radio show to say they saw me on it and they liked all that stuff about old restaurants.

And if one person calls me on the air about an old restaurant, it's inevitable that the next person on the air will ask, "Talking about restaurants that ain't dere no more, how about that little seafood joint that used to serve . . . ?" And away we go. Sometimes that day's radio show never returns to the present.

The catchphrase "ain't dere no more" is now a permanent and immediately understood local idiom, thanks to Benny "Grunch" Antin's song about all the lost New Orleans institutions. We never get tired of talking about places that "ain't dere no more."

So, why not a book? Here it is.

Places to eat outside the home began to appear in New Orleans in the 1830s, when the prosperous port city was the seventh largest in the United States. New Orleans kept up with the vogues from Europe, one of which was a hot new idea called a "restaurant." That French word means "a restoring place." In the late 1700s in France, the former chefs of the Revolution-deposed aristocracy were looking for a new way to make a living. They discovered that enough people would pay to have a meal cooked and served for them to make a business of it.

In this country, the first restaurant was Delmonico's in New York. It opened in 1828 and quickly became the talk of the town. It triggered a wave of similar establishments that spread to other major American cities. It was so influential that "delmonico" almost became the generic term for a grand eatery instead of the French "restaurant."

New Orleans was right behind New York in opening restaurants. And with the city's French culture, the idea took root easily. French-Italian immigrant Antoine Alciatore opened his namesake restaurant in 1840. It's still here, under the ownership of Antoine's fifth-generation descendants. Antoine's inspired the opening of many similar establishments. The Civil War greatly attenuated the fortunes of New Orleans, but by the 1880s the first substantial population of permanent restaurants was firmly in place.

Restaurants have opened at an increasing pace ever since. Inevitably, many of them closed. Relating all the advents and departures would make a very thick, dense book. History and culinary buffs would find it of great interest.

Our aim is more limited and, I think, more delightful. This book is about extinct restaurants remembered by a fair number of Orleanians still living as of 2011, when we composed it. Fortunately, that limitation more or less coincides with my career of writing about New Orleans restaurants. I took up that pen in 1972, wrote a review every week since (or more often), and still have all of those reviews. Almost no noteworthy restaurant open since the late 1960s escaped my firsthand observation and notes.

Another lucky coincidence: Peggy and I are both members of the first generation of middle-class Orleanians who frequently went to restaurants for entertainment purposes. Only well-heeled members of the prior generation dined in restaurants often. (My own parents never did, as in not ever.) The Baby Boom generation triggered an explosion of new restaurants in the late 1960s and beyond. Many of those ended up . . . well, in this book.

We have been yet one degree more selective. A lot of bad restaurants ain't dere no more. Many of those are remembered fondly by a lot of people, because of what I call the Wistful Palate Effect. The longer it's been since a restaurant closed forever, the more wonderful we remember its food having been. If we could climb into a time machine and try the eats in these places as they really were, we'd be severely disappointed.

It even happens to me, I'm ashamed to admit. In going back through old reviews of restaurants I haven't thought about in a long time, I was often astonished by the lack of regard I had for their food back then. I thought I liked it better.

That's why I left one or more of your favorite lost restaurants out of the book. My initial list included more than two hundred restaurants. We brought it down to a more manageable (and more interesting) one hundred plus, largely by favoring those for which we had the best documentation and artifacts.

In a few cases, an old restaurant closed, then reopened (sometimes many years later) with the same name and location but different owners, styles, and menus. The old Delmonico on St. Charles Avenue was so different from the new (and excellent) Delmonico operated by Emeril Lagasse that we consider the old place a lost restaurant.

Finally, a restaurant's appearance in this book doesn't mean that it's gone forever. Restaurants can and do return from the dead and go on as if nothing happened.

To add fun and controversy, I'm rating all the lost restaurants on my usual five-star scale. The ratings are for how good the restaurants were when they were at their peaks. (Five stars—Among the Best Locally, Four—Excellent and Ambitious, Three—Worth Crossing Town For, Two—Recommended, and One—Acceptable.)

I hope our look back at the way we ate in the past decades gives you goose pimples of pleasure. Please write to us about stories you have about these and other lost restaurants of New Orleans. We lose a few more (fewer than in any other major food town) all the time, and I have no doubt that we'll create a second edition of this book someday. It's too much fun for us not to.

—Tom Fitzmorris

The documentary *Lost Restaurants of New Orleans* is the program I've gotten the most viewer reaction from. That wasn't a surprise, since one of New Orleanians' favorite pastimes is talking about food and dining, and often such conversation occurs during a meal.

So it wasn't a huge leap to consider doing a book inspired by the program and expand on the topic. It also made perfect sense to ask Tom Fitzmorris to collaborate. Tom has been reviewing restaurants since the 1970s for his *New Orleans Menu* newsletter and now Web site, in various publications, and on WWWL (1350 AM) and WWL (870 AM) radio.

Tom has compiled forty-one rare recipes connected to lost restaurants, many being printed for the first time. We've gathered more than two hundred images! I've included interviews with folks associated with some of the restaurants mentioned and peppered the book with "Bites of History," in recognition of eateries that we wanted to cover from the more distant past.

I have also included memories from the 1984 World's Fair. Having worked at the Fair as a producer/host for WDSU-TV, I had ample lunchtime opportunities to dine just about everywhere at the Fair.

We hope *Lost Restaurants*, the book, will be like a good menu, filled with tempting selections and, in the end, satisfying.

—Peggy Scott Laborde

LOST RESTAURANTS of NEW ORLEANS

Acy's Pool Hall, located in New Orleans' Lower Garden District off Magazine Street, was renowned for its poor-boy sandwiches. (Photo © Mitchel Osborne MMX)

★★
Acy's Pool Hall
Lower Garden District: 1925 Sophie Wright Place
1960s-80s

Acy's had a sign over its bar that said it offered the best poor-boy sandwiches in the world. That may have been going a little far—but only a little. The roast beef sandwich they made was certainly one of the best around. The beef component was on the verge of falling apart—just this side of debris.

But the gravy was something else. It was darker and more intense than most, and when it mixed with the mayonnaise (a natural process that seems to occur on a well-made roast beef poor boy, without any assistance from the maker or the eater), it got me right between the eyes. The fact that they toasted the whole sandwich a bit before sending it out made it everything a roast beef poor boy should be.

As luscious as that was, the dominant image that remains in my brain about Acy's was how they dressed their tables. Red-checked tablecloths covered a half-dozen or so tables between the billiard tables (this was a full-fledged pool hall). The sandwiches came out on plastic plates, and when you ate them the inevitable occurred: some of the gravy-mayo surplus would drip onto the tablecloth. After you were finished, the waitress would clean up the detritus, pull the tablecloth off, whip a good pop on it, turn it over, and put it back. The next customers ate their roast beef poor boys, made just as big a mess, and the waitress did the same thing afterwards. The same tablecloths were turned over and over until, one imagines, they were on the verge of getting up and playing a game of pool under their own power.

Acy's also made all the other standard poor boys, plus a few rarities (such as the pastrami). And muffulettas. It was among the first sandwich shops to heat muffulettas, a bad idea that has become almost universal. Oh, well.

A BITE OF HISTORY

A & G Cafeterias
California Building
Gentilly Shopping Center
Westside Shopping Center
Carrollton Shopping Center
Clearview Shopping Center

Restaurants
Canal Street at North Broad Street
Loew's Theatre Building
(Canal Street)
Texaco Building
(1501 Canal Street)

A & G Cafeterias and Restaurants was a locally owned chain. This one was located on the riverside corner of Canal Street and North Broad Street. (Courtesy of the Louisiana Division/City Archives, New Orleans Public Library)

Many locals' first visit to a cafeteria was to an A & G. They were all over town, and for growing families during the Baby Boom, the price was right. A & G also owned Mrs. Drake Sandwich shops, but by the sixties the sandwiches were being distributed to grocery stores, schools, and businesses. The business was founded by R. L. Atkinson and Clifton L. Ganus in the 1930s.

In the cafeterias, there was the choice of either the green or light brown tray. The colors signified whether or not you wanted a waiter to carry your tray to your table. You usually found your check wrapped around your water glass. Among the favorites on the menu were carrot salad, eggplant dressing, and baked fish.

Ray McNamara played the organ at local movie theatres and A & G Cafeterias and Restaurants for many years. (Courtesy of the Louisiana Division/City Archives, New Orleans Public Library)

—Peggy Scott Laborde

The place was almost always busy at lunch, and you just figured on waiting for a table. Or you got the things to go, which wasn't quite as good, because they were best eaten immediately.

★★★

Alonso & Son
Old Jefferson: 587 Central Avenue
1939-2003

The New Orleans neighborhood restaurant and bar as we came to know it began appearing in substantial numbers in the 1920s, when the population started moving into the parts of the city we know now as "the wet zone," thanks to Hurricane Katrina.

They reached their peak in the 1950s, when almost every modern neighborhood in New Orleans was in place. Particularly in the older sections, a combination "bar & rest." appeared every few blocks in any direction, all over town.

Then began a downturn, as fast-food restaurants began to take over the job of providing quick, inexpensive lunches and dinners. By the 1980s, neighborhood cafes were becoming rare, and only the best of them survived.

Alonso's was one of those. It was a classic of the genre: a small, stark building well off the arteries. Central Avenue was the old main route for getting from Jefferson Highway to Airline Highway. After the much wider Clearview Parkway opened all the way from Lake Pontchartrain to the Huey P. Long Bridge, traffic on Central Avenue fell to very little. The presence of four trunk-line railroad grade crossings in less than a mile of Central was also discouraging.

None of that mattered. Alonso's had a well-established reputation for terrific seafood, poor boys, and platters (what we used to call "short orders") even before it moved to Central Avenue. Its original location was a few blocks away on Jefferson Highway. It was there for a quarter-century before Hurricane Betsy blew it down in 1965.

Al Alonso opened his new location quickly. It was even better than the old shack on the highway. My memories of this are particularly acute, because I was a teenager living two blocks away. I worked at the Time Saver store on Central at Jefferson Highway, and we were constantly going over to Alonso's for roast beef poor boys or fried oyster loaves.

If we could leave the store for lunch, we'd walk the long block to Alonso's for red beans and rice, seafood gumbo, a bowl of chili (Alonso's was one of the last restaurants around town to offer chili, and it was pretty good), daily plate specials, and seafood platters.

The latter were the best. Alonso's fried everything to order, and it came out crisp and too hot to eat immediately. I remember thinking, years after I'd left the neighborhood, that Alonso's was a candidate for Best Fried Seafood in Town. It really was that good.

They also had excellent boiled seafood all the time. In the 1980s, it was almost unthinkable that any seafood joint would not have boiled crabs, shrimp, and crawfish; nowadays, boiled seafood is a rarity in restaurants. (Reason: people eating boiled seafood make a mess and occupy the table for a long time.)

The only problem with Alonso's in its heyday was that it was always full. Like most neighborhood restaurants of that era, a disproportionate amount of space was given over to the bar, which was fully stocked and well decorated with signs that would probably pull a pretty penny on eBay these days. (Some were made of iridescent butterfly wings.) The waitresses were always running around shouting, and the kitchen was always running behind—mainly because they really did cook everything to order. That was the standard in those days.

Al Alonso chose, for some reason, not to let the restaurant pass to the next generation. He sold it in the late 1990s to some regular customers who had a business up Central Avenue. But it was more work than they realized, and the tide and traffic had turned against restaurants like this. Alonso's closed for good in 2003. The premises have been at least four other eateries since then.

★★★

The Andrew Jackson Restaurant
French Quarter: 221 Royal Street
1963-82

When the Andrew Jackson Restaurant opened in 1963, if you wanted to dine in unusually beautiful surroundings, the pickings around New Orleans were rather slim. We had more than our share of restaurants with the antique charm of many decades. But only a handful of restaurants could be called fancy in any contemporary way.

The Andrew Jackson was one of those. Although it would be considered laughably corny now, in the 1960s it was considered sophisticated and highly atmospheric, decorated in a frilly but modern style.

The food was up to date as well. It was inspired as much by French cooking as by New Orleans cooking, and the style in which the food was served was significantly more polished than we were used to seeing. Its radio commercial (with a background music track of Robert Goulet singing "You Stepped Out of a Dream") made the point that if you wanted a romantic dinner, the Andrew Jackson was the place for it.

By day, the Andrew Jackson had a substantial lunch business among businessmen who wanted an auspicious midday meal but for whom the likes of Antoine's and Galatoire's were a bit too set in stone or too full of blue bloods.

Owned by the Sevin family, the Andrew Jackson had as a menu consultant no less an authority than Warren Leruth, who was in the early years of operating his own restaurant on the West Bank. While the Andrew Jackson's food was never on a par with that of LeRuth's, it was very good and distinctive compared with the interchangeable menu used in most other first-class restaurants of the time.

Like other restaurants trying to establish themselves as more French than Creole, the Andrew Jackson placed a great deal of emphasis on its

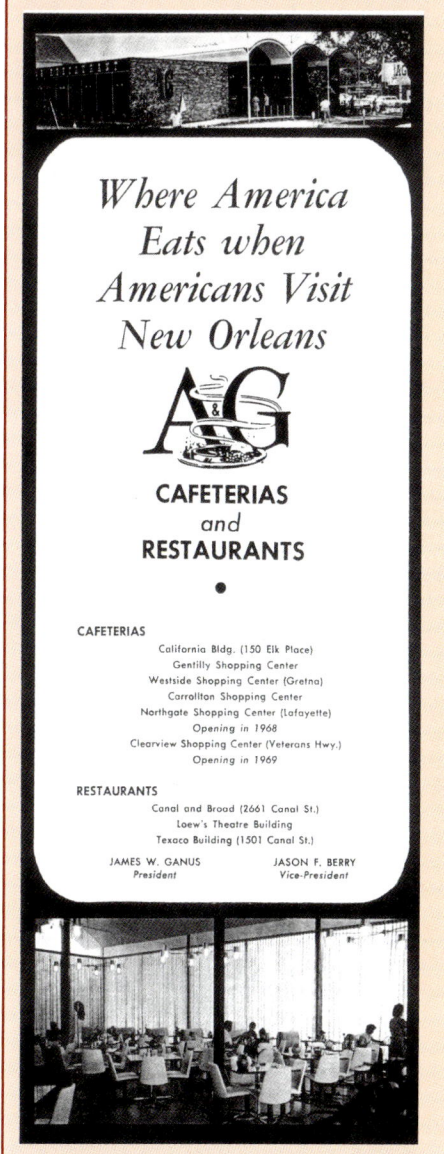

An advertisement for A & G Cafeterias and Restaurants indicates that many of the cafeterias were located in local shopping centers. (Courtesy of Clifton L. Ganus, Jr.)

During its time, the Andrew Jackson Restaurant was one of the few contemporary fine-dining establishments in the French Quarter. Turkey poulette was a popular lunch dish. (Courtesy of New Orleans Magazine*)*

sauces, particularly the thick, rich ones. Egg-based sauces were much more commonly used then than now. If you can imagine most of the cream sauces we see today replaced by variations on hollandaise, you have a good idea of the kind of food that upscale restaurants purveyed back then. Veal with béarnaise and crabmeat, crabmeat all by itself with hollandaise—the Andrew Jackson's menu was full of such dishes..

The dish many Andrew Jackson customers ordered at lunch was turkey poulette. While that dish would now be considered a throwback, many people thought of it as gourmet cuisine then. It was slices of turkey breast topped with slices of bacon, flooded with a light béchamel sauce with mushrooms and melted cheese over the entire thing. The restaurant that was famous for turkey poulette was the Roosevelt Hotel's cafe. But the Andrew Jackson made it better.

They flamed a lot of desserts here. The waiters looked like the kind who would flame desserts, dressed as they were in tuxedos with more than a little bit of frill—particularly in the 1970s.

The end of the Andrew Jackson was a familiar story. The management's formula was successful enough for long enough that they never altered it. But when the gourmet bistros began to set the style for dining out in New Orleans, restaurants like this looked pretentious, especially to those of the Baby Boom generation, who became the major market force in the Andrew Jackson's last years.

The place was revived as Café Anglais, a British-Creole restaurant operated by Café Sbisa's Dr. Larry Hill and David Tardo. But even that was too much for the new age, and it only lasted a couple of years.

The Andrew Jackson Restaurant's Turkey Poulette

Sliced turkey with a hot sauce, cheese, and bacon—this is an old luncheon favorite that is now nearly extinct. But I get asked for sources for it and recipes all the time. So here it is, the way they used to serve it at lunch at the Andrew Jackson.

½ stick butter
3 Tbs. flour
1 cup warm whole milk
1 cup sliced fresh white mushrooms
1 oz. dry sherry
⅛ tsp. white pepper
¼ tsp. salt
2 onion rolls
8 large slices roast turkey breast, about ⅛ inch thick
8 slices bacon, fried crisp
⅔ cup shredded sharp Cheddar cheese
¼ cup thinly snipped green onions

Preheat the broiler to 450 degrees.

1. Melt the butter in a small saucepan and stir in the flour to make a blond roux. When the roux just begins to color, lower the heat to the lowest setting and add the warm milk. Whisk until the mixture pulls away from the side of the pan.

2. Add the mushrooms, sherry, white pepper, and salt. Stir until the sherry disappears. Simmer, stirring every now and then, until the mushrooms are soft. Remove the sauce from the heat.

3. Slice the onion rolls from top to bottom to make slices about ½ inch thick. Toast them until medium brown. Divide the slices on 4 plates.

4. Top the onion roll toasts with 2 slices per plate of the turkey. Divide the sauce over the turkey. Top each plate with 2 slices of bacon and a fourth of the Cheddar.

5. Put the plates under the broiler until the cheese melts and the sauce bubbles. Remove the hot plates to liner plates. Garnish the turkey poulettes with green onions and serve.

Serves 4.

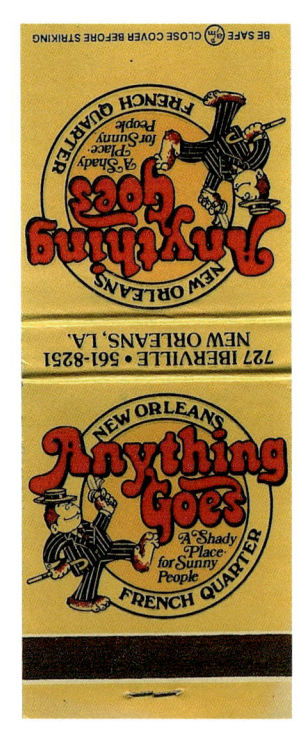

Anything Goes was located in the French Quarter and run by the Brennans of Brennan's Restaurant. (From the collection of Peggy Scott Laborde)

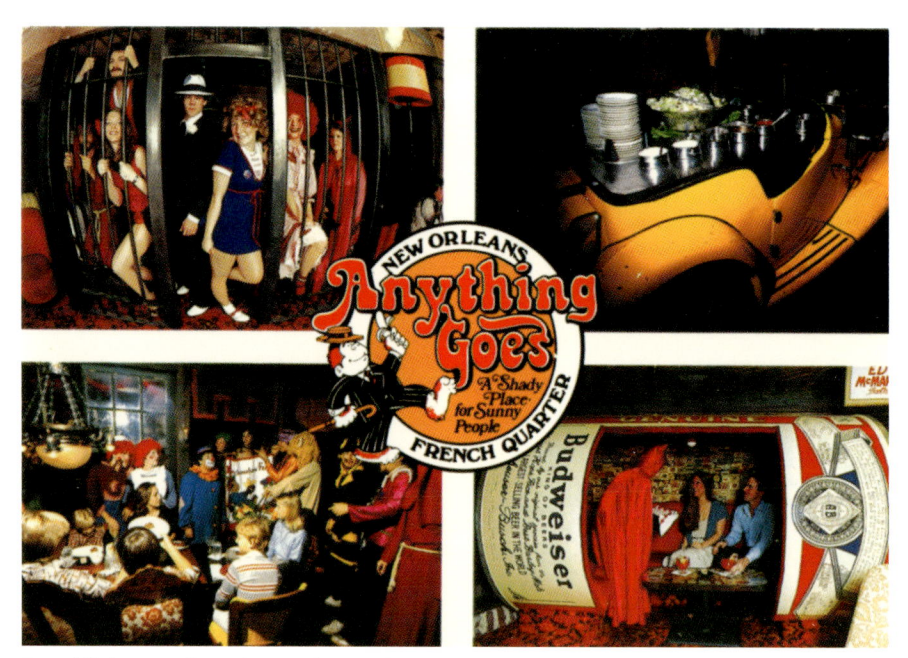

In addition to the eclectic décor of Anything Goes, the wait staff wore costumes. (From the collection of Reno Daret III)

★★
Anything Goes
French Quarter: 727 Iberville Street
1975-81

Although Anything Goes lasted only a few years, anyone who dined out in the 1970s remembers it. How could one forget it? It tops the all-time list of Most Preposterous Restaurants in New Orleans.

The gimmicks were outrageous and relentless. Each table was in a strange environment. One was in a giant Budweiser can. Another was in a jail cell. The servers were costumed in equally unconventional getups and were encouraged to get as wacky as they liked as long as the table was entertained and the food served timely.

What few people remember about Anything Goes are the two things that actually made it worth a visit. First, it was the work of no less than Pip, Ted, and Jimmy Brennan. A couple of years earlier, after the infamous Brennan family split, they became sole owners of Brennan's on Royal Street—at the time one of the most profitable restaurants in the world. Brennan's was free of the money-losing satellite restaurants in Dallas and Atlanta, among other lesser restaurants in the Brennan orbit. They had to do something with the money, and Anything Goes was that.

It's also forgotten (because it seems so unlikely now) how good the food was at Anything Goes. Some of it was served unconventionally. Their soup and salad bars, for instance, were ensconced in a boat and in an antique car, in keeping with the studied nonconformity of the place. But the groceries were of good quality, and the chefs from Brennan's were used to turning out delicious eats.

The concept was inspired by a still-running chain of restaurants in Texas called the Magic Time Machine. It was successful here at first, but New Orleans is a different place from San Antonio, Dallas, and Austin. (Much more so in the 1970s than now.) Locals who were delighted on the first visit (when they went on their own) and the second (when they brought uninitiated friends) were less charmed on the third and fourth visits. After that, the joke was old. Since the gimmick was so dominant, you thought about whether you wanted to sit in the pyramid again before thinking about the food.

Being in a prime tourist location didn't help. Visitors to New Orleans come to have a New Orleans-style dining experience, not an evening of amusement-park-style goofiness.

Side note: The previous occupant of the Anything Goes location was the New Orleans outpost of the Playboy Club. The building was also later used for a "gentleman's club," no longer there.

★★★★
Bali Ha'i at the Beach
Pontchartrain Beach, Lake End of Elysian Fields Avenue
1959-86

For New Orleanians of the Baby Boom generation, the experience of having dinner at the Bali Ha'i with one of the first people you ever dated is almost universal. The number of us who went there for dinner before the prom is legion. I did, three times, in the late 1960s.

Ad for Bali Ha'i. (Courtesy of New Orleans Magazine)

Bali Ha'i was known for its tiki-style drinks. (Courtesy of New Orleans Magazine)

BALI HA'I MEMORIES

Imagine if your playground was an amusement park. Bryan and Jay Batt are members of the family that operated Pontchartrain Beach, New Orleans' much beloved fifty-five-acre oasis on the shores of Lake Pontchartrain that included the Zephyr rollercoaster, Laff in the Dark, and the Wild Maus.

The Batt brothers' grandfather, Harry Batt, Sr., together with his father started Pontchartrain Beach. Bryan and Jay's father, John Batt, and uncle Harry Batt, Jr., ran the Beach from the late 1960s until it closed in the 1980s.

In addition to the hamburger and hot-dog stands along the midway, there was the fancier Bali Ha'i, inspired by the movie *South Pacific* and part of a tiki craze around the country. "I thought it looked like something out of an old movie or if Mr. Howell had opened a fine restaurant on Gilligan's Island," recalls actor/interior designer Bryan Batt. "The thatched walls and roofs, bamboo everywhere, giant clam shells and stuffed blowfish and glass buoys hanging from the ceiling, all very South Seas. We would often have family dinners there for birthdays, holidays, or entertaining, and often sat in the secluded 'huts.' The big rattan queen's chair was the seat of honor and I remember feeling very special when it was my turn to sit there."

Local businessman Jay Batt remembers the libations: "My favorite drink was a Flaming Zorro, which was a fruit-juice drink, but what set it apart was the 151-proof

The Bali Ha'i was located on the midway of Pontchartrain Beach amusement park. (Courtesy of Bryan and Jay Batt)

The Bali Ha'i was one of many restaurants across America that copied the style of Trader Vic's and Don the Beachcomber, two wildly popular restaurants that began in San Francisco. "Trader" Vic Bergeron (who, despite his name, was from nowhere near New Orleans) said his food was Polynesian, with hints of Hawaiian. It was no such thing, because Polynesians could not be said to have had a cuisine. Trader Vic's served Chinese food, really, with lots of frying and sweet sauces and without all those puzzling Chinese names, along with rum drinks whose potency was hidden by appealing, sweet fruit juices, served in unusual cups and glasses with island motifs.

Bali Ha'i was located on the midway at Pontchartrain Beach, the place where we had incomparable fun in our childhood years that we weren't quite ready to relinquish completely. The restaurant was so fancy that you couldn't enter it wearing a swimsuit, as you could everywhere else at the Beach.

Also, during the heyday of the Bali Ha'i, most classy restaurants were serious places, bound by rules of etiquette that most of us knew so little about that we were afraid of doing the wrong thing. The Bali Ha'i, on the other hand, was obviously a fun sort of place. How could it not be? It was at the Beach! That alone made it unintimidating. We were sixteen and seventeen. The whole category of places like Houston's did not exist. The Bali Ha'i was perfect.

The dining room was dark, hung with Hawaiian stuff, with bamboo everywhere. There should have been open flames, like on the *Survivor* set, but there weren't. However, you could get a flaming cocktail, which many people did. It was all exotic enough to translate as romantic.

My most vivid memory of the Bali Ha'i involved a girl named Sandy, who asked me to her prom. There we were, both underage, ordering the Tiki Bowl, a china tub held up by three round-bellied little china guys, filled with about a quart of a pale orange-colored drink from which extended two straws. I took a sip; I loved it. Sandy also said she liked it. Soon it was drained. What I didn't know was that Sandy was not really drinking at all and that I had sucked almost

Using extra-long straws, Bali Ha'i customers drank from Tiki Bowls filled with rum and fruit juice. (From the collection of Edward Piglia)

all of it down myself. The next thing I didn't know was where I was, who I was, or what I was doing.

"Are you okay?" Sandy asked.

"Yes," I said, slowly. "Just . . . give me a minute . . . and I'll . . . be . . . just fine." It was my first experience with intoxication. No drink has ever slammed into me with the force of that one.

The food came. Sandy had some shrimp dish. I ordered a filet mignon, because that's all I knew. I'd never eaten Chinese food, or whatever that other stuff on the menu was supposed to be. I remember that it was pretty good and that Sandy was impressed (or appalled— I've never decided which) that I ordered it. As I ate, the fog cleared. We stayed there a long time, looking at each other with the eyes of love—a new experience for both of us.

When I looked at an old Bali Ha'i menu a few years ago, I was surprised by how much like any other Cantonese restaurant's menu it was: rumaki, fried rice, sweet-and-sour chicken, shrimp on skewers, sweet ribs—all that stuff. And a big filet mignon.

The rumor among my friends was that the most devastating drink at the Bali Ha'i was the Fogg Cutter. But I learned my lesson and kept to the safe side of the drink menu on the two or three more times I went there.

The Bali Ha'i was open year round, but its business took a tumble

rum-soaked lemon, which floated on top of the drink and was set on fire. I also liked the Fogg Cutter."

As for the food, Jay's favorite dish was cellophane noodles in a sweet and savory sauce.

Then there were the characters. "My favorite thing to do was to hang out with Miss Laverne," says Bryan. "She would check the coats and sell the gifts behind the greeting counter, but I loved it when she would let me assist her in spraying the floral leis with gardenia perfume. She had bright red hair, which she wore in a high beehive, so sweet. I also liked hanging near her because her station was near the bar area, which featured a painting of a topless native girl. To a fourth grader, that was so risqué!"

Celebrities visited the Bali Ha'i, and Jay recalls meeting Dan Blocker, best known as "Hoss" on the *Bonanza* television series. "I remember him putting me on his shoulders and walking me around the restaurant—that was special!"

A fire snuffed out the Bali Ha'i,

Pontchartrain Beach owner Harry Batt, Sr. (standing at left), was the mastermind behind the Bali Ha'i. Standing next to him is longtime New Orleans television personality Mel Leavitt. Seated on the right is Mrs. Harry Batt, Sr., and Mrs. John (Gayle) Batt, who was active in the local theatre community. (Courtesy of Bryan and Jay Batt)

but what can't be snuffed out are memories and photos of the giant turtle shells hanging on the wall and fishing nets suspended from the ceiling. To many former patrons, the memory of Bali Ha'i is still calling.

A night out at the Bali Ha'i. In the left foreground is John Batt. On the right are Harry Batt, Jr., and Mrs. John (Gayle) Batt. (Courtesy of Bryan and Jay Batt)

—Peggy Scott Laborde

during the eight months of the year when Pontchartrain Beach was closed. During the off months, they met you in the parking lot with a golf cart and drove you to the front door of the restaurant through a special gate.

When Pontchartrain Beach closed down, the Bali Ha'i remained open for special events until it burned in 1986. We've never had a restaurant like it since. Now, there's a small revival of these "hula restaurants" around the country. Trader Vic's is still around but much diminished. Maybe this is something we need again.

Rum-based drinks such as mai tais and Fogg Cutters were served in these tiki-style glasses at the Bali Ha'i. (From the collection of Peggy Scott Laborde)

★★★
Barrow's Shady Inn
Hollygrove: 2714 Mistletoe Street
1943-2005

Finishing at or near the top of the All-Time Best Fried Catfish in New Orleans list, Barrow's Shady Inn opened during World War II in the predominantly black Hollygrove neighborhood—although, like many neighborhoods in New Orleans in those years, it was really pretty well mixed.

William Barrow knew a couple of important things in 1943. First, he could make his place a center of social life in his neighborhood by making it attractive and classy. Practically from the time he opened, he began renovating and adding on to the restaurant. When the Beverly nightclub and casino in nearby Old Jefferson shut down in the 1950s, Barrow bought a lot of the neon signs and installed them over his door.

Second, he knew how to fry catfish. He bought wild fish from Des Allemands and fried them whole, after marinating them in a recipe that would pass down to two generations of his descendants, never shared with anyone else.

In the 1960s, Barrow's created a controversy among its customers when it began serving filleted catfish. That would ultimately push the whole fish off the menu. The filleted fish may or may not have been as good as the whole fish, but it's hard to imagine how any catfish could have been much better than Barrow's fillets. They were fried to order (it took longer to come out than in the mass-production places) after spending time in the secret marinade and being coated with an incomparably light cornmeal hybrid. Billy Barrow (second generation) told me that it was "cream meal"—a mixture of cornmeal and corn flour.

He told me that while we shot a television piece on the restaurant in the 1980s. While wandering around the kitchen, I saw a large tub of catfish fillets in a reddish marinade—the secret stuff! So there was hot sauce in it. Or was that ketchup? I don't know. Billy Barrow kept his father's secret.

When the fish came to the table, it was the definitive golden brown and so hot you shouldn't have eaten it right away. But there was no way to keep from diving in. It was so good and light, with that background glow of red pepper, that you wanted to inhale it. A friend called it "popcorn fish," so irresistible was it. You could eat it with your fingers like popcorn, too. This fish needed no sauces or lemon—no salt or pepper, even. It was perfection.

Catfish was about all they had for a long time, until Billy Barrow's mother said she thought some home-style pot food would be well received. She cooked that up on weekdays for lunch until she retired. Even then, no menu was needed or ever printed. Signs on the wall told you the current price for the catfish platter, with handmade potato salad (also great) and a couple of slices of Bunny bread. The price was always a little higher than you were used to paying for fried catfish, but the goodness was incomparably better.

Barrow's was little known to people outside Hollygrove. Mistletoe was a back street you wouldn't likely travel unless you lived around there. Then the Earhart Expressway was cut through in the late 1970s, a half-block lake side of Barrow's. With its neon stars, it was very visible from the new thoroughfare, and many new customers discovered what a place it was.

The premises were a bit unusual. The main items of decoration were lava lamps from the original era of those fixtures—long before they became cool again. The walls were hung with photographs of shoes, of all things. Billy Barrow liked being well heeled. He was a force in bringing up the neighborhood and bought up a lot of nearby houses to renovate them.

For a long time, children weren't allowed at Barrow's. Billy told me that this was because the bar wasn't separated from the dining room, and there was a city ordinance about that. I told him I could think of a lot of neighborhood restaurants where the bar and the tables were in the same room and kids were allowed. He gave me a look I understood immediately. You don't get slack if you look black.

Billy Barrow died in the late 1990s, when he was hit by a car as he crossed the street in front of the restaurant. His daughter and her husband took over the restaurant and ran it without any drop in quality (they had the secret marinade formula) until Hurricane Katrina. The Hollygrove neighborhood was not only deeply flooded by the levee breaks, but the water flowed through the area, doing unusually great damage to all the homes, and Barrow's, too. Barrow's reopened briefly on the West Bank after the storm, but it didn't catch on there. It's one of those places we hope comes back, but as each year passes it seems less and less likely.

★★★

Bart's Lighthouse Inn
Lakefront: 8000 Lakeshore Drive
1950s-94

As casual seafood restaurants go, Bart's was literally set apart—by the New Basin Canal, to be exact, which separated Bart's from the concentration of seafood restaurants in West End Park. But in every other way, dining there was the same experience as in West End. It had a view not only of Lake Pontchartrain but the century-old lighthouse that stood next door until Katrina knocked it over.

The original Bart's was a big, rambling frame building with beacon-like neon signs on its facade. Its prices were low and its portions were large. That combination alone kept it full most of the time. The main limitation on its business was parking, but its regulars were happy to park in the bays along Lakeshore Drive and hoof it a block or two. Especially during the summer, this added an after-dinner interlude on the seawall, where you could watch the sun go down.

My recollection of Bart's food is that it was pretty good but not so good that anyone accused it of having the best in town of anything.

People went there mostly for the view and the family-style dining.

The place burned to the ground in 1976. A few years later, a new Bart's with new owners and a new menu went up on the site. The setting was even more atmospheric: a second-floor dining room and a balcony gave even better views of Lake Pontchartrain than the old place. (Of course, customers of the old Bart's claimed to like that one better.) Tapping into a long-established tradition of romance in nearby waterside bars such as the Port Hole and the Hong Kong, the lounge at the new Bart's was almost as large as the dining room. On most nights, a lively young singles scene swung deep into the night.

The new Bart's menu was more ambitious than the old one. Indeed, it seemed gourmet compared with the simple food at the West End Park restaurants. They were grilling fish here before any other lakeshore restaurant, for example. Dishes such as shrimp Clemenceau and seafood with hollandaise tried to head upscale. But for most customers, the thing was a fried seafood platter.

The second Bart's closed in 1994. The new place was torn down and replaced in the early 2000s by Joe's Crab Shack, a chain out of Houston. After Katrina, still owned by the same chain, it reopened as a Landry's.

★★★
The Bean Pot
Old Jefferson: 4100 Jefferson Highway
Riverbend: 8117 Maple Street
Chalmette: East Judge Perez Drive
1972-98

Ignacio "Chico" Vazquez ran utterly unique Mexican restaurants during three decades around New Orleans. Neither he nor his cantinas were ever prominent. But his fans were so devoted that I'm still asked where Chico's cooking these days, even though it's years since he passed on.

Chico was born July 31, 1927, in Aguascalientes in central Mexico. He came to the United States soon enough to serve in the U.S. Army in the Korean War. He moved to New Orleans in the 1960s and spent most of his forty years in his crusade to get people to eat authentic Mexican food.

It was time well spent. Chico never looked to the marketplace to decide his menu. Instead, he served the kind of Mexican food he liked and tried to talk his customers into liking it, too.

Chico could really talk. Every dish on his menu had a story. If you expressed even a little interest, he would flesh the story out, often adding tales not much related to food but always fascinating. He'd talk to you as long as you would listen and as long as he had the time, which was most of the time. None of the Bean Pot's several successive locations was ever especially busy. That was a good thing, since most of the time Chico was nearly the entire staff, doing both the cooking and the serving.

This would lead to one of his main topics: why don't more people come here to eat real Mexican food instead of all that Americanized stuff?

It was a good question. And it had a good answer. Most people who went to the Bean Pot expecting what they had been fooled into thinking was Mexican food by the chain restaurants would be at least puzzled by Chico's real deal.

Another explanation was obvious, but you'd keep it to yourself. The Bean Pot, in all its locations, was atmospherically challenged. It wasn't dirty, just really worn out and cheaply furnished. We Orleanians don't seem to mind that too much (think Uglesich's and Charlie's Steak House). But it prevented a lot of people from going (or staying) there for the first time. That, plus the unique menu, was too much for the unadventurous.

The first time I met Chico, he was in a former drive-up burger joint in front of the Jeff Drive-In Theater. (Long gone, that complex was across Jefferson Highway from Haydel's Bakery.) I had just begun to write about food. Chico was cooking—and raving about—cabrito, barbecued baby goat. It was the most exotic thing I'd ever eaten up to that time. The next time I saw him, Chico said he was having a hard time finding goat meat locally. "In Texas and of course in Mexico you can get cabrito everywhere," he explained. "In Louisiana, I just found out it's against the law!" He was as disappointed as I was.

Chico's menu was largely an invitation to mix and match various proteins (chicken, beef, pork, crabmeat, shrimp) with what he called his "gravies." Chico was a master at making sauces. He had the familiar chili and ranchero sauces plus mole, which you might expect if you'd ever been in a real Mexican place.

But he didn't stop there. He made an avocado gravy and a tomatillo gravy—this at a time when few Orleanians had ever heard of tomatillos, the little green tomato-like fruits from Mexico. He explained that tomatillo gravy was very good with crabmeat enchiladas. Those who tried it became fans for life, even making the trek out to Chalmette to his predictably stark restaurant there.

Chalmette was the last stop for Chico. It seemed to me the people in St. Bernard Parish took to him and his shabby cafe more enthusiastically than people from other parts of the city. It would not be until the influx of Hispanic people and taco trucks after Katrina that we would taste anything like what he cooked.

The Bean Pot's Green Enchiladas with Crabmeat

The green is in the sauce, which has many green ingredients with a wide range of flavors. The flavor is Mexican and a fine foil for the local crabmeat. It's inspired by Chico's Bean Pot, which served this sort of thing for decades.

1 banana pepper
1 small hot pepper
2 fresh jalapeno peppers
½ cup chopped white onion
2 cloves garlic, chopped
6 sprigs cilantro
12 tomatillos, husked and boiled 15 minutes
1 avocado, just under ripe
1 Tbs. lime juice
½ tsp. salt
1½ cups chicken broth
2 Tbs. olive oil
1 lb. claw crabmeat
¼ cup sour cream
12 small soft corn tortillas
1 cup shredded Monterey Jack cheese or queso fresca
Sour cream and guacamole for garnish

1. Remove stems, seeds, and internal membranes of all peppers, and rinse.

2. Combine peppers, onion, garlic, and cilantro in a food processor. Pulse until finely chopped. Add tomatillos, avocado, lime juice, and salt; process until smooth. Pour in chicken broth in a slow thin stream while continuing to process.

3. In a large saucepan, heat the olive oil over medium heat. Add the mixture in the food processor all at once. Bring to a boil, then reduce to a simmer. Cook for 15 minutes.

4. Blend the crabmeat and sour cream together.

5. Spread some of the tomatillo sauce on a tortilla. Spoon about 2 Tbs. of the crabmeat filling across the middle of it, then roll it up. Place the tortilla seam side down in a shallow casserole or baking dish. Repeat until all tortillas are filled, reserving some sauce for topping.

6. Pour tomatillo sauce over enchiladas, covering all the way to the edges. Sprinkle cheese over all and bake in a 350-degree oven for about 15 minutes—until cheese melts and begins to bubble. Serve hot with sour cream and guacamole.

Makes 6 appetizers or 4 entrees.

★★★
Bechac's
Mandeville: 2025 Lakeshore Drive
1885-1993

The most colorful exemplar of the grand New Orleans Creole lifestyle in the early 1800s was Bernard de Marigny de Mandeville. In his glory years, Marigny built a second residence on the north shore of Lake Pontchartrain—a thirty-mile sail from his main digs in the Faubourg Marigny.

Many other New Orleanians followed Marigny's lead and built their own summer and weekend homes in the town that grew around his place. Others took steamboats across the lake for the day. The resort town of Mandeville, developed by Marigny, was incorporated in 1840.

In 1847, a two-story Greek revival plantation home went up on the lakefront, on Lot #1 in Marigny's 1834 town plan. In 1885, the prominent Bechac family opened a restaurant in the building. For most of its history, Bechac's served the New Orleans escapees with food a lot like what could be found in the restaurants at home. It was less formal and had a simpler menu, dominated by seafood pulled out of the lake across the street.

Bechac's flavors were unambiguously Creole. You began with shrimp remoulade, baked oysters, turtle soup, or gumbo. The many configurations of fried seafood platters were far and away the most popular entrees. Broiled fish, sometimes with sauces but usually not, was also popular. (This was before the advent of grilled fish.) My first review of Bechac's in 1974 expressed some dismay at the prices, which seemed right for so scenic an ambience but more than a little high for fried seafood. I thought it was less good than, say, the West End Park average. That's about what I remember from succeeding visits.

But people who lived (full or part time) in Mandeville had few restaurants of significance, and if you wanted a nice evening out, you went to Bechac's, where at least you knew the view of the lake would be marvelous.

One certainly was likely to meet just about anyone there. Novelist Walker Percy was part of a group called "The Sons and Daughters of the Apocalypse" that had lunch at Bechac's every Thursday in the 1970s and 1980s. On one of my dinners, I saw Willie and Anna May Maylie, the owners of Maylie's on Poydras Street in downtown New Orleans. Their weekend house was a few blocks away, and where else could they go?

The main dining room was on the ground floor, with its low ceiling and small windows. Less often, for some reason, the much more spacious second-floor rooms were used. All were served by a well-dressed, all-black staff whose style was reminiscent of Pullman dining-car waiters, or the waiters at the Elmwood Plantation, or even the Camellia Grill.

Paradoxically, the old Bechac's faded and then closed when St. Tammany Parish began to grow explosively. Most newcomers thought nothing of crossing the lake to dine, since they were probably commuting to work anyway. At the same time, many new restaurants opened in the area, lessening the captive-clientele appeal of Bechac's.

The Bechac family still owns the building but has been leasing it to others since the 1990s. Even though most of these have been quite good (notably Pat Gallagher's Camelia [sic] Beach House and Alex Patout's Cajun-flavored interregnum), the tenants came nowhere close to matching Bechac's century. The current restaurant is the Lake House, with an ambitious new Creole menu and the same old great sunsets.

★★★
Beef Baron Steak House
Mid-City: 2501 Canal Street
1965-92

Only the most focused diners with the best memories can recall much about the food at the Beef Baron. I had to dig up my old reviews to remember any menu details beyond the obvious one that the place was a steakhouse.

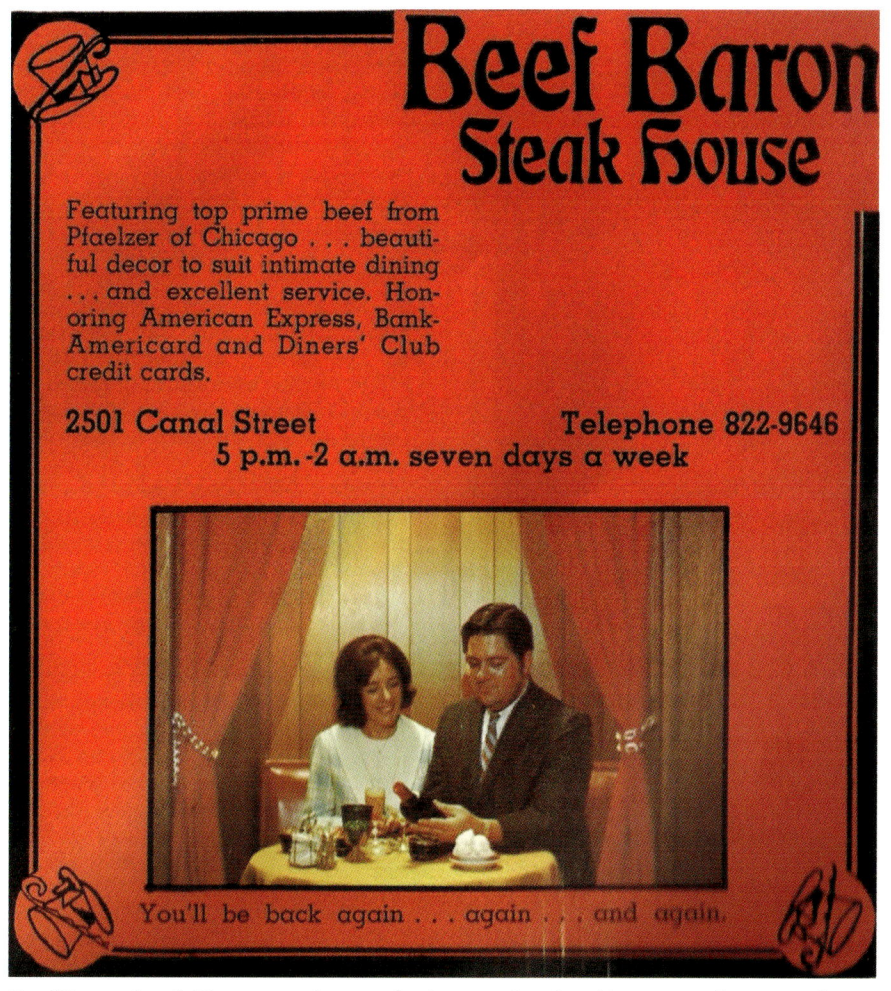

Beef Baron Steak House was known for its cozy booths. (Courtesy of New Orleans Magazine*)*

This culinary amnesia seems to have been caused by the distinctive atmosphere of the Beef Baron. And everybody who dined there remembers that vividly.

Along two walls, the dining room had enclosed, curtained booths, each with a table for two. Four people could have used them if they were willing to snuggle up close. But snuggling is what couples do, and the booths were made for them. They'd draw the curtains closed and dined—or did whatever else they pleased—out of sight.

Not even the waiters bothered these sequestered guests. A light switch inside turned on a little red light above the booth's archway to let the waiter know he was needed.

When the Beef Baron opened in the 1960s, this gimmick was building business for restaurants around the country. The idea seemed to have been hatched somewhere on the West Coast in the 1940s. Nor was it unique to the Beef Baron in New Orleans. Both Chris Steak House (before Ruth arrived) and the Crescent City Steak House also had the booths. (They are still in use at the Crescent City.) But they weren't as elegant nor as private as those at the Beef Baron. The Beef Baron's dining room was also much darker than most restaurants, adding another level of mystery.

Speaking of mystery, why were the only three New Orleans restaurants with private booths all steakhouses, within a seven-block radius? Could it have been where that day's winners from the nearby Fair Grounds Racetrack would go to celebrate?

The Beef Baron's steaks were not quite as exciting as those of its neighbors, but it always did serve USDA Prime beef. In a series of commercials starring WWL-TV weatherman Don Westbrook, the point was made that all of the steaks at the Beef Baron were Prime. This came with the heavy suggestion that maybe this was not the case at the competing steak joints in the Private Booth District.

The two most memorable dishes at the Beef Baron involved onions. The onion soup was made in the style of Les Halles in Paris. A cap of melted cheese over a crouton covered the crock. And in lieu of French bread, the Baron served crusty, hot onion rolls. It was almost worth going to the restaurant just for those.

The Beef Baron suffered from a downward trend in its neighborhood in the 1980s. Pan-American Life Insurance Company across the street moved to new headquarters. This hit the Baron hard. It closed, then reopened in the early 1990s in an unfortunate location on Oaklawn just river side of Veterans Boulevard—right behind a Burger King. It built the new place with many private booths, but it made them just a shade too small. The restaurant closed after a few years. Petra, also now gone, took over the space and ultimately pulled out the booths.

Meanwhile, back on Canal Street, a unique restaurateur named Dale Wamstad took over the old Beef Baron location. It was the second New Orleans location of his steakhouse, called Del Frisco's. That would not be long term, but when he moved the concept to Dallas, it was so popular that after a few years he sold the place to Lone Star for $23 million. There are Del Frisco's all over the country now.

In the summer of 1967, I congratulated myself for being named interim manager of the Time Saver in River Ridge by having dinner at the Beef Baron, still then in its original location. I had no date, no booth, and a thick filet mignon with all the trimmings. The total check was $6.78. This seemed like an unconscionable splurge. But I think I've had my money's worth of memories from it.

★★★★
Berdou's
Gretna: 300 Monroe Street
1950s-88

Berdou's looked like a neighborhood restaurant, the kind of place you'd go for a poor boy and a beer. It was a plain brick building almost directly underneath the original span of the Mississippi River Bridge.

The dining rooms were pleasant, and the tables had white tablecloths. But they weren't what you'd call fancy. Nevertheless, Ida Berdou wanted to impress upon you that this was a restaurant of substance. She maintained a strict dress code that often surprised first-timers. Jeans—regardless of their expense—were forbidden, even on little kids.

Mrs. Berdou, who herself always seemed a bit overdressed, enforced a few other rules. She did not like late diners, and if you weren't in the house by seven thirty, you were just out of luck. She once told me that the extra butter the waiter had brought me at my request was too much cholesterol and I'd better watch it. (I was in my twenties at the time.)

Mrs. Berdou wasn't being a martinet for its own sake. She believed that her customers wanted a civilized establishment, and to give it to them she required them to stick with her rules. Her husband, George, loved her for this and chewed me out after I referred to her once on the radio as "the old lady at Berdou's."

George Berdou was a great chef. He'd worked in the kitchen at Galatoire's for quite a few years before opening his own place. The food at Berdou's was from the same precinct of the Creole culinary world that Galatoire's was, and darn near as good. And it was ambitious, too. Berdou's most famous specialty was pompano en papillote—pompano baked in a parchment bag. It's so complicated a preparation that no restaurant prepares it regularly anymore.

Making this even more amazing was Berdou's pricing. A review I wrote in 1977 shows the pompano en papillote at all of $4. That's a *dinner* price. A shrimp remoulade appetizer (a good one) was $1.50. Turtle soup or gumbo was a buck. Crabmeat Berdou, a great casserole with a satisfying tinge of garlic, was $4. Trout Marguery with a very well made sauce of shrimp and mushrooms was $4; chicken Clemenceau, $3.50. Two broiled lamb chops (complete with those little paper things that looked like chef's hats slipped over the bones) were $4.50. For $2 more, they'd make the entree part of a four-course dinner.

When Berdou's was in its prime in the 1960s and 1970s, a reservation was hard to come by. Fortunately, they stayed open all afternoon, and those hours had food as good as at any other time. You might even catch one of the lunch specials. Mr. Berdou liked field peas, for example, and featured them once a week.

A line from my 1977 review: "You wonder whether there will be a philanthropist who will jump in and change nothing should Mrs. Berdou ever decide to lay down her reservation book." That proved to be Mr. Berdou, but even he was able to keep the place open only for a few more years after his beloved wife's death. The neighborhood was in steep decline, and the decline of the oil business kicked the wind out of the West Bank economy. It closed in 1988, barely in time for me to get George to show me how to make crabmeat Berdou in a report on WVUE-TV.

Since the demise of Berdou's, no restaurant anywhere has come close to filling its gap. It was one of a kind.

Crabmeat Berdou

George Berdou demonstrated this great recipe on my television show. It will appeal especially to garlic lovers. This is also a great dish made with crawfish tails or small shrimp.

Béchamel:
4 Tbs. butter
3 Tbs. flour
1 cup milk, warmed
½ tsp. salt

1 stick butter
½ cup chopped green onions
½ cup sliced mushrooms
1 Tbs. chopped garlic
Pinch cayenne
½ cup sherry
1 lb. lump crabmeat

Preheat the broiler with the rack about 4 inches below the heat.

1. Make the béchamel by heating the butter in a saucepan until it bubbles. Stir in the flour to make a blond roux; don't allow it to brown. Whisk in the milk over low heat until the sauce thickens. Add the salt and keep warm.

2. In a second saucepan, heat the butter until it bubbles, and in it sauté the green onions, mushrooms, garlic, and cayenne until the mushrooms are tender. Add the sherry and bring to a boil. Lower the heat and cook until all the liquid is absorbed.

3. Carefully add the lump crabmeat and combine with the rest of the ingredients by agitating the pan, so as not to break the lumps. Spoon the mixture onto 4 oven-proof serving dishes.

4. Nap 2 or 3 Tbs. of the béchamel over the top of the crabmeat on each dish. Put the plates into the hot broiler for about 1 minute. Serve immediately, warning that the plates are hot.

Serves 4.

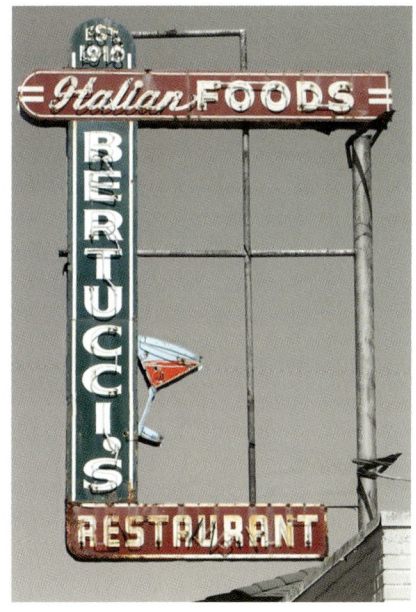

★★★
Bertucci's Restaurant
Harvey: 3300 Fourth Street
1918-2005

For a restaurant with as long a history as Bertucci's enjoyed, it wasn't nearly as well known as it should have been. However, those who lived on the West Bank—especially if they lived anywhere along the old main traffic corridor that was Fourth and Fifth streets—not only knew about it but raved about it.

Because it had been around as long as it had, Bertucci's had most of the qualities we cherish most in our restaurants. It had the menu and prices of a neighborhood cafe. But it also had tablecloths and a certain old-style formality not often seen in that category.

Like the many other Italian restaurants that opened in New Orleans just before and after World War I, Bertucci's cooking was Sicilian. But local prejudices against Italians were still current. To ingratiate itself with non-Italians, the place served many of the dishes you'd find in other local restaurants. It was as famous for its red beans and rice as it was for its spaghetti and meatballs.

And that was saying something. Bertucci's had as luscious a red sauce as any other restaurant in the area, bar none. It made a great

Bertucci's Restaurant was a fixture in Harvey for nearly nine decades. (Photo by Rachel Favoloro)

After John Bertucci had a heart attack in 1948, his two daughters and their spouses took over the operation of Bertucci's. From left, Vincent Territo, Marie Bertucci Territo, Frances Bertucci Bruce, and Dave Bruce. (Courtesy of Vincent Territo, Jr.)

John and Christina Bertucci opened their restaurant in 1918. Among their many specialties was Spaghetti Bertucci, which consisted of angel-hair pasta served with a rich tomato gravy, with mushrooms, meatballs, and generous pieces of chicken breast. (Courtesy of Vincent Territo, Jr.)

gumbo and an even better turtle soup. Seafood never filled a large part of the menu, but it was there, cooked in the New Orleans way.

When the main flow of east-west traffic moved to the West Bank Expressway in the 1950s, what inevitably happened to old main drags across America happened to Fourth Street and Bertucci's. However, Bertucci's was close enough to the Jefferson Parish Courthouse to get a good deal of lunch business from it.

Still, Bertucci's slowly declined in the 1980s, faster in the 1990s. A combination of family attrition and the aging of the regular customers took its toll. In 2003, Bertucci's closed but was soon after taken over by some former employees, who promised to keep everything the same. That didn't work out for long, and the restaurant came to an end after almost nine decades of deliciousness.

★

Beverly Dinner Playhouse
Old Jefferson: Labarre Road at Jefferson Highway
1972-83

Everybody wanted the Beverly Dinner Playhouse to be a big hit. The appeal of combining professional theatre and restaurant food and service into one big evening out was tremendous. And the venue was ideal. The Beverly had a long history as a nightclub from the 1920s onward. After World War II, the building was dressed up with a plantation-like facade and a glittering interior. Its theatre was big enough to accommodate big-name acts, and it did.

For a time, the Beverly Country Club was a casino—legal in Jefferson Parish in those days. This caught the attention of various local and national crime fighters, and the Beverly went through a period of close, reopen, repeat through the 1950s and 1960s. Even when the gambling was gone, a lot of people assumed it continued, thereby giving the place a slightly tawdry reputation.

In 1972, dinner theatres were on the rise around the country, and investors reopened the Beverly to that end. The plays were usually light fare—a mix of classics, long-running Broadway hits (*The Fantasticks*), and a lot of Neil Simon. Most of the shows featured a recognizable performer, often best known for their television work. The entire cast was professional.

Before each play, of course, was the dinner. I was a reviewer of everything at the *Figaro* weekly during most of the Beverly Dinner Playhouse's career, and I covered many plays there.

The best comparison would be to the secondary Sunday brunch buffets in the outlying hotels around town. The food was simple and ample. There was always a haunch of beef being carved. But nobody ever went to the Beverly to eat. Sometimes the kitchen would have a great night, but that was the exception that spotlighted the rule.

The Beverly ended with a disastrous fire in 1983. There was talk of reopening it, but it remains an empty lot. Other dinner theatres have opened and closed. I'm asked about them now and then by people

Theatre goers dined buffet style at the Beverly Dinner Playhouse. (Courtesy of New Orleans Magazine*)*

who think that there must be such a thing somewhere around here. But there usually isn't. Show biz and cookery have never got along as well as the customers would hope.

★★★★
Bistro Steak Room
Westwego: 1098 Fourth Street
1969-88

People who dined in this highly improbable restaurant all talked about the same two dishes. Both of them were free. Fried parsley—"French popcorn"—was coated with a dusting of seasoned flour before going into the fryer. It came to the table in a coffee-filter-lined basket that also held "Bistro bread," crescent-shaped pieces of French bread spread with a concoction that resembled a very herbal pizza sauce and a bit of Parmesan cheese, then baked.

Improbable, I said. The Bistro was on the old, superseded, and (in spots) super-seedy main route through the communities on the other side of the river from New Orleans. The Bistro's entrance—marked by a small neon sign whose script said *Bistro*—was inside a casual eatery called the Riviera. With big windows and bright fluorescent lights, the Riviera fed truck drivers and other hard workers with the likes of poor boys or fried chicken.

Walking through the Bistro's door revealed a radical change in atmosphere. Inside it was cool, dark, and romantic. The tables were set richly. Art hung on the walls. Stained-glass panels glowed here

In addition to its steaks, the Bistro Steak Room was known for such dishes as bowtie pasta with crabmeat and cream sauce and poached eggs with hollandaise over smoked salmon. Diners were given fried parsley and Bistro bread when they arrived. (Photo by Bonnie Warren, courtesy of New Orleans Magazine*)*

and there. Finding a first-class restaurant in such a place tickled one's sense of the absurd enough to add something to the meal—or even make you giggle.

The Bistro was the creation of the Bitoun brothers, Moroccan Sephardim named Jacques, Andre, Maurice, and Simon. All had substantial résumés. Andre in particular was well known in fine-dining circles, having worked both on the front door and in the kitchen at the Rib Room and Brennan's.

Although the menu and style of the Bistro bore the unmistakable mark of Andre Bitoun—the most talented chef among the brothers—for most of its history the Bistro was run by Maurice. He was the chef and host and good at both jobs. He was always there, with a big smile under his big black mustache. He knew everybody, and since most of his customers came from Uptown (hard to believe now, but true), his currency spread. Simon, whose offbeat sense of humor added further entertainment to the meal, was the maitre d' and lead waiter.

After the fried parsley and Bistro bread, you moved on to the bowtie pasta with crabmeat and cream sauce, the poached eggs with hollandaise over smoked salmon ("Kosher Eggs Benedict," Maurice called it), or the baked oysters.

Steak was the restaurant's specialty, and they handled it well, even in the absence of the most expensive beef. Maurice told me that the trick was to sear steaks in the pan on top of the stove and then finish them in the oven. However it was done, the Bistro's steaks were always bulging with juiciness. They made an assortment of sauces to go with the steaks; the best of them was the peppercorn-encrusted steak au poivre. They came out with what amounted to potatoes au gratin in the jacket.

Seafood here was also good. The list started with a fried seafood platter, lifted from the West End level by an excellent version of the brown, opaque, Arnaud's-style meunière sauce. Other specialties included veal Normande, very tender, served atop noodles in a great apple-brandy-flavored sauce. You finished dinner with the Bistro jubilee—cherries jubilee made in the kitchen instead of flamed in front of you, but with no loss of flavor.

The Bistro was most popular in the 1970s. It declined along with all the other restaurants on the West Bank after the oil bust in the early 1980s. At the same time, the new wave of Mr. B's-style gourmet cafes began opening throughout Uptown, siphoning away many of the Bistro's regular customers.

After the Bistro closed in 1988, vestiges of its style cropped up now and then, when Andre, Maurice, and Simon all opened other restaurants here and there. Andre and Maurice joined their big brother Jacques in the Big Kitchen in the Sky in the 1990s. Simon is still living but hobbled and retired. In their prime, these men built one of the most distinctive, most memorable, and most surprising restaurants ever to operate in New Orleans.

Bistro's Eggs Bitoun

"Kosher Eggs Benedict" is what chefs Andre and Maurice Bitoun called this dish. Made with a single egg and smoked salmon in place of the ham of a standard Benedict, it was an appetizer at their Bistro Steak Room in the 1970s and 1980s. A garnish of fried capers completes a real original derived from a familiar classic.

Hollandaise:
2 egg yolks
1 Tbs. red wine vinegar
1 Tbs. warm water
1 stick butter, softened
1 tsp. lemon juice
Pinch cayenne

Garnish:
2 Tbs. olive oil
2 Tbs. small capers

Eggs:
2 Tbs. salt
2 Tbs. vinegar
8 very fresh jumbo eggs
8 slices cold-smoked salmon, about ¼ inch thick
4 English muffins, split and toasted

Hollandaise:

1. Whisk the egg yolks and the vinegar briskly in a metal bowl set over a saucepan with about 1 inch of simmering water at the bottom. If you see even a hint of curdling in the eggs, take the bowl off the heat, but keep whisking. Keep going back and forth from the heat until the mixture turns thick and lightens in color. Whisk in 1 Tbs. of warm water.

2. Begin adding the softened butter, a pat at a time. After about a fourth of the butter is in there, you'll begin to see a change in the texture of the sauce. At that point, you can step up the addition of the butter a bit, and keep going till all the butter is incorporated.

3. Whisk in the lemon juice and cayenne. Cover the bowl with plastic wrap and set in a bigger bowl of warm (not hot!) water.

Garnish:

Heat the olive oil until fragrant. Add the capers and fry in the oil until crisp—about 1 minute. Drain on a paper towel and keep warm.

A BITE OF HISTORY

B. Montalbano Italian Delicatessen
724 St. Phillip Street

B. Montalbano Italian Delicatessen owner Biaccio Montalbano revered St. Joseph so much that he built a shrine to the saint in a back room he called the Roma Room. It was covered with holy pictures and featured an altar to St. Joseph on a large table in the center. Every year, Montalbano erected an enormous altar filled with Lenten dishes and baked goods in the saint's honor on St. Joseph's feast day, March 19. The delicatessen, which operated in the French Quarter from the 1930s to the 1950s, was famous for its "Roma Sandwich," kin to a muffuletta. (From the collection of Peggy Scott Laborde)

—Peggy Scott Laborde

Eggs:

1. Use a large stainless-steel skillet filled with water about 1½ inches deep. Bring it to a boil while dissolving the salt into it and adding the vinegar.

2. The hard part of poaching eggs is keeping them intact as you add them to the pan. The best trick is to use a coffee cup—the kind that narrows at the bottom. Being careful not to break the yolk, break 1 egg into each of 4 cups (or 8, if your skillet is big enough to fit all those eggs).

3. When the water comes to a boil, lower the heat to the lowest possible setting. Slide the eggs carefully into the pan, 2 (or 4, even) at a time. Let them simmer for 3 to 4 minutes, depending on the size of the eggs.

4. The best tool to remove the eggs with is a round skimmer with holes in it or a large slotted spoon. Carefully remove 1 at a time, and let the excess water drip off.

5. Repeat the poaching process with the remaining eggs.

6. Place 1 slice of smoked salmon atop each English muffin half, then top with 1 egg. Cover with a generous flow of hollandaise. Garnish with the fried capers.

Makes 4 entrees or 8 appetizers.

★★★

Buck Forty-Nine Pancake and Steak House
French Quarter: 216 Bourbon Street
Metairie: 1927 Airline Highway
Riverbend: 734 South Carrollton Avenue
Gretna: West Bank Expressway at Stumpf Boulevard
1961-98

"Never name a restaurant after a price!" said Joe Riccobono, the creator and owner of the Buck Forty-Nine Steak House. I never met him, but I wish I had.

His son Vincent quoted the line. Vincent owns the Peppermill, the Metairie restaurant his mother opened in 1975. Josie Riccobono wanted a restaurant that was more feminine and stylish than her husband's steakhouses. It was the sixth restaurant in a local chain that included the four Buck Forty-Nines and Rick's Pancake House on Canal Street.

The name makes the Buck Forty-Nine sound like the last place a steak lover would go. They really did have a steak dinner that sold for $1.49 as late as the midsixties. It was a sirloin (probably top sirloin, not a strip), and it came with fries and a salad for that price. It was not a great steak, but it's hard to argue at a price like that. Among the

Buck Forty-Nine, owned by the Riccobono family, was known for its inexpensive but good-quality steaks that at one time actually sold for $1.49. This one was located at the corner of South Carrollton Avenue and Maple Street. (Courtesy of Teresa Riccobono-Johnston and Vincent Riccobono)

many jokey advisories on the Buck Forty-Nine's menu was another quotation from Joe Riccobono: "People ask how we can serve such great steaks for such a low price. Frankly, I have an uncle who is a cattle rustler."

The décor completed the down-market, cowboy image, with stark, kitschy, Western-themed dining rooms.

But it could not be said that the Buck Forty-Nine was a bad place to eat. The other steaks on the menu were reasonably decent. I never heard anyone call them the best in town. With steakhouses like Chris and the Crescent City, we knew better. But the Buck Forty-Nine kitchens went far beyond cheap steaks. They offered the full range of casual New Orleans eating: as much seafood as a seafood house, red beans and other favorite local lunch specials, poor-boy sandwiches, bread pudding, and caramel custard. They served the distinctive "cap bread," a crusty loaf that was about the size and shape of a first baseman's glove, a distinctly local variety of bread served only in ancient places such as Arnaud's and Tujague's.

The seafood was probably the best part of the menu, actually. They fried catfish especially well and served trout amandine with the brown New Orleans-style meunière sauce that the Peppermill still uses. The stuffed crab was first rate, and the shrimp remoulade was beyond reproach. The daily specials were as good as could be found anywhere else in town at that price.

Particularly at the Carrollton Riverbend location, the Buck Forty-Nine functioned as a neighborhood restaurant. Everybody there was local, the food was Creole, and only the cowboy décor differentiated it from any other big locals hangout. Some people were so loyal to the place that they ate three meals a day there, seven days a week.

Three? See, breakfast was a big deal. The list of pancakes ran to dozens of varieties, served with a rack of six differently flavored syrups. Omelettes, fancy poached eggs with hollandaise, grits and

Matches from the Buck Forty-Nine. (From the collection of Edward Piglia)

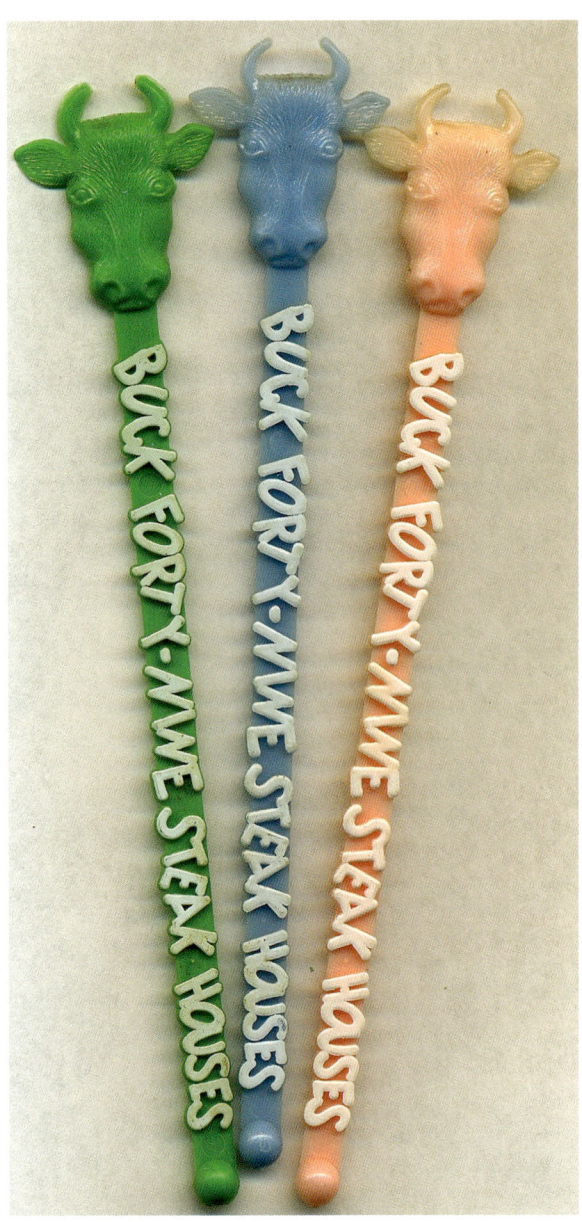

sausage and bacon and lost bread—it was all here and well turned out.

Restaurants like the Buck Forty-Nine went out of vogue east of the Mississippi in the 1970s, and it happened here, too. They closed one by one. The Gretna location hung on years longer than the others.

The Carrollton Buck Forty-Nine evolved (with much the same menu) into The Riverbend. That was a classic fern restaurant of the 1970s. It was wildly popular as a slightly upscale, slightly dressed up neighborhood hangout for over a decade. It was so well known that its name came to describe the whole neighborhood, and it still does. The Riverbend went out of vogue in its turn, and the location ceased to be a restaurant.

Maybe that's another lesson that Joe Riccobono learned. If you try to keep up with restaurant vogues but you're not careful, they can leave you behind. The Peppermill too has experienced this, although it has outlived its predecessor by many years.

I have fond personal memories of the Buck Forty-Nine. In it I discovered the pleasures of dining out—something my parents never did. I worked at the Time Saver on Carrollton and Oak during my teens and had dinner at the nearby Buck Forty-Nine a few times a week. I ate an unvarying menu of onion soup, salad with the unique, garlicky vinaigrette, a chopped sirloin steak with a baked potato and the works, and a caramel custard. Soon I found that the pursuit of pleasure is not in discovering the thing you like best and sticking with it but trying new dishes all the time. At the Buck Forty-Nine, I learned how to get the most out of a restaurant.

Nothing like the Buck Forty-Nine exists now. I can't help thinking that with a new look it could attract a strong clientele again. Or maybe I'm just being wistful for my first time.

These swizzle sticks were a reminder that beef was a featured item on the Buck Forty-Nine menu. (From the collection of Edward Piglia)

★★★
The Bull's Corner
Broadmoor: 4440 Magnolia Street
Laplace: 1036 West Airline Highway
1966-2009

Restaurants in the immediate vicinity of a hospital can count on a steady clientele of hospital staff. Restaurants serving hamburgers and beer in the near environs of a large college can also expect to see a consistent flow. The Bull's Corner enjoyed both of these advantages. Not only did it give owner Doug Depp a successful restaurant, but it created an engaging scene. The memory of it glows.

The original Bull's Corner was across the street from the former

Doug Depp was the owner of the Bull's Corner. (Courtesy of New Orleans Magazine*)*

Southern Baptist Hospital (now a campus of Ochsner). When it opened in the 1960s, the restaurant reminded a lot of people of the well-established Bud's Broiler. The Bull's Corner grilled good hamburgers over charcoal and served them with a variety of sauces specified by numbers, like at Bud's.

But the Bull's Corner was much more sophisticated and comfortable than Bud's. In addition to the hamburgers, it served steaks—USDA Prime steaks, at that. It had a full bar. A lot of customers—particularly the younger ones—went there on dates, liking the dim lighting and the easy-to-dig food. No doubt quite a few people had the first cocktail of their lives at the Bull's Corner. I am one of them. The drink was a banana banshee—spelled on the order board as *abanche* for some reason.

One regular customer liked the Bull's Corner enough to sell Doug Depp on the idea of franchising. Mike Norton opened his edition of the Bull's Corner in Laplace in 1985—far enough away that it wouldn't affect the original. Laplace had such a dearth of eateries that its Bull's Corner evolved into a full-service restaurant with a wide-ranging menu. It expanded into the adjacent shopping mall to pull in groups and parties.

Not long after, street construction and expansion of the hospital made the original Bull's Corner hard to get to for an extended period.

Depp closed the place but kept the name and the spirit alive, with at least the hope of reopening in the future. He and his burgers have long been a fixture at the Audubon Zoo To-Do.

But with no open Bull's Corner in New Orleans, Mike Norton opened a second location of his version in Bucktown. There was some legal maneuvering between Norton and Depp because of this, but it became moot when the Bucktown building was bought from under the restaurant and torn down.

The Bull's Corner kept selling Bull burgers and steaks in Laplace, but a downturn there put the place in distress. Norton closed it in 2009. And that was that. But with upscale hamburgers becoming popular, the thought of having the Bull's Corner again sounds good.

★★★
Buster Holmes
French Quarter: 721 Burgundy Street
1944-83

A tease line on the front cover of the first edition of *The Underground Gourmet* said that a good meal revealed in its pages could be had for twenty-seven cents. In 1970, when the book first appeared, I burrowed through its pages to find the source of this "best underground meal in town." It was Buster Holmes, on the corner of Orleans and Burgundy.

In this, and in several other reviews, Richard Collin made the most audacious recommendation in his very bold book. He said that white people were missing essential Creole food if they failed to dine in black-owned restaurants, in black neighborhoods, with dining rooms full of black people.

The front door of Buster Holmes. (Photo by Philip M. Denman)

Buster Holmes was known for his delicious home-style food at great prices. His French Quarter restaurant was popular with musicians and artists. (Photo © Mitchel Osborne MMX)

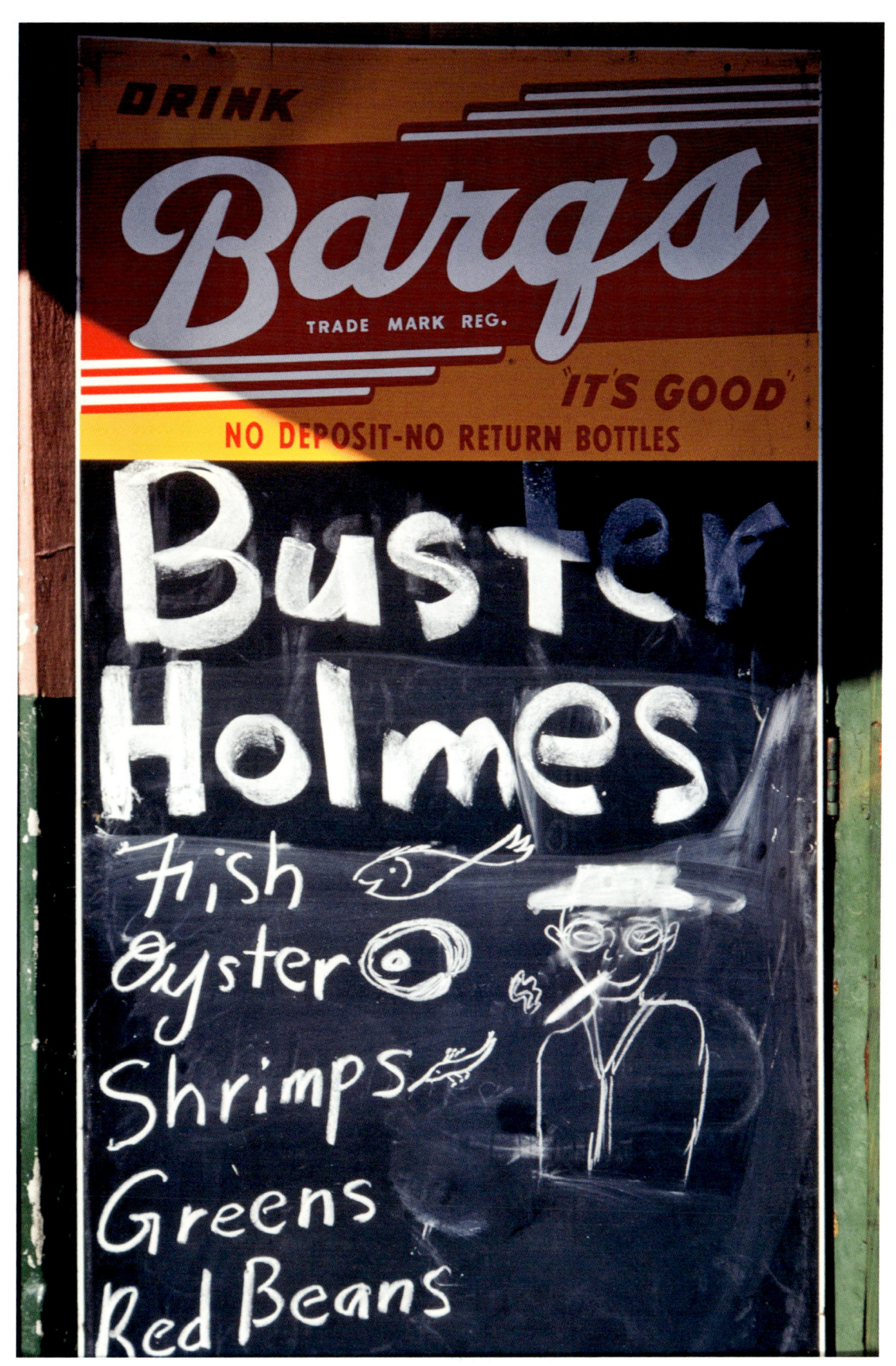

The menu sign outside of Buster Holmes. (Photo © Mitchel Osborne MMX)

A plate of Buster Holmes' famous red beans and rice. (Photo © Mitchel Osborne MMX)

Much of my life until then was spent in a segregated society. I remember total racial separation, in bathrooms, buses, and restaurants. No African-American kid shared any of my classrooms—not even in my first school, St. Augustine, founded by free people of color in a well-mixed neighborhood—until I reached high school.

But 1970 was a liberal-minded time. Even Richard Nixon now seems liberal. Black culture, then as now, was very cool among young white people. It goes without saying that we all listened to black music. As Collin said in one of the history courses I took with him at the University of New Orleans, "Why would anyone listen to Perry Como when you can listen to Aretha Franklin?"

Still, going to a black restaurant was a step over the line for most whites in 1970. It was one thing for black people to enter white institutions. It was quite another to reverse the process.

Of course, my friends and I went. It was exciting, probably a little too much. I suspect we came across as patronizing. We made an absurd show of delight over food that was actually very familiar to us. Creole cooking—although it's usually credited to the French and Spanish colonizers of New Orleans—received most of its inspiration from the Africans who cooked it.

The part of the French Quarter along Burgundy Street was still largely a black neighborhood in the 1970s, as it had been for most of the century. It was where a lot of old jazz musicians had lived, and it had a sense of community. The Morning Star Baptist Church, one of the city's best-known centers of gospel singing, was a centerpiece. So was Buster Holmes restaurant.

Buster's had two dining rooms. The front room had the bar, so it was air conditioned and had tables. The first time I went, the front room was full, so I went to the back room. This was really the kitchen, with screen doors providing ventilation and a fan blowing the warm air around.

After Buster Holmes closed his restaurant, he catered for many years. (Photo by Peggy Scott Laborde)

On my memorable first visit, I took a stool at the counter. After a few minutes, a large lady wearing an apron stood opposite me. She turned her eyes to the ceiling and recited, "We gots red beans, butterbeans, crowder peas, hot sausage, smoke sausage, chicken, backbone, hambone, pork chop, turnip greens, spinach, and po' boys."

I ordered fast, so as not to seem like a fussy white boy (as if that weren't obvious). "Butterbeans," I said. She turned around, grabbed a plastic plate like the ones we had in the school cafeteria, and dished up a mountain of rice. Then she ladled up a massive quantity of tan beans—the really big ones—studded with pieces of auburn pickled pork, in a light sauce. She cut six inches off a loaf of poor-boy bread and put it in one of the unoccupied pockets of the plate. She stuck a knife in a block of margarine and scraped it off onto the side of my plate. My order was complete.

The beans were delicious, heartwarming, and familiar. As I would discover every time I dined in a black-owned restaurant, the food tasted like my mother's. On that first visit, it was really more than I wanted, but I was nineteen and ate all the beans anyway—and all the bread. The lady brought me another hunk. I didn't need any more margarine. I forgot to ask for something to drink, and the lady forgot to ask. I just let myself get thirsty. And I sat there, a long time. Nobody asked me anything. It became clear that many of the customers came in to take a load off for as long as they could, and the ladies working the counter were in no hurry, either.

I stood up and asked how much. "You had the butterbeans, right?" said the lady. "Nothing to drink? You didn't drink nothin'? Okay. Let's see. Fifty cent plus tax . . . fifty-two cent."

I gave her a dollar. "I heard you can eat here for twenty-seven cents," I said, smiling.

Her face didn't change. "Yeah. Some people do that. Butterbeans fifty cent."

"What's twenty-seven cents?"

"That not for you, honey," she said, her tone turning almost motherly. "That for poor people. I know you got fifty cent. Now you come back and get chicken with the beans and spend that whole dollar next time."

I was not the only white person at Buster Holmes that day. But it wasn't long before whites would outnumber blacks. Buster's pricing system would reveal many tiers, with the same plate of beans costing as much as $1.50 if you were a well-dressed white person with an out-of-town way of talking and insisted on eating in the front room.

A floating price system was hardly unique to Buster's. It was part of his solidarity with his community, which continued to be a priority even as his new fame began to fill his place with tourists.

After that very substantial lunch, I went to work at the Time Saver. I was still full at dinnertime. Not only that, but I was jet propelled, if you know what I mean. I think of that every time I eat butterbeans, even really good ones.

★★★
Café Atchafalaya
Uptown: 901 Louisiana Avenue
1991-2004
★★★
Dante by the River/Tea 'n' Tiques
Uptown: 723 Dante Street
1977-86

These three rather different restaurants belong together in this recollection because of the unique woman who connects them. Iler Pope moved to New Orleans from the Mississippi Delta country in the late 1970s, bringing with her a classic Mississippi speech rhythm (the word "wine" came out of her mouth in three syllables) and a love of Southern cooking.

New Orleans might seem to be the perfect place for a restaurant serving Southern cooking. But what people eat in the Mississippi Delta and what people eat in New Orleans are almost as different Creole and Yankee cooking are.

"Rather Southern, slightly sophisticated" was the slogan of Café Atchafalaya. You'd go there not for the usual New Orleans crabmeat ravigote but for crabmeat West Indies, a classic dish from the Mississippi Gulf Coast. Not for red beans and rice but for crowder peas and speckled butterbeans Iler bought from Rolling Fork, Mississippi. Not for chicken Clemenceau but for chicken and dumplings. Fried chicken livers, too, and lots of greens and grits.

All the while, Iler sat in a corner of the dining room, smoking cigarettes and holding court with her friends. At times, she would jump up and correct a problem with a decisiveness so much in contrast with her genteel country-South persona that you'd be taken aback. Where did that tough old broad come from?

Iler's Café Atchafalaya was the second, most famous, and most distinctive of the four restaurants to bear that name on the corner of Louisiana Avenue and Laurel Street. The building was inherited from Petrossi's Seafood Restaurant and had been a restaurant since the 1920s. It was long and narrow, with high ceilings and a bit beat up. But that suited the style perfectly, once Iler put up the right mix of paintings and plants.

In its heyday, Café Atchafalaya was exceedingly popular. After Iler left it behind for health reasons, I'd get frequent calls from both locals and New Orleans visitors who were distressed to learn that she wasn't there anymore.

Iler had this fan club already assembled when she opened Café Atchafalaya. Her first New Orleans restaurant, Dante by the River, was a blend of Southern and Creole. It was more along the lines of the traditional New Orleans bistros that were beginning to open Uptown in the early 1980s.

It had much else going for it. The location was in the cluster of shops and cafes in a neighborhood that had only lately become known as Riverbend (replacing the former "around the Camellia Grill"), near where the St. Charles streetcar makes its sharp turn onto South Carrollton Avenue. The building was one of the old houses that had been built out of planks and beams from dismantled river barges. Hundreds of those came down the Mississippi. They were easier to build new than to pull back upstream.

Dante by the River had been Tea 'n' Tiques, a combination dining room and antiques store. Everything in the restaurant—including the entire restaurant itself—was for sale. Iler bought it in 1981. The antique furnishings were just what she had in mind, and it was all very charming.

She also had a major asset in the kitchen. Chef Richard Hughes would later go to New York and open a hit Louisiana-style restaurant called Memphis. Since 1990, he's been the owner-chef of the Pelican Club, a five-star gourmet place on Exchange Alley in the French Quarter. Iler hired him from Baton Rouge. He already spoke with a nice Southern cadence. And he was a terrific cook.

Dante by the River was full most of the time, even though some interpreted Iler's personal style as a little pushy. (Even if she liked you, Iler never candy-coated what she felt she had to tell you.) After a few years, she had had enough of trying the please all of the people all of the time and took a break. In 1986 Frank and Marna Brigtsen, fresh out of K-Paul's, took over the place and opened their current restaurant there.

Iler came back five years later to open Café Atchafalaya, where she stayed for thirteen years. She died at age sixty-eight, right after Thanksgiving 2007. People still write me to ask where her restaurant is these days. I expect to be answering that question for the rest of my life.

Café Atchafalaya's Crabmeat West Indies

Spring brings the really good crabmeat at affordable prices. At this time of year, it may be true that the ultimate jumbo lump-crabmeat experience is to open the tub, reach in, and just start eating. Here is a popular dish all along the Gulf Coast that is about as close to naked as a lump of crabmeat can get.

1 lb. lump crabmeat
¼ cup chopped white onion
½ cup olive oil
¼ cup cider vinegar
1 tsp. lemon juice
1 Tbs. very small capers
¼ cup water
¼ tsp. salt
4 drops Tabasco

Blend all ingredients in a nonmetallic bowl. Cover and refrigerate for 2 hours to overnight. Serve cold over a thick slice of ripe tomato.

Serves 4 to 6.

★★★

Café Pontchartrain (The Silver Whistle)
Garden District: The Pontchartrain Hotel, 2031 St. Charles Avenue
1927-2005

From the smallest hamlet to the biggest city, there's always one restaurant where the big names in the community go to have breakfast with others of their kind. For many decades in New Orleans, that place was the coffee shop of the Pontchartrain Hotel.

Every morning at seven, a changing cast of highly recognizable men (they were all men, at least on all the occasions when I saw them there) sat down with chicory coffee, the hotel's famous (but overrated) blueberry muffins, and perhaps a serious breakfast. The latter ran the full gamut from the standard bacon, eggs, and grits to hollandaise-topped poached eggs with crabmeat. The coffee shop's kitchen could do it all, because its other job was to feed the customers who came in for the excellent lunches and dinners in the hotel's vaunted Caribbean Room.

No matter what you ordered or when, chances are that you'd linger much longer than you would over breakfast anywhere else. The elite diners at the round table replaced one another as the hours ticked by. Everybody knew everybody else, if only by reputation. I was often tempted to just walk up and sit down there, but I never had the guts to do it. These guys were mostly attorneys and politicians. I never saw a journalist with them.

The cafe originally opened as the Silver Whistle. Sometime in the 1960s, it was renovated into a much more handsome space and became Café Pontchartrain. In later years—after the founding Aschaffenburg family lost control of the hotel—the new management tore out all the dark paneling and found the old, charmingly retro décor under it. It was a little beat up, but they left it that way. And the name changed back to the equally antiquated Silver Whistle.

But the food service was in decline by then. About a year before Hurricane Katrina—with the Caribbean Room extinct—the Silver Whistle became Lafitte's, a touristy parody of New Orleans food. It never came back after the hurricane. The hotel has been converted into apartments for senior citizens. Café Pontchartrain may return— and maybe even the round-table breakfasters.

★★★★
Cafe Sbisa
French Quarter: 1011 Decatur Street
1899-2005

Cafe Sbisa became a historic restaurant at least twice. It may be one again someday.

Through most of the 1800s, the building—then as now across the street from the French Market—housed a chandler, selling food and other supplies to the many ships calling at the busy Mississippi River docks. It's reputed that it also served other needs of the seamen and was a bordello for a good while (hardly the only one in the vicinity).

The French Quarter became the de facto Italian Quarter in the late 1800s, particularly in the French Market area. The Sbisa family took over the chandler's store and made it into a restaurant. The customers were waiting: they were the many bankers, shippers, and other businessmen in the neighborhood. After the main port action moved to other parts of town, Sbisa's declined from a meeting place for busy people from everywhere in the world to a worn-out joint whose primary customers were longtime regulars. By the 1970s, it was more a bar than anything else, serving the last of a dying clientele.

In 1978, Dr. Larry Hill—formerly a partner in the hip Marti's restaurant—acquired Sbisa's. He performed an inspired restoration of the building, keeping the oversized exposed wooden beams but cutting through the second floor to create a mezzanine. This aired out the space considerably. He kept the ancient bar and its mirrors and installed furnishings that made the place look as old as it was. The wood-framed mirrors in the dining room added dimension as well as suggesting the atmosphere of renowned old restaurants such as Antoine's and Galatoire's.

But Hill's bigger achievement was in the food at Cafe Sbisa. Although it would be considered traditional by today's standards, the

Cafe Sbisa had balcony dining in addition to its Old New Orleans bistro-style interior. (Photo © Mitchel Osborne MMX)

menu was dramatically and delightfully different from those of the other French-Creole restaurants around town.

That menu included an innovation that soon spread to almost every restaurant in town. Cafe Sbisa was the first restaurant in the modern age to grill fish over an open fire (charcoal, at that). Hill got the idea from Bud's Broiler, the local hamburger chain. "I tried to find out where they got that charcoal grill," he said, "but they wouldn't tell me. Finally I tracked down a metalworking plant right here in the Quarter and they built one for me."

Also here was a raw bar with not just raw oysters but mussels and clams on the half-shell. Maryland-style crab cakes made their first New Orleans appearance at Cafe Sbisa. Beloved home-style Creole dishes that people knew well from home cooking, but that had never been seen in a restaurant, were numerous on the menu.

The chef who executed all this was Jason Clevenger. His mother, JoAnn Clevenger, was the owner of the nearby Abbey bar, and he

The mural behind the bar was painted by George Dureau. (Photo by George Long)

was familiar with the neighborhood scene. When JoAnn opened the Upperline five years later, Jason went with her as its first chef. The Upperline was in the front line of the gourmet Creole bistros that opened right and left Uptown in the mid-1990s. Most of them owed an inspirational debt to Cafe Sbisa.

Cafe Sbisa became very chic almost immediately after opening. Everybody went there. It was especially popular among the French Quarter's gay and arts communities, which made the place a headquarters.

That went on for a decade. Then Cafe Sbisa declined, probably because there were by then many restaurants copying its playbook. It closed in the early 1990s but returned shortly after. Charles and Craig Napoli—who owned The Boot Lounge near Tulane—bought it at an auction. They originally intended to sell the restaurant business and keep the real estate, but they came to like the dynamics of the place and kept it going. However, Cafe Sbisa never regained its hip edge and became a traditional Creole restaurant serving food that bordered on cliché, which wasn't a bad business move in that neighborhood, heavily trafficked as it is by visitors.

Cafe Sbisa attempted to reopen after Hurricane Katrina, but none of the several efforts stuck. It's such a fine restaurant property that it's hard to imagine that it won't be back. But at this writing, it's at best in suspended animation.

Cafe Sbisa's Trout Eugene

Pan-sautéed speckled trout with a lemon butter sauce, crabmeat, and shrimp is not a rare dish in white-tablecloth restaurants around town. It originally became famous under the name trout Eugene at the Caribbean Room at the Pontchartrain Hotel and, many years later, at Cafe Sbisa.

Sauce:
2 Tbs. extra-virgin olive oil
2 Tbs. chopped French shallots
12 medium (20-25 count) shrimp, peeled
½ cup dry white wine
3 Tbs. lemon juice, strained
½ cup shrimp or crab stock
1 stick butter
8 oz. lump crabmeat
6 sprigs flat-leaf Italian parsley, leaves only, chopped

1 Tbs. salt
¼ tsp. black pepper
1 cup flour
4 fillets speckled trout, about 6-8 oz. each
½ stick butter

1. Make the sauce first. Heat the olive oil in a skillet over medium-high heat. Add the shallots and shrimp, and cook until the shrimp turn pink. Lower the heat to medium.

2. Add the wine, lemon juice, and stock, and bring to a boil. Reduce the liquid to about one-fourth the original volume, then lower the heat to as low as it will go.

3. Cut the stick of butter into pats and whisk them in to make a creamy-looking sauce. Add the crabmeat, and agitate the pan until the crabmeat is heated through. Cover the pan and turn off the heat.

4. Mix the salt and pepper into the flour. Dust the trout fillets liberally in the seasoned flour.

5. Heat the ½ stick butter over medium-high heat until it shimmers. Sauté the trout, 2 fillets at a time, until golden brown—about 3 minutes per side.

6. Place a trout fillet on each serving plate and top with the sauce. Garnish with fresh chopped parsley.

Serves 4.

The atmosphere at the Caribbean Room in the Pontchartrain Hotel was a mix of Old World charm amid contemporary surroundings. (Photo by C. F. Weber, courtesy of Bergeron Photography)

★★★★

Caribbean Room
Garden District: Pontchartrain Hotel, 2031 St. Charles Avenue
1930s-94

For most of the history of New Orleans dining, only a few hotel restaurants had a serious local clientele. Of them, the most revered was the Caribbean Room at the Pontchartrain Hotel.

Created by Lyle Aschaffenburg—the hotel's founder, world traveler, and dedicated gourmet—the C-Room was one of the handsomest, most comfortable, and most romantic restaurants in town. The rooms had a soft glow: a color scheme of plush pink among walls of rich wood paneling that went a long way up to the ceiling. A fountain splashed in the center of the main room, and you could hear it, so quiet was the environment. Everything about the place spoke of luxury in the old manner.

The Caribbean Room's two longtime chefs were legendary practitioners of Creole cooking. Nathaniel Burton and his successor and protégé Louis Evans were unusual in having celebrity status in a time when few African-American chefs were known at all. They were encouraged by Aschaffenburg and his son Albert to maintain an unambiguously Creole flavor, and they did. At the same time, they also prepared a number of classic French dishes (one of which, trout Veronique, became the house specialty) and other dishes that Aschaffenburg found in his travels.

My favorite dish at the Pontchartrain (the hotel's name was synonymous with that of the restaurant) was crabmeat Remick, made with bacon, mustard, and chili sauce in an au gratin sort of way. They also made a great fish-with-everything (oysters, crab, and shrimp) dish called trout Eugene.

Many New Orleans families gathered for special occasions at the Caribbean Room in the Pontchartrain Hotel. (Photo by C. F. Weber, courtesy of Bergeron Photography)

The two most famous dishes at the C-Room, however, were both sweets. The first was the blueberry muffins that came in the bread basket. Those were so popular that they should have been on the hotel's crest. They were also much liked in the Pontchartrain's coffee shop at breakfast.

The other signature was mile-high ice cream pie, now widely copied by other restaurants. It had vanilla, chocolate, and peppermint ice cream in layers, with a meringue on top and chocolate sauce all around. It was designed to be split by at least two people. In my early twenties, I somehow managed to eat an entire slice of it. "My God!" said the waiter. "Do you know what we do to anyone who eats a whole piece of mile-high pie?" What? I asked. "We give you another slice on the house!"

For years, the Caribbean Room was famous for its Sunday-night buffets. That style of dinner service was almost unheard of in New Orleans. It was popular but—as all the regulars knew—not as good as the regular menu.

Service at the Caribbean Room was orchestrated by its incomparable maitre d', Douglas Leman. Douglas (many longtime customers never knew his last name) was the apotheosis of hospitality and style, always ready with an effusive gratefulness for the customers for just showing up. Douglas was at the front door of the Caribbean Room for most of his adult life. It seemed to me that his death was the final nail in the coffin of the Caribbean Room. The earlier departure of Chef Louis Evans didn't help.

The restaurant was already fading when the Aschaffenburgs sold the hotel in 1987. The new owners cut back the C-Room to a third of its former size, and the handwriting was on the wall. When it finally closed, few people noticed, so marginal had the restaurant become.

The Caribbean Room figured in many high moments in people's lives and the history of New Orleans dining. I have one myself: my first date with my wife, Mary Ann, was at the Caribbean Room, as Douglas smiled on.

Caribbean Room's Shrimp Saki

Shrimp Saki, despite the name, does not have any sort of Polynesian or Asian aspect. The name is the nickname of a Mrs. Sakowitz, who used to stay at the Pontchartrain Hotel every time she came to town. Shrimp Saki was on the menu at that hotel's restaurants for a long time.

Compound butter:
½ lb. softened butter
1 tsp. chopped garlic
1 tsp. chopped fresh basil
½ tsp. chopped fresh thyme
½ tsp. chopped fresh oregano
1 leaf fresh sage, chopped (optional)
1 tsp. paprika

2 Tbs. olive oil
24 medium (20-25 count) peeled, deveined shrimp
Salt
White pepper
3 oz. dry vermouth
½ cup softened compound butter

1. To make the compound butter, blend all ingredients together and refrigerate. It's better if blended a day or more before you use it.

2. Heat the olive oil in a small skillet until it smokes, then sauté the shrimp until they turn pink—about 2 minutes. Sprinkle on salt and pepper while sautéing.

3. Add the vermouth to the pan and remove the pan from the heat. Stir in the compound butter until it coats the shrimp. Spoon the extra sauce on the plate, and serve the shrimp in a row on top of the sauce.

Makes 4 to 6 appetizers or 2 entrees.

Mile-High Ice Cream Pie

The famous dessert at the Caribbean Room was really very simple: three kinds of ice cream layered under a thick crown of meringue. It's funny that nobody ever pointed this out, but mile-high ice cream pie was really an extravagant variation on baked Alaska. You do indeed bake it, ice cream and all. The Caribbean Room made its own chocolate sauce, and that was a big part of the goodness of the dessert.

The trouble with making it the way the Pontchartrain did involves the bottom layer of ice cream. The flavor was peppermint, and you will not find that in many stores, if at all. However, my daughter has been making her own peppermint ice cream since she was a tweener, and hers is perfect for this. We would make our own ice cream for that layer, certainly. She would also make the chocolate and vanilla layers. But there's nothing stopping you from using store-bought ice cream. Nor is there any reason to limit oneself to the Pontchartrain's flavors. It's really great using Angelo Brocato's spumoni.

I despise making piecrust, so I buy the kind that comes in sheets and fit it into a ten-inch pan, with enough overlap around the edges to hold the bottom layers in place.

1 qt. plus 1 pt. vanilla ice cream
6 standard peppermint candy canes
Flour
1 pkg. piecrust
1 qt. chocolate ice cream
10 egg whites
½ tsp. cream of tartar
½ cup sugar
2 tsp. vanilla extract

Chocolate sauce:
12 oz. Baker's semisweet chocolate squares
1¼ cups sugar
1½ cups heavy cream

1. Make the peppermint ice cream first. (In fact, it's best to do this a day or two ahead of time.) Take 1 qt. vanilla ice cream out of the freezer and allow it to soften on the counter for about 10 minutes. Meanwhile, put the candy canes into a food-storage bag. On a plastic cutting board, pound the bag of candy with a meat mallet until the canes are broken into tiny pieces.

2. Scoop about two-thirds of the softened vanilla ice cream into a bowl. Stir the crushed candy canes into the softened ice cream until well distributed. Cover with plastic wrap and put the bowl into the freezer.

3. When you're ready to make the pie, preheat the oven to 425 degrees. Clean the counter and dust with flour. Unroll the pie dough and lay it out on the counter. Place a 9-inch pie pan upside down on top of it,

and cut a piece of dough in a circle 1 inch beyond the edge of the pan. (Use 2 sheets of pie dough if necessary.)

4. Grease the pie pan lightly. Push the pie dough into it. Squeeze pleats in the part that extends above the edge, so that it forms an upright collar above the pan. Sprinkle ½ cup dry red beans or pie weights into the crust, and bake the crust until light brown. Remove from the oven and allow to cool for ½ hour.

5. When the crust is cool, remove all the ice creams from the freezer and let them soften a bit in their containers on the counter.

6. In the meantime, put the egg whites into a clean bowl. Make sure no yolk has gotten into the whites. Add the cream of tartar to the bowl.

7. Clean the beaters of your electric mixer to remove any fat that may be on them. Beat the egg whites with the bowl tipped a little, with the beaters right in the pool of liquid egg whites at the bottom. Beat until the foam forms soft peaks. Add the sugar and the vanilla and continue beating until the peaks get stiff.

8. Preheat the oven to broil (top heat only) at 425 degrees. Remove the beans from the cool pie shell. Put the peppermint ice cream into the piecrust, and spread it out to a uniform layer with a rubber spatula. Next, layer in about three-fourths of the chocolate ice cream. (Save the rest for a guilty late-night snack.) Cover the chocolate ice cream with the vanilla ice cream. Finally, spoon the egg-white meringue over the top, forming a high dome of meringue, preferably with a lot of a little peaks.

9. Put the pie into the oven. Broil for 1 or 2 minutes, until the meringue peaks are distinctly browned and the rest of the meringue lightly brown.

10. Immediately put the pie into the coldest part of the freezer, and leave it there for at least 3 hours, until all the ice cream has hardened.

11. To make the chocolate sauce, put all of the sauce ingredients into a bowl set on a pan of simmering water (or a double boiler). Stir constantly as soon as the chocolate starts to melt, and continue until the sauce is smooth.

12. To serve, remove the pie from the pan and place it on a flat plate or serving board. Heat a French chef's knife in hot water, and cut the pie into 6 slices. Each slice will serve 2 people. Drizzle the chocolate sauce over the top and serve with salad forks and tablespoons.

Serves 6-12.

Ad for Castillo's. (Courtesy of New Orleans Magazine)

★★★
Castillo's
French Quarter: 620 Conti Street
1964-2000

When Castillo's opened, Mexican food was not much eaten around New Orleans, save by a few adventuresome gourmets, transplants from Texas and the Southwest, and Latinos. For most Orleanians, Mexican food meant hot tamales—specifically, the very un-Mexican kind sold by Manuel's and other street-corner vendors.

The few Mexican restaurants in those years did little to encourage growth in their market. The discovery by Chi-Chi's and its ilk that Mexican food could be pasteurized for American tastes was still in the future.

Nevertheless, a few good Mexican places could be found in 1960s New Orleans if you looked for them. The best was Castillo's.

Owner Carlos Castillo was a unique character. Well educated, he maintained a small library of books on many abstruse subjects next to his table in the dining room. He could talk for a long time on the history of Mexico and its cuisine and give you full dogma about how authentic Mexican food needed to be cooked.

The restaurant was also distinctive. It was in an 1820s building on the corner of Conti and Exchange Alley. Windowed doors lined two of its walls. If it had been legal back then, it could have had a great sidewalk dining scene under its balcony and on the alley. When I first went there in the 1970s, it already seemed much in need of a renovation. No such renovation ever came.

None of the regular customers seemed to care. Almost all either lived or worked in the French Quarter. A place like this was a hard sell to tourists, who come to town for Creole cooking and seafood.

The menu didn't change much over the twenty-five-year span during which I dined at Castillo's. That menu was unintentionally prophetic. Many of the ingredients, dishes, and styles are now hot stuff in the nouvelle restaurants of our day. The first place I ever saw the word "cilantro" was on Castillo's menu. He also used an ingredient called "culantro" and said it was so important to the house soup that he grew it himself. This was not a typo in cilantro but an entirely different herb.

The soup involved was caldo xochil—a light chicken broth with a very slight spiciness and a hard-to-pin-down herbaceousness. It must have been the culantro.

Castillo's was one of the earliest Mexican restaurants in New Orleans. (Courtesy of New Orleans Magazine)

Most of the menu would be familiar now. But even the most prosaic dishes were prepared distinctively, with a good deal more work done in the background than is typical. The enchiladas de res, for example, sound like plain old beef enchiladas. Their filling, however, consisted of a beguilingly seasoned ground beef that tasted much different from standard taco meat. The sauce was a fresh ranchera sauce, redolent of tomatoes and peppers.

Castillo was precise about the provenance of his cuisine. The description of the enchiladas Texanas, for instance, all but apologizes for the fact that they're covered with chili con carne. Which, Castillo wanted you to know, is not Mexican but Texan. Other dishes are attributed to the northern provinces, the Maya, the Yucatan, or the coast.

The great dish at Castillo's is still a rarity around New Orleans. Mole poblano, made from scratch from cocoa, peppers, peanuts, sesame, oil, and herbs, accompanied roast chicken or cheese enchiladas and lifted both to an astonishing goodness.

Chilmole de puerco used another unique, jet-black sauce. The peppers in it were roasted to that color before entering the saucepan. The resulting sauce was spicy with an edge of caramelized pepper fruit. "That's strictly a Mayan dish," Castillo told me.

Pollo pibil was also Mayan. It included achiote and orange peel in the sauce. It's served stew style over rice. The only other place I ever encountered anything like it was in the Yucatan.

Even the eggs were worth ordering. Huevos rancheros weren't scrambled but shirred (baked in a casserole) before being topped with ranchera sauce.

Castillo's downfalls were inconsistency and terrible service. Although its fans said that both of these complaints were overreactions to the authentic Mexican lifestyle, that didn't help business. Still, even with sparse crowds, Carlos Castillo kept it going until his health declined. For awhile, his son operated a second Castillo's in the building where Restaurant August is now.

If Castillo's were still around, even with the same menu, it would still be on the cutting edge by New Orleans standards. And it would still be a contender for best Mexican restaurant in town.

★★★
Chez Helene
Downtown: 1540 North Robertson Street
1964-95

In the early 1970s, when Richard Collin encouraged a lot of white people to go to black-owned restaurants for the first time in their lives, Chez Helene was one of the three great New Orleans soul-food restaurants. (The other two were Buster Holmes and Dooky Chase.)

Chez Helene's Chef Austin Leslie was famous for his fried chicken. (From the collection of Phil Johnson)

REMEMBERING CHEZ HELENE

An Interview with Austin Leslie

Here are excerpts from a 2002 interview recalling Austin Leslie's early career, his days at Chez Helene, and the New Orleans black dining scene before the Civil Rights Bill was passed:

Q: What's the origin of Chez Helene?

A: It was named after the original owner, my Aunt Helen. It means the "House of Helen." My aunt's name was Helen Pollock. She had four restaurants, including one on Rampart, before she opened Chez Helene. My aunt had never worked downtown in her life but a fella called Joe Mancuso recognized the quality that she was doing. She always worked hard and so he decided to finance her in a restaurant. He provided, in fact, not only the place, he provided the house next door for her to move in. There was a little apartment next door to the restaurant.

Q: Describe Chez Helene's décor.

A: When we first started we had pictures of some French Quarter scenes. We had red and white checkered tablecloths.

Q: Weren't your customers primarily black at first?

A: It was all black and very few whites. I had a lot of friends who worked at Pat O'Brien's. They would come in after work. And so they went out and spread the word to out-of-towners. The out-of-towners would ask them,

Towards the end of his long career, Chef Austin Leslie worked at Jacques-Imo's Cafe and Pampy's Restaurant. (Photo © Kevin R. Roberts)

Its chef, Austin Leslie, was an icon of Creole cooking until his life ended in September 2005, in one of the worst Hurricane Katrina tragedies in the culinary world.

Chez Helene's roots go back to 1942. Austin's aunt Helen Pollock began a cafe in the Central Business District called Howard's Eatery. From the time he was a very young man, Austin helped his aunt, then began cooking full time. His first job supplied him with the secret of great fried chicken. Chef Bill Turner taught him that at a restaurant called Portia's (it was on the corner of Lafayette and South Rampart and was terrific until it closed in the 1980s). He also worked in the kitchen at D. H. Holmes department store, which had a major restaurant operation on Canal Street.

Austin's Aunt Helen shut down Howard's Eatery and opened Chez Helene in 1964. She brought Austin in as the chef, and from that moment on it was essentially his restaurant. He bought it outright when his aunt retired in 1975.

By then, Chez Helene's clientele had grown far beyond the African-American community, and even New Orleans. People came from all over the world to eat there. Food writers also gave it a lot of glowing attention. In 1987, Chez Helene became the model for the network television comedy *Frank's Place*.

The food lived up to Chef Helene's fame. The menu was large, and many of the dishes on it seemed more appropriate for a gourmet French-Creole establishment in the Quarter than the neighborhood place that Chez Helene was. You could start with gumbo, or you

"Where's a good restaurant?" They'd say Chez Helene. We were at 1540 North Robertson Street, fifteen blocks from the Mississippi River and fifteen blocks from Canal Street, so it was really a nice short distance. We opened in '64, then in 1971 Richard Collin put out a book called *The New Orleans Underground Gourmet* and he made us number one. Before *The New Orleans Underground Gourmet*, writer Calvin Trillin came; in fact, *Redbook* wrote us up first. I started to put on the menu dishes I'd learned from working at D. H. Holmes. I started off with oysters Rockefeller and trout Meunière, trout Marguery. It was very new to blacks, but the whites heard about it, and they had a fella from the *Times-Picayune* named Jack Duarte, who wrote me up. So people just started coming, but we were ready for them. When they had the Black Shriners in town, in 1975, they spent some money! I was able to put another dining room next door and so everything was working out nicely. Then the neighborhood got kind of rough around there.

Q: Tell me about the CBS comedy *Frank's Place*.

A: CBS sent Tim Reid and his wife, Daphne, down to the French Quarter to pick out a restaurant. He had his own idea and he came to me on a Thursday night and I had such a "rainbow" atmosphere. People were waiting in the bar and we had every nationality. Reid and his wife were sitting in the bar and we recognized them. They went into an extreme corner of the restaurant so they could get a nice view of everything and called me to the table. They asked if I would like to go to Hollywood. I said yes, and they said they were going to send a ticket. So I went and on the set they had a man dressed like me and everything. And I was in the kitchen showing them my mannerisms and showing how to make dishes. It was real wonderful. They wanted a lot of stories and everybody that was in the sitcom came to the restaurant. So it was real good fun.

Q: How did fried chicken come to be your specialty?

A: The fried chicken came from Portia's. The owner, Mrs. Ethel Williams, has a daughter named Portia. She had two restaurants, Portia's Number One and Number Two. Her husband's name was Bill Turner and had me working at the Portia's on Rampart Street. I started cutting his chickens. Everybody used to beg this man, asking how to fry or what he does to fry this chicken. And all of a sudden he told me, "Come here; let me show you something," and he showed me how to fry chicken.

Q: You are also known for your stuffed bell pepper.

A: Working at D. H. Holmes taught me how to make a dressing, I mean from paying attention. I used to watch this fella that was really the "dressing man." He used stale French bread and all the seasonings, some eggs in it, and I would put ground beef and shrimp in it.

Q: Describe what the dining scene was like for somebody who was black who lived in New Orleans during the 1940s, '50s, and '60s. What was it like; where did you go to eat?

could have oysters Rockefeller and Bienville. The main course could be (and probably was) the famous fried chicken or trout Marguery. Austin really could cook all of that, and sometimes he did it better than the fancy places.

Back to the fried chicken. Chez Helene's style was set before the time when crispy coatings came into vogue for fried chicken. Their chicken was greaseless and far from soggy, but the crust was light and thin, never crunchy. What made the chicken good was the flavor of the seasonings in the coating, which was both spicy and herbal.

Chez Helene also predated the advent of Popeyes and its much spicier chicken. The balance was just right.

The classic Chez Helene chicken platter included a stuffed pepper and potato salad. My own preference was for the chicken and the equally good red beans, a perfect combination.

They also fried and broiled excellent fish, oysters, and shrimp. The menu was a catalog of New Orleans everyday dishes, made better than anywhere except your own mother's kitchen (if you were lucky). All of this was abetted by the personality of Austin Leslie, who in his captain's cap and with his mutton-chop sideburns became a familiar and friendly face.

All this great food and widespread fame were not enough to overcome the decline in the neighborhood. When cabdrivers refused to go to Chez Helene, the place found it hard to make ends meet. Austin closed Chez Helene in 1995 and tried reopening in a couple of other locations, none of which worked. He became an itinerant freelance chef, making particular marks in the early days of Jacques-Imo's (his fried chicken recipe lives on there) and on frequent tours to Europe, especially Denmark. He was the chef at Pampy's in Gentilly when the hurricane hit.

Austin was trapped in the attic of his house during the floods following Katrina. The temperature rose to 120 degrees. He was in bad shape when rescuers pulled him out. A month later, he died in a hospital in Atlanta. He was seventy-two.

★★★★

Christian's
Mid-City: 3835 Iberville Street
1973-2005

Among Hurricane Katrina's restaurant victims, none is more lamented than Christian's. Beyond being a great place to dine and socialize, it was also unforgettable. I mean, really: a restaurant named Christian's in a former church? With family connections to Galatoire's, to boot? Its fame was inevitable.

As memorable as Christian's was, its early history is largely forgotten. Latter-day customers were surprised to learn that it originally opened in a nondescript, hidden building off Veterans Boulevard, near Bonnabel Boulevard. The menu was the same as the one that became famous in the church a few years later, cooked by the same chef and every bit as well.

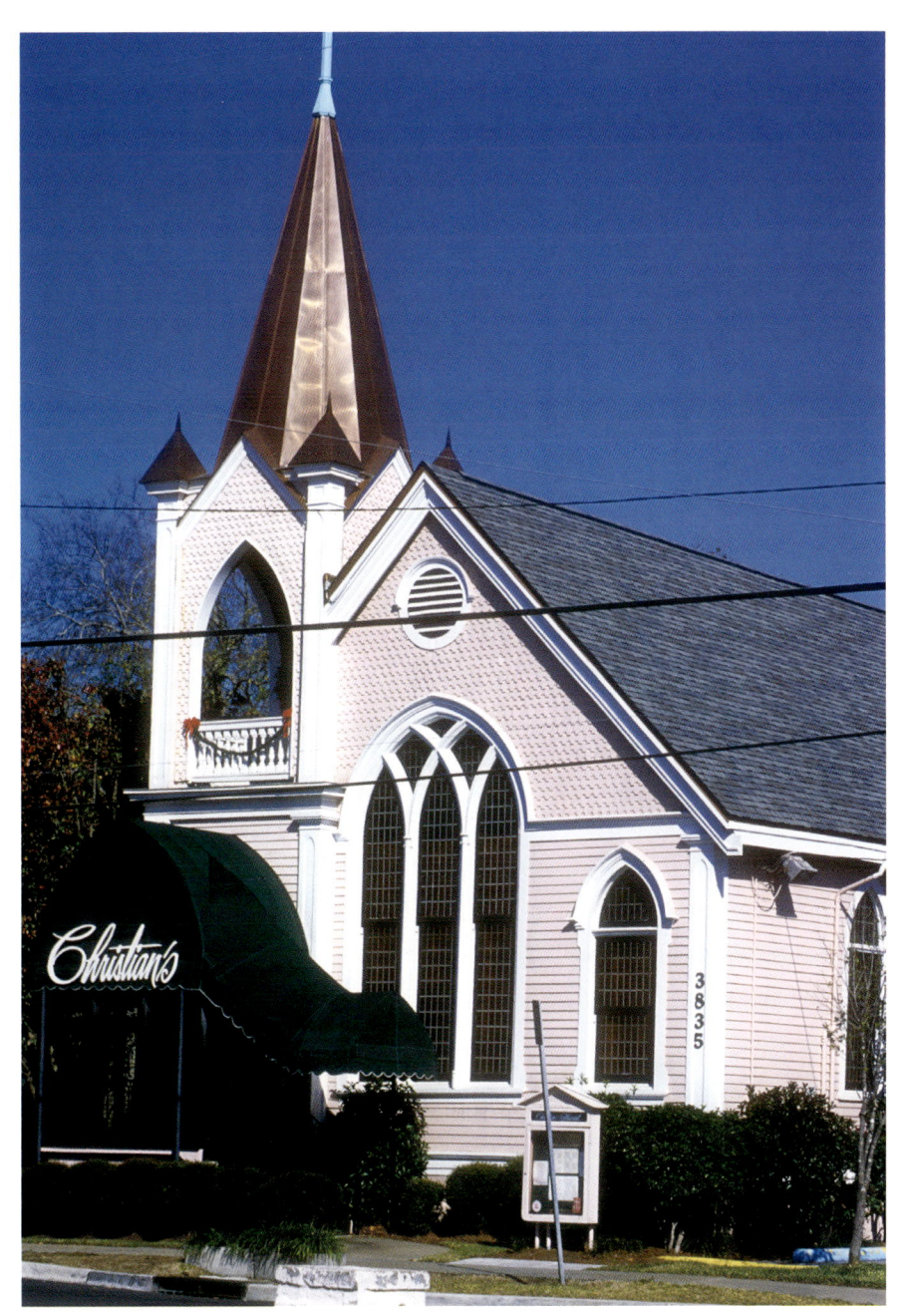

The exterior of Christian's. Truly a coincidence were the facts that one of the owner's names was Christian (Ansel) and the restaurant was located in a former church. (Photo © Kevin R. Roberts)

Christian's never caught on in Metairie. It suffered an effect familiar to other suburban restaurant operators. If a Metairie or West Bank or North Shore restaurant serves exactly the same food in exactly the same environment as a restaurant Uptown or in the French Quarter, it will be expected to charge something like a third less for it. And people wouldn't dress up to go there. After all, it was "only in Metairie."

There never was any question about the restaurant's credentials. Christian Ansel is the grandson of Justin Galatoire, who was part of the early management of the vaunted namesake restaurant. Chris (I never heard anyone call him Christian) was one of the managers

A: When I was a kid we didn't have appetizers; we didn't have any such thing as an appetizer. When we went to the table we just kept eating the gumbo until it was gone. We had other food, like fried chicken, baked macaroni. In black restaurants you would get the gumbo or red beans and rice; they call it soul food but at the time we were just calling it food that sticks to the ribs: pickled tips, pickled tails, ham hocks, cabbage, spareribs, barbecue ribs. I mean that was all over the city and it was plentiful, so there was no such thing as not going out. The weekend was really the time for blacks to really go out, and they went to places like Dooky Chase or Peck's on Orleans Street. They had Levata's and Portia's. They had a fella way ahead of his time, Hayes with Hayes Chicken Shack. It was on Louisiana Avenue. He made a beautiful dining room; a man had to come in there with a coat. The place was all blue with white tablecloths. There was also Paul Gross' Chicken Coop, right there on Bienville and North Roman.

Q: Tell me about South Rampart Street.

A: Portia's was on the 300 block. They had Little Jane across the street from Portia's. Then they had the Sunset Grill, up on Howard Avenue right across from the train station. They must have had about thirty restaurants. They had a restaurant called Sam's that you went to for beautiful roast-beef sandwiches. They had another place on Rampart called Eli's. You had blacks on one side, and whites on the other side. Only air-conditioned place in that block.

Then they had another place called Virginia Kitchen right at Dauphine and Iberville. They sold a hell of a roast-beef sandwich—real juicy, you know, thin sliced, and the meat was so tender. That was the sandwich you got when you went there and then you'd go right to the Palace movie show with it wrapped up.

—Peggy Scott Laborde

of Galatoire's for years, even though his real profession was as an engineer.

Chris tried to push Galatoire's forward a bit. He met with stony resistance from older family members. He decided that the future as he saw it would not come anytime soon at Galatoire's. He left the family business and opened his own restaurant, in partnership with fellow engineer Henry Bergeron.

In Christian's kitchen from the outset was Chef Roland Huet. He was from Pau, France—not far from the ancestral hometown of the Galatoires. Roland had worked at Galatoire's and understood perfectly where Chris was coming from.

Chef Roland was among the last of his breed of chefs. French cuisine was being modernized, and chefs who stayed with the classic Escoffier-era styles were disappearing. Chef Roland could cook anything and did—even if a recipe took two days. He laid down a foundation of French-Creole dishes in the style of Galatoire's. Then he began inventing the dishes that made Christian's famous.

At the center of his menu was one of those two-day recipes. When Christian's opened, no restaurant in New Orleans routinely made its

Christian's owners retained the church's yellow stained-glass windows. (Photo © Kevin R. Roberts)

own demi-glace—the classic reduction of veal stock to a near jelly, the essence of beef flavor. In fact, almost nobody knew what demi-glace was. Roland used it as the base for a brilliant signature dish, filet mignon à la Bayou la Loutre. The filet was stuffed with oysters, and more oysters were poached in the intense demi-glace sauce. Oysters and beef are a rare but marvelous combination. No restaurant ever did it better than Christian's.

Another of Chef Roland's dishes that will survive him (he died in 2009) was his smoked soft-shell crab. It took the chef months and four different kinds of smokers, but he finally developed a method. He put live soft-shell crabs into a cold smoker for about fifteen minutes. They would come out smoked but still alive. Then he'd fry them and serve them with a Galatoire's-style brown butter. They were so delicious and light that you inhaled them.

The menu was riddled with other great and unique creations: oysters Roland (baked with mushrooms, breadcrumbs, parsley, and garlic), stuffed fish (rolled around a filling of rich, crabmeat-and-shrimp-riddled béchamel), braised veal sweetbreads with port and demi-glace, and veal with morel mushrooms.

As brilliant as all this was, Chris and Henry knew Metairie wasn't the place for it. They began looking for a new location. They found a small, vacant church in Mid-City. They took a look, got some opinions from architects, and worked out a price with the congregation (which had moved to bigger quarters).

"The big question was, could we get away with opening a restaurant named Christian's in a church, without offending a lot of people?" said Chris. "We decided to go for it. Nobody ever told us anything untoward."

That was probably because the church aspect was soft-pedaled. Pews were turned into banquettes, and the pulpit became the maitre d's stand. But waitresses didn't dress in nuns' habits or anything like that. How hard does one need to sell the concept in a place with a steeple above its entrance?

The new Christian's won architectural awards. And the customers were delighted. Tourists heard there was a must-try restaurant in a church and booked tables at Christian's before they knew where it was or what it served. All this, with the existing great cooking, turned Christian's into a tremendous success.

Maybe a little too tremendous—reservations were hard to come by. The tables were jammed in the way they were at Galatoire's, which is to say that you were practically in the lap of the person next to you. This was especially true in the pew-banquettes. For this and other issues, some people complained. The reviews were less than reverent. Chris and Henry reacted at one point by banning restaurant critics—myself included—for a few years.

They mellowed later. A number of tables were removed, and the restaurant became much more pleasant. Meanwhile, Chef Roland kept inventing his French-Creole food.

Christian's peaked just before the Uptown gourmet Creole bistros took over the dining scene. It began a long, slow decline—not in quality but in volume. In the late 1990s, Chris Ansel retired and sold his half of Christian's to Henry. Chris then became involved in Galatoire's again, behind the scenes. He was to a great extent the force behind the tremendous changes at Galatoire's at the turn of the twenty-first century.

Hurricane Katrina did major flood damage to Christian's. Henry Bergeron—who by that time was in his seventies—was so depressed by the disaster that he never reopened the restaurant, even though he and his family don't consider Christian's dead. They did, however, sell the iconic building to a Baton Rouge seafood merchant, who has reopened the place as Redemption.

Christian's Oysters Roland

½ cup water
4 dozen medium oysters
1 bunch curly-leaf parsley, bottom stems removed
3 cloves garlic
8 oz. small mushrooms, well washed
1 tsp. salt
1 tsp. black pepper
Generous pinch nutmeg
1 lb. softened butter
1 cup French-bread crumbs

Preheat the oven to 400 degrees.

1. Bring 1 water to a light boil in a small skillet. Add the oysters and poach for 2 minutes. Strain the pan contents, reserving the liquid. Return the liquid to a light boil and reduce by about a third.

2. Put the parsley, garlic, mushrooms, salt, pepper, and nutmeg into a food processor, and process into a very fine mixture. Add the butter and process into a coarse, gritty puree.

3. Add the breadcrumbs and the reduced stock from the oysters and process only long enough to mix everything thoroughly.

4. Place 6 oysters in the bottom of each of 8 small gratin dishes. With a spatula, lightly pack down enough sauce to cover the oysters completely, filling the dishes nearly to the top. (You can prepare the dish to this point ahead of time and hold in the refrigerator. Take them out of the refrigerator a half-hour before baking.)

5. Bake the gratins of oysters until the tops are distinctly browned and crusty and the sauce is heaving and steaming. Serve immediately with hot French bread for getting up the extra sauce.

Makes 8 appetizers.

★★★
Clarence and Lefty's
Gentilly: 1934 Almonaster Street
1932-77

Clarence and Lefty's looms large in my personal culinary annals. It was the place where I had my first roast-beef poor boy, when I was about ten years old. That sandwich would set the standard for me for the rest of my life. I also credit it as the first step on my long road of eating for pleasure and talking about it.

Clarence and Lefty's was in the center of the Eighth Ward, in a wedge-shaped block between Almonaster and Franklin at Prieur. It made Uglesich's look like Commander's Palace: concrete floors, a bar full of whiskey and cigarette smells, and the kind of characters that Bunny Matthews captures in his cartoons on all the stools and at all the tables. (In fact, Bunny's Vic 'n' Natly series was modeled on Clarence and Lefty's.)

My parran, Uncle Billy, was one of those characters. He was a longshoreman, burly, gregarious, and always laughing. Clarence and Lefty's was where he drank beer with his buddies every weekend. Dozens of bars like that were scattered throughout the city. Most of them served some kind of food.

Uncle Billy had me in tow one night and took me along to Clarence and Lefty's. He thought I was too skinny. "I'll give you something to put some meat on your bones, Tommy!" he said and ordered up a roast-beef poor boy. And there it was: a good foot long, thick with roast beef and drooling with brown gravy.

I took a bite. Uncle Billy smiled and went back to the bar and his beer. I ate the whole thing—and half of another one. I couldn't remember loving the flavor of anything this much.

Fifteen or so years passed. I ate many poor boys before I was in Clarence and Lefty's again. I was there to check out a rumor that this was the best roast-beef poor boy in town. It indeed had what I thought of as the classic flavor profile: the perfect balance of meat, gravy, mayonnaise, pickles, etc. In fact, there was something vaguely familiar about the sandwich and the place, but I couldn't dope it out.

I gave a glowing report about Clarence and Lefty's on the radio. A couple of days later, Uncle Billy called me. "Hey! I heard you went back to Clarence and Lefty's! Remember that night I brought you there and you ate two po' boys?" He started laughing. "I told you it was good!"

Fast forward to 1987. Sometime in the 1970s, Clarence and Lefty's went away. I kept talking about it now and then on the radio with people who liked to reminisce about favorite but extinct restaurants.

One morning I got a call from Alma Bourgeois. "I think you'd know who I am if I told you I'm Mrs. Lefty, of Clarence and Lefty's," she said. She then went on to tell me the real recipe for the roast beef as she cooked it. And she was the one who did, every day. It had nothing to do with Coca-Cola in the gravy (a widespread rumor) or anything like that. Her recipe involved fifty pounds of beef, plus other ingredients by the beer mug (a standard measure at Clarence and Lefty's).

It's a lot of work, but it's the only way to reproduce what I still

---

A BITE OF HISTORY

Chris Steaks
(Near the Fair Grounds)
1100 North Broad Street

Chris Matulich ran Chris Steaks on North Broad Street for more than thirty-five years. According to The New Orleans Underground Gourmet, Matulich served "spectacular steaks at reasonable prices." Lyonaise potatoes was a signature dish. When Matulich decided to retire, he sold his business to Ruth Fertel, who went on to develop a national steak restaurant chain. (Courtesy of Nick Matulich)

The exterior of the original Chris Steaks on North Broad Street at Ursulines Avenue. (Courtesy of Randy Fertel)

—Peggy Scott Laborde

think of as the definitive roast-beef poor-boy flavor. Here's the recipe as she gave it to me.

Clarence and Lefty's Roast-Beef Poor Boy

The critical difference between Mrs. Lefty's recipe and others I've seen was this instruction: "Don't be afraid to use a lot of water. The beef should almost float." It's a pot roast, really.

6-8 lb. beef chuck or round (preferably inside round)
5 cloves garlic, quartered
1 medium onion, sliced thin
3 Tbs. salt
1 cup standard barbecue sauce (not smoke flavored)
½ cup Worcestershire sauce
2 bay leaves
Mayonnaise
French bread
Lettuce
Sliced tomatoes
Sliced pickles

Preheat the oven to 350 degrees.

1. With the point of a knife, punch slits into the top of the beef. Insert the quartered cloves of garlic.

2. Cover the bottom of a large Dutch oven with the sliced onions. Place the beef atop the onions. Scatter the salt, barbecue, and Worcestershire sauce over the beef.

3. Pour ½ gal. water around (not over) the beef. Put the pan into the oven, uncovered, and roast until the top of the beef turns noticeably brown—about 45 minutes.

4. Turn the beef inside the pan 180 degrees. Add enough water so that the beef seems nearly weightless, as if it were about to float. Continue cooking, turning the beef about 90 degrees every 45 minutes, for 3 hours.

5. Check the doneness of the beef. It should have a blush of pink in the center—about 160 degrees on a meat thermometer. If it's not there, keep going, but know that the speed of the cooking will increase, so check it more often.

6. Remove the beef from the Dutch oven onto a pan, to collect the juices. Pour the stock from the Dutch oven into a large saucepan. Add the juices that come out of the roast. Add the bay leaves and bring the pan contents to a simmer. Cook until reduced to about one-quarter of what you started with—about 6-8 cups of liquid. Strain.

7. Optional: Make a medium-dark roux with ½ cup each flour and vegetable oil. When done, add about ½ cup reduced stock to the roux and whisk until smooth. Use this mixture to thicken the stock to gravy consistency.

8. Adjust the gravy seasoning with salt and pepper. To make 1 poor boy, slice the roast beef as thinly as you can, and dip into the gravy before putting the beef onto one-half of a mayonnaise-spread French bread sliced end to end. Spread the other side with mayonnaise and add the lettuce, tomatoes, and pickles. Put the sides together and place the whole sandwich into a preheated 450-degree oven until toasted. Eat with a root beer or a not-so-root beer.

Serves about 20 to 24.

★★★
Compagno's
Riverbend: 7839 St. Charles Avenue
1925-2001

Over the years, seven restaurants named Compagno's have opened around New Orleans. Most were Uptown. Two were on Fern Street. Some family connections existed among them, but it didn't show up in the food, at least not at the three Compagno's in business when I started covering the restaurant scene. All were neighborhood cafes, mixing New Orleans and Italian dishes. One Compagno's was on the corner of State and Magazine streets, where WOW Wingery is now. One of the two on Fern was on the corner of Panola. I lived two blocks from that one in the early 1970s, but after a couple of meals there I never went back.

The best of the Compagno's—on St. Charles Avenue two blocks from South Carrollton Avenue—survived years after all the others were gone. It not only had good food but one of the most personable chefs in that segment of the biz. Sal Compagno took the restaurant over from his parents, but it was his wife, Maria, who made Compagno's a great place to eat.

Compagno's menu had two specialties, and Maria was adept at both. The Italian food was the Sicilian-inspired New Orleans kind but with a distinction. Maria always made her own pasta for things such as ravioli, at a time when almost no other restaurant did that. Everything in her kitchen was made from scratch, from the sauces to the fantastically garlicky, herbal olive salad on the muffulettas.

The other emphasis was seafood. Compagno's served as much variety there as any local seafood restaurant. A sign in the dining room declared that no seafood was seasoned or breaded—let alone cooked—until someone ordered it. That was very clear in what came to the table. It was always golden brown, greaseless, fresh, and light.

The dining room looked almost exactly as Vincent's does now: a brick divider ran through the center of the room, dividing the bar (where there were always a few regulars having a drink or a beer) from the tables.

Compagno's was inexpensive and generous—a combination of merits that made it a perennial favorite among Tulane and Loyola students and faculty. It was particularly busy on Sunday nights, when it was one of the few restaurants open Uptown.

No matter when you went, Sal and Maria were there. In a way, they still are. Maria was very pleased to sell the restaurant to Vincent Catalanotto, who, she says, continued to run the kind of restaurant she could be proud of, even with a different style of food and service. She loved her restaurant and its regulars and still talks about them all the time. It took a few years, and it's hard to find, but her cookbook is an accurate rendering of the kind of food Maria Compagno cooked.

★★★
Corinne Dunbar's
Lee Circle Area: 1716 St. Charles Avenue (later 1617)
1935-87

Corinne Dunbar's was unique. Its customers found the restaurant's story so engaging that they kept it full all the time, not minding that the food, environment, and service were much less than memorable. The effect was so pervasive that, a quarter-century after it served its last meal, people still ask me about it often.

Oysters Dunbar was a signature dish of the restaurant. (Courtesy of WYES-TV)

Corinne Dunbar ran an antique-filled restaurant that made patrons feel more like guests in someone's home than in a restaurant. (Courtesy of Cheri Banos Schneider)

Corinne Dunbar opened a restaurant in the grand parlor of her own home, not because she wanted to but because she had to. It was the middle of the Great Depression and her husband was ill. Corinne was a cultured member of New Orleans society and wanted to remain part of it. So she brought her skills as a hostess to bear in the service of dinner to whoever was willing to pay for the pleasure.

Hence was born—well, let's not call it a gimmick, although it would appear to be that in its later years. Corinne Dunbar served her customers as if they were guests at a party in her home. Everyone arrived at the same time, was greeted by a maid and a butler, and was seated in one of the Belle Epoque-style parlors. Then the set menu of the night was served to every guest. Guests paid discreetly on the way in, preserving the illusion all the way through the evening.

This conceit was so delightful for so many diners that a reservation at Corinne Dunbar's became impossible to secure on short notice. This was especially true in the decade following World War II, when gourmets flocked to New Orleans for a taste of Europe. (Europe itself was out of business at the time.) Dunbar's was declared by a wide range of famous people to be the best restaurant in New Orleans and perhaps the entire world.

It wasn't, not, at least, if you were primarily interested in the goodness of the food you ate. Although it does seem that Corinne Dunbar's chefs in its prime years could cook with the best of them, the creative flow had stopped long before I was able to get there.

Corinne Dunbar died in 1947, but the restaurant had many years ahead of it. Her daughter took over. She altered nothing. The restaurant changed hands again (although still within the family) in 1956. Jimmy Plauche was the final owner. He is best remembered for moving the restaurant a block away to a somewhat larger but just as authentically Creole mansion. He also instituted the sale of alcoholic beverages at Dunbar's for the first time.

DUNBAR'S

1617 St. Charles Avenue
New Orleans, La. 70130

Distinctive Creole Cuisine
525-0689 Reservations Requested 525-23
James J. Plauché, Jr., Owner & Manag

A St. Charles Avenue mansion was the home of Corinne Dunbar's. (From the collection of Peggy Scott Laborde)

The local customers (although not the tourists) drifted away in the 1960s, a decline accelerated by reviews from Richard Collin in 1970. Few restaurants received commentary as harsh as Collin dealt Corinne Dunbar's, which he thought was outmoded, corny, and tasteless. The invective was so strong that Plauche ran retaliatory ads in the newspaper. They didn't name Collin, but it was clear who the ads' target was.

Nevertheless, Corinne Dunbar's managed to hang on to a semblance of culinary reputation because of a single, undeniably excellent dish. Oysters Dunbar brought the bivalves together in a sauce involving artichokes, mushrooms, and breadcrumbs. Even Collin admitted it was delicious. And unlike most of the ever-changing menu, it was available every night. Dunbar's was also famous for gumbo z'herbes—the gumbo made with more greens than anything else. Indeed, it was one of the few restaurants that kept that dish alive into a new generation of eaters.

If Corinne Dunbar's were resurrected now as it was in its glory days (the building is still there, ready for service), it's hard to imagine that even its most avid fans would go there much. It was just chugging along when it closed in the late 1980s. By that time, dining styles had changed dramatically from what they were just a decade before. Old-fashioned formality was waning fast. But past diners who didn't have to see that happen carry nothing but golden memories of the restaurant where you dined as if you were in an old, formerly wealthy friend's home.

Corinne Dunbar's Oysters Dunbar

Corinne Dunbar's most famous dish was an oyster-and-artichoke casserole. The original recipe is floating around out there, but I've made it often enough that I've polished it a little, this way:

2 Tbs. salt
Juice of ½ lemon
4 large artichokes
1 stick butter
2 Tbs. flour
¼ cup thinly sliced green onion
Oyster water, up to 1 cup
2 dozen oysters
Salt and pepper
¼ tsp. Tabasco
½ cup breadcrumbs

Preheat the oven to 350 degrees.

1. Bring a large pot of water to a boil with 2 Tbs. salt and the lemon juice. Cook the artichokes until tender, then remove from the water and allow to cool.

2. Scrape the meat from the outer artichoke leaves. When you get to the hearts, pull them apart and keep the whole leaves. Also chop the artichoke bottom into medium dice.

3. In a skillet, heat the butter until it bubbles, and stir in the flour to form a loose blond roux. Add the green onions and cook until tender.

4. Lower the heat to medium low. Add the oyster water and whisk until the pan contents are as thick as molasses. Add the oysters, and cook for another 2 minutes. Add salt, pepper, and Tabasco to taste.

5. Scatter the reserved artichoke pieces in a baking dish. Add the skillet contents. Top with breadcrumbs. Bake for about 12-15 minutes, until the breadcrumbs are browned and the rapid bubbling of the liquid contents has begun to slow.

6. Allow to cool for about 5 minutes. Serve in small dishes with pasta Bordelaise or as an appetizer.

Serves 4 to 6.

★★

The Cosmopolitan
Metairie: 1918 Veterans Boulevard
1977-78

The left side of the menu was a substantial collection of Greek dishes. The right side enumerated just as many Mexican platters. There were two chef-owners, one Greek, one Mexican. Both went on to open their own restaurants, each with only his own cuisine. The world was a better place for it.

★★★★★

Crozier's
New Orleans East: Lake Forest Boulevard at Bundy Road
New Orleans East: Read Lane off ReadBoulevard
Metairie: 3216 West Esplanade Avenue
1976-2000

Chateaubriand Steakhouse
Mid-City: 201 North Carrollton Avenue
2001-5

Chef Gerard Crozier and his wife, Eveline, accomplished a feat unmatched in the annals of French cooking in New Orleans. They operated restaurants at the top level for almost thirty years and never once served a Creole dish.
Coming from Lyon, France and a few intermediate cities (chefs move

Eveline and Gerard Crozier made their mark with classic French cooking at Crozier's and Chateaubriand restaurants. (Photo by George Long)

around a lot early in their careers), the couple came to New Orleans when Gerard signed on to the kitchen brigade at the Royal Sonesta Hotel. He worked with Chef Willy Coln there through the early 1970s. In 1976, both Crozier and Coln (see index for Willy Coln's Chalet) left to open their own restaurants. The Croziers had a rough time doing that, as one bank after another rejected their loan applications. They finally opened in a location so incongruous that I remember laughing at the prospect when I saw it for the first time.

Crozier's Restaurant Français, said the marquee over a space in a new, isolated, spartan strip mall in New Orleans East. I didn't expect much, but it was suppertime, and there I was. The spare, pleasant room was decorated only with French travel posters. The chairs were the bolt-upright stackable kind, but the tables were covered with good napery.

The menu sounded great. I had escargots, aromatic with garlic butter. A salad of whole romaine lettuce leaves came out with a simple but strikingly good vinaigrette, then tournedos Gerard, a filet mignon topped with a round of pate de foie gras and surrounded by a cream sauce with small shrimp. I'd never seen the likes of that dish. I couldn't believe how good it was.

On my radio restaurant review the next morning, I rashly gave Crozier's a ten out of ten rating, one of only four such in the whole city. And I returned a few days later to have another spectacular meal. Eveline, who managed the dining room with irresistible charm, remembered me. Sure she would. She didn't know who I was or what I did, but I had wandered into Crozier's on the second day they were open.

At first, Crozier's was open for lunch and dinner, because they needed every nickel they could bring in. The lunch menu offered a hamburger, even though Gerard hated cooking them. He reached critical mass one lunch while I was there. Someone in the room (not me) ordered the burger. When the waitress brought the order into the kitchen, I heard a shout in a French accent, "No more f——g ham-bur-*guerre!*" And that was the end of American cooking at Crozier's.

It was also the beginning of a menu that stayed with the restaurant for the rest of its history and even a bit beyond. Gerard added a few more items, staying with French classic cookery. He cooked in simple ways with pretty good but inexpensive ingredients. But he did so with such perfection and consistency that one bite was enough to convince a diner of Crozier's command of flavor.

Among his best dishes were his homemade duck pate (still unequaled locally), coq au vin, sautéed veal with lemon and wine butter sauce, steak au poivre, fish with fennel or capers, and pommes de terre dauphinois. That last item was a side dish—the last word in potatoes au gratin. Many customers went to Crozier's just for that. Gerard's rice pilaf appeared to be just rice but had a flavor I still am trying, in vain, to reproduce.

Gerard's omelettes were apotheoses: perfect golden yellow, without so much as a fleck of brown; moist and fluffy at the same time. They were so spectacular that Crozier's shutdown of lunch service (the only time he made omelettes) was a disaster for many of his regular customers.

After a few years, the Croziers bought their own larger, more comfortable building—still in New Orleans East. It was a full house almost every night for years. Then a few developments made business decline. A large percentage of their customers came from Uptown. But rigorous enforcement of anti-DWI laws began. How could you eat food like this without wine and Cognac? At the same time, the chic new Creole bistros multiplied Uptown, taking even more business away.

The Croziers relocated again, to another anonymous strip mall in Metairie. This was closer to where many of their customers lived. The new restaurant was nicer than either of the two in the East, and full reservation books returned.

Meanwhile, the consistency of the food remained inviolate. Tournedos Gerard tasted and looked exactly the same nearly twenty-five years after that first time I had it. So did everything else. There was a downside: the menu hardly ever changed. When the cult of name chefs with their floods of new dishes became the vogue, Crozier's trade softened, even though he was serving better food than most of the new chefs were.

Still, Crozier's remained a busy place until Gerard and Eveline sold it in 2000, saying they were going to retire. The people who bought it got all the recipes, kept most of the staff, and continued with the same menu. But it was never the same after Gerard left, and after several renamings and retoolings, it finally gave up the ghost in 2004.

Meanwhile, the Croziers came out of their premature retirement with Chateaubriand Steakhouse. Steak had always been a major specialty at Crozier's, and Gerard built upon that, in a much larger restaurant than his old bistro.

But the stars were aligned against it. Chateaubriand opened right before 9/11. As soon as that depression played out, the city began ripping up Carrollton Avenue in front of the restaurant for the new streetcar route. When that major inconvenience ended, the mad-cow problem caused beef prices to double. That was just starting to ease when Katrina put two feet of water into Chateaubriand.

The Croziers threw up their hands, gave up the business, and retired to Knoxville. Gerard never returned to cooking. To stay active, he signed on as a greeter at Walmart, a job he enjoyed. He continued running (both he and Eveline were marathoners, which explained their wiry frames) and playing golf. On September 30, 2009, Gerard died suddenly and inexplicably while watching television. He was not quite sixty-four.

Crozier's Veal with Crawfish

This is one of the few dishes Gerard Crozier ever cooked that had a (slightly) New Orleans flavor, as opposed to being pure French (although I can hear him dispute this from the grave as I write these words). It's simple enough to make, once you have nice veal (make sure it's sliced across the grain). When crawfish aren't in season, you can use crabmeat, shrimp, or even lobster.

1 Tbs. salt
¼ tsp. white pepper
1 cup flour
8-12 thin slices veal round, about 2-3 oz. each
2 Tbs. vegetable oil
4 Tbs. butter
12 oz. fresh mushrooms, sliced
½ cup white wine
1 lb. fresh Louisiana crawfish tails
1 pt. heavy cream

Preheat the oven to 200 degrees.

1. Blend 1 Tbs. salt and ¼ tsp. pepper into the flour.

2. Lightly pound the veal scallops. Dust lightly with the seasoned flour on both sides.

3. Heat oil and 2 Tbs. butter in a large skillet over medium-high heat. Add the veal and cook for 90 seconds to 2 minutes (depending on thickness) on each side, until browned around the edges. Pick up the veal with tongs, let it drain over the pan for a few seconds, then put it onto 4 plates. Put these in oven to stay warm.

4. Pour off excess fat from the pan, but don't wipe it. Add the rest of the butter and the mushrooms. Cook for 1 minute. Add the wine and reduce the liquid by half over medium-high heat.

5. Add the crawfish tails and cream, plus salt and pepper to taste. Agitate the pan and cook until cream thickens.

6. Spoon the crawfish and mushroom sauce over the veal and serve. This is good with rice on the side, with some of the sauce running into it.

Serves 4.

★★★
Delerno's
Old Metairie: 619 Pink Street
1940s-90s

Can you imagine a New Orleans-style restaurant that never serves crawfish? Strange as it seems, that was the case in most New Orleans eateries above the level of boiled-and-fried seafood houses in the 1960s and earlier. Crawfish—even in polite dishes such as bisques, etouffees, and gratins—were simply not on the menu in most white-tablecloth restaurants.

The few better establishments that made crawfish a house specialty did very well with it. The Bon Ton Café became world famous for serving great Cajun-style crawfish dishes. Out-of-towners found it exotic and delicious, back then and still.

Delerno's was on a crawfishing par with the Bon Ton but focused almost entirely on local diners. J.B. Delerno (I never heard anyone—not even his wife—call him by anything other than his initials) spent some years in other people's restaurants before opening his own in Old Metairie. He was quite a host and built up a clientele so regular in their visits that Delerno's made a lasting impression.

If you mentioned Delerno's to those people, they would almost instantaneously reply, "J.B. makes the best crawfish in town!" They wouldn't mention which dish, exactly. J.B. cooked crawfish a lot of ways. Not only were these delicious, but they were presented more beautifully than I've seen crawfish served before or since.

The etouffee was a great example of that. An island of rice on the plate was surrounded by a tremendous number of crawfish tails in a singular, deep-orange sauce with a huge flavor. It was more a Creole etouffee than a Cajun one, but crawfish live in New Orleans, too.

That traditional dish was only the beginning. Crawfish turned up in various sauces next to or around all sorts of other things: soft-shell crabs, veal, chicken. Crawfish appetizers were rife, notably an oddity called crawfish topas. These were essentially crawfish tostadas, with crawfish etouffee on flour tortillas, topped with cheese and green onions, all run under the broiler. (The name was a misspelling of *tapas*. It and the dish spread to a few other restaurants, evolving into *Topaz* somewhere along the way.)

Delerno's cooked just about everything else well, particularly in the seafood department. It was a classic New Orleans neighborhood restaurant in the category of Mandina's or Manale's, with modest but comfortable dining rooms and chummy service.

Delerno's closed when J.B. passed away in the early 1980s. It has been a number of restaurants since—two of them called "Delerno's." Mrs. Delerno owned the building and lived upstairs. When asked by a tenant, she'd give advice on how to run the place. The location is now the Sun Ray Grill.

Crawfish prepared in a multitude of ways was the specialty at Delerno's. (Courtesy of New Orleans Magazine*)*

Delerno's Crawfish Topas

The Old Metairie neighborhood restaurant Delerno's created this dish. It did not fit any rigorous definition of tapas—way too filling and cheesy and messy to eat for that—but it was delicious. I got the recipe a few months before the place closed and messed with it a little.

4 Tbs. butter
¼ cup flour
½ cup chopped onion
¼ cup chopped bell pepper
¼ cup coarsely chopped celery
¼ cup dry white wine
1 cup crawfish or shrimp stock or water
Pinch dried thyme
1 bay leaf
⅓ tsp. chopped garlic
1½ cups crawfish tails, with fat if possible
½ cup diced tomatoes
1 Tbs. chopped flat-leaf parsley
⅓ cup sliced green onions
¼ tsp. salt
1 tsp. salt-free Creole seasoning
8 small flour tortillas
2 cups shredded pepper jack cheese

1. In a large saucepan, melt the butter and heat it to a bubble. Add flour gradually and stir constantly over medium-high heat to make a light-brown roux.

2. Lower heat to medium and add onion, bell pepper, and celery. Cook until the vegetables soften, while stirring to keep the roux from burning.

3. Add the wine, stock, thyme, bay leaf, and garlic, then bring to a boil. Simmer 2 or 3 minutes, until thickened.

4. Add crawfish tails, tomatoes, parsley, and green onions. Simmer for about 8 to 10 minutes, until sauce can be picked up with a fork. Adjust seasoning with salt and Creole seasoning.

5. Heat a griddle or a black iron skillet over medium-high heat. Grill the tortillas on both sides until they are brown in spots. Sprinkle cheese over tortillas. Put them on a pan or baking sheet 3 inches under the heat in a broiler until the cheese melts. Top with the hot crawfish sauce in the center (don't spread it around pizza style). Cut each into 4 pieces and serve hot.

Serves 6 to 8.

★★★
Delmonico
Lee Circle Area: 1300 St. Charles Avenue
1895-1998

All restaurants that manage to pile up long histories evolve over the years. Sometimes this is hard to see (Galatoire's), other times obvious (Commander's Palace). Arnaud's underwent a revolution when Archie Casbarian bought it from Germaine Wells, Count Arnaud's daughter, but the main effect was to reverse a long, steep decline. The new Arnaud's looked and cooked much as it had done at its peak.

But the old Delmonico was not really the same restaurant that Emeril Lagasse now operates under the same name in the same location. His 1998 renovation changed the way Delmonico looked and cooked. The restaurant's before and after can't be compared. I very much liked both of them. But the old Delmonico is unambiguously extinct, so I thought it fit well into this book.

Delmonico was founded in 1895 by Anthony Commander, with the help of his brother Emile—the man who, a decade before, opened Commander's Palace. Anthony named it for Delmonico's in New York City, considered by most historians to be the first grand restaurant in America. The New York Delmonico's was so influential that when other would-be restaurateurs copied its style, they often went ahead and took the name, too. "Delmonico" came close to becoming the generic term for what came to be known as a restaurant.

The Commanders ran a much less grand restaurant than the New

Delmonico was a St. Charles Avenue fixture for many years. In the 1990s, Emeril Lagasse purchased the restaurant, so it's now known as Emeril's Delmonico. (Courtesy of New Orleans Magazine)

One of the many elegant dining rooms in Delmonico. Among the restaurant's specialties were stuffed trout and eggplant casserole. (Photo by C. F. Weber, courtesy of Bergeron Photography)

York namesake, serving sandwiches and plate lunches in modest surroundings at low prices. But Delmonico's location—in a high-culture part of town—demanded more. Particularly after Anthony LaFranca bought Delmonico in 1911, a series of renovations and additions made it a restaurant as formal as any other in New Orleans at the time.

Delmonico was at its peak when LaFranca's daughters Angie Brown and Rose Dietrich took over in the 1960s. Its stretch of St. Charles Avenue was chic, full of shops and other restaurants, and an easy streetcar ride from Uptown and Downtown both.

The restaurant's culinary style was thoroughly Creole, and it had many specialties. Most of those seem home style now, but that's how every Creole restaurant cooked back then. The turtle soup was one of the best; until the end, it was not uncommon to find actual turtle bones in the bowl. Delmonico's stewed chicken with brown gravy and rice, its eggplant casserole, its grilled veal liver with bacon, and its stuffed trout all set the local standards. Even its house salad was distinguished. It was a collection of greens and poached vegetables (carrots, cauliflower, and broccoli), all held in a sort of bowl made from a big iceberg lettuce leaf.

Delmonico was as well known for its pricing as for the goodness of its food. A review I wrote in 1977 shows six oysters Bienville for $3.75, turtle soup for $2, and trout Leonard (with a seafood dressing) for $6.75. Lunches could be had for under $5. Yet the place was so elegant (if in an old-fashioned way) that most people dressed up to go there.

The two sisters presided over their restaurant with a graciousness that brings a tear of nostalgia to my eye now. One or the other of them (but usually both) was always there. All their customers loved them. Miss Angie and Miss Rose (that's what everybody called them, even customers much older than they were) always seemed to be on the verge of expiring with delight that you came in to dine with them.

The kitchen staff at Delmonico had astonishing longevity. In the 1990s, Miss Angie and Miss Rose allowed me to hold a series of charity dinners in their dining rooms, with the help of their regular staff. The younger of the two main cooks went by the name "Jitterbug." He was seventy-eight. Chef Leonard was eighty-four. They moved slowly but with such efficiency that they always kept up with the orders from what was really a large restaurant. Meanwhile, they maintained one of the cleanest kitchens I ever saw.

The neighborhood had changed a lot by the time Delmonico celebrated its century anniversary. Business was way off, and that scourge of long-running, successful restaurants—the aging of their customers—kept a lot of younger new customers away.

Emeril came along at the perfect time. He was near the peak of his local popularity, and Miss Angie and Miss Rose were thrilled with what he wanted to do to their daddy's restaurant. The deal was quickly made, and Delmonico undertook the process of rebirth.

As of this writing, both sisters are still alive and active. I see them in restaurants often. They look exactly the same—and are still smiling all the time.

Creole Eggplant Gratin Delmonico

I had this dish for the last time at Delmonico two days before the old regime closed down. It was the night of the Babylon parade, which passed right in front on St. Charles Avenue. We had most of our dinner, went out to watch the parade, and came back in for dessert with Angie Brown and Rose Dietrich, the sisters who owned Delmonico. The combination of that Mardi Gras experience with one of the best meals I ever had there (the old place was good to the last) is forever engraved in my memory.

2 eggplants, peeled and cut into large dice
2 Tbs. butter
1 medium onion, chopped
2 ribs celery, chopped
1 cup small peeled shrimp
½ lb. claw crabmeat
1 tomato, chopped
¼ tsp. Tabasco
¼ tsp. Worcestershire sauce
¼ tsp. marjoram
3 sprigs parsley leaves, chopped
½ tsp. lemon juice
½ tsp. salt
¼ cup breadcrumbs

Preheat the oven to 350 degrees.

1. Bring a large pot of water to a rolling boil and drop the eggplant in for about 2 minutes. Remove and drain.

2. Heat the butter in a large skillet and sauté the onion, celery, and shrimp until the shrimp turn pink. Add all the other ingredients except breadcrumbs and cook, stirring very lightly, until everything is heated through.

3. Load the mixture into a baking dish and top with the breadcrumbs. Bake for about 15 minutes or until the breadcrumbs are toasty.

Serves 4 to 8.

★★★
DiPiazza's
French Quarter: 337 Dauphine Street
1989-92

Three years is a brief lifetime for a memorable restaurant, but I think this one ought to be in this book, because it tied together two eras of New Orleans Italian dining. It's sort of a missing link.

The story begins in the 1960s with a tiny Italian cafe called Eva's Spot. Two sisters who looked and acted as if they'd been cooking for decades operated it. Eva's was one of the last of many inexpensive trattorias that dotted the French Quarter at the time. It was home-style New Orleans-Sicilian food all the way, lunch only: red beans, gumbo, spaghetti and meatballs, and the like. All that sold for prices under $2. This made the house specialty stand out: four-cheese lasagna, $5. Everyone was curious as to why this was so much more expensive. Not everyone satisfied the curiosity, but I did. It was a fantastic, meatless lasagna, served in a perfect cube. I may have had a better lasagna in my life, but I can't remember it. I do remember Eva's lasagna to this day.

Eva's finally closed in the 1970s. The space was so small and out of the way that it sat empty for awhile. Then Anthony DiPiazza came along. He had an interesting credential: he'd worked for Carlos and Joe Marcello in a number of situations, most notably Broussard's. Broussard's is a half-block away from 337 Dauphine, which must explain why he knew it was available.

What Anthony did here strained one's credulity. In a space that would hardly be big enough for a stove and a cook, he served the thirty or so people he could fit into the dining room an entirely new generation of Creole-Italian food.

The eats were good, but what brought the customers in was the ordering protocol. DiPiazza's was a "feed me" restaurant. For a tab ranging between $15 and $25 per person (depending on how hungry you were), a procession of the day's specials would come to the table, along with plates for splitting them with dining partners. Six to eight courses was typical. All were delicious; some of it was rather unusual.

A lot of Anthony's creations were unheard of then but common now. For example, he grilled slabs of marinated giant squid—translucent white steaks cut from the squid bodies. An oval baking dish had baked oysters with garlic, breadcrumbs, and bacon on one end and spicy roasted red and yellow peppers with mozzarella on the other. Quail flew into position with spinach and mushrooms in a very buttery sauce. Broad noodles ran among white beans and lentils with herbs. Veal sirloins—never a common cut of meat, but one the Marcellos always liked—came out with mushrooms, peppers, and onions.

Then, one day, the food went down in interest, people stopped coming, and it closed. Reason: Anthony had moved on. But we were hooked on his food. He would reappear now and then, here and there. The word would get out that he was back to his delicious tricks. His last stand was at Eleven 79, working with Joe Segreto, Anthony's old boss at Broussard's. He was there for about four more years, and then he passed away. But this time his food lived on at Eleven 79, which still serves most of it.

As for the funny little hole in the wall on Dauphine Street, it's now the Louisiana Bistro. It has attracted a crowd a lot like what DiPiazza's did and for the same reasons. But that's outside the purview of this volume.

Too bad Anthony's career ended early. (He was barely in his fifties when he died.) He set a lot of trends in motion that we now take for granted.

Eva's Spot Lasagna with Six Cheeses

The trick with this is picking out the right cheeses, the kind that will melt nicely without turning the whole thing greasy. That means no Cheddar or Swiss. The pasta should be cooked only long enough to take the stiffness out. And the sauce is cooked very briefly—you don't want the eight-hour sauce in here.

Sauce:
2 28-oz. cans whole Italian plum tomatoes
2 Tbs. olive oil
2 tsp. chopped garlic
½ tsp. crushed red pepper
½ tsp. dried basil
¼ tsp. dried oregano
¼ tsp. salt

1 Tbs. salt
1 Tbs. olive oil
8 oz. lasagna noodles (or, better, 12 oz. fresh pasta sheets)
10-oz. bag fresh spinach, picked and well washed
8 oz. Fontina cheese, sliced
¾ cup finely grated Pecorino Romano
8 oz. ricotta cheese
4 oz. Provolone cheese, shredded
8 oz. mozzarella cheese, grated
½ cup finely grated Parmesan cheese

Preheat the oven to 350 degrees.

1. Make the sauce first. Drain the tomatoes (reserve the juice) and put them into a food processor; chop to a rough puree. (You can also do this with your fingers in a bowl.)

2. Heat the olive oil in a saucepan over medium heat till the oil shimmers. Sauté the garlic and crushed red pepper for about 1 minute—until you can smell the garlic.

3. Add the tomatoes, ½ cup of the reserved juice, basil, oregano, and salt. Bring to a boil, and lower the heat to medium low. Simmer for about 20 minutes, uncovered. Then keep on the lowest possible heat while you continue with the rest of the recipe.

4. Bring a large pot of water to a boil with the salt and olive oil. Add the lasagna noodles and boil for about 2 minutes or until the noodles are no longer stiff. Reserving the water, remove the noodles to a bowl of cold water for a moment, then remove and drain. (Leave this step out if using fresh pasta sheets.)

5. Cook the spinach in the same water you used to cook the pasta, just for 1 minute. Remove with a slotted spoon, drain, and spread out.

6. Coat the inside of a glass or ceramic baking dish (about 9" x 13" x 4") with olive oil. Pour about ¼ cup of the sauce on the bottom. Make the following layers, alternating the direction of the pasta with each layer:

Pasta
⅓ cup sauce
Fontina cheese
¼ cup Romano
Pasta
⅓ cup sauce
Spinach
Ricotta
¼ cup Romano
Pasta
⅓ cup sauce
Provolone
¼ cup Romano
Pasta
⅓ cup sauce
Mozzarella
Pasta
Remaining sauce
Parmesan

7. Cover the casserole with aluminum foil and bake in the center of the oven for 40 minutes. Remove the foil and return to the oven until a light crust has formed on the top.

8. After removing from the oven, let the lasagna rest for at least 15 minutes before attempting to slice. Serve with a wide metal spatula to keep it together (almost impossible to do with the first slice).

Serves about 8.

★★★★
Dragon's Garden
Metairie: 6415 Airline Highway
Metairie: 4417 Veterans Boulevard
Metairie: 3100 17th Street
1970-2004

From a diner's standpoint, the Dragon's Garden was the most important restaurant in the history of Chinese cooking in New Orleans. Its owner, Andy Tsai, introduced local diners to the spicy dishes of Szechuan, the elaborate creations of the Mandarin cuisine, and many exciting dishes that are now staples in every Chinese restaurant in town.

Imagine going to a Chinese eatery and not being able to order hot and sour soup, pot stickers, shrimp toast, kung-pao chicken, Peking duck, or Szechuan beef. That's how things were before the Dragon's Garden opened. Every restaurant here cooked more or less the same menu of mild Cantonese dishes and those created by the early Chinese immigrants to America.

Andy Tsai didn't invent the dishes with which he wowed adventuresome New Orleans palates. Szechuan and Mandarin food was already commonplace in cities with growing Chinese communities. But the New Orleans Chinatown (there was one—near where the main public library is now) was long gone by the 1970s, and the Chinese restaurant community was at best static.

The original Golden Dragon was a lunch counter in the Airline Park strip mall. It might well have lived a short time and died there, but Richard Collin—who'd spent enough years in New York to know an adventuresome Chinese menu when he saw one—touted it highly in his "Underground Gourmet" column. Soon the place was so jammed that Andy moved to a larger, upstairs space with a view of Clearview Mall. After a few years, he moved again to a new building on the corner of 17th Street and Ridgelake Drive. (The previous location almost immediately reopened with a very similar menu as the Golden Dragon, the first of numerous spinoffs of Andy Tsai's innovation.)

If you didn't know any better, the Dragon's Garden was much like all the other Chinese restaurants in your past experience. Most customers of Chinese restaurants hit on one dish they like and order the same thing forever. Andy would cook won ton soup, moo goo gai pan, egg foo yung, and fried rice if you asked. But if you started asking about the more unfamiliar dishes, Andy's face would light up (he was always in the dining room), and the next thing you knew a feast the likes of which you never imagined was coming out.

You'd start with the high-piled shrimp toast, great with plum sauce, or the pot stickers, or the brilliant hot and sour soup. From there the spicy dishes (stir-fried pork strings with hot garlic sauce, to name a favorite of mine) would alternate with the milder, more elegant ones (such as moo shu pork, which you'd assemble yourself on thin "pancakes" and eat like burritos). Every dish was dramatically different from all the others.

A little planning (because it took a full day to prepare) would bring Peking duck to one's table. The big platter had piles of meat on one side and crisp skin on the other. Again, you'd tuck the duck, green onions, and hoisin sauce into pancakes. People at adjacent tables, their same-old chop suey in front of them, would ask what in the world you were eating. You'd tell them with great enthusiasm, and another convert to the new dishes was made.

Andy delivered not only the food of a gourmet restaurant but the service, wine, and atmosphere, too. Dining there was as special an event as going to Galatoire's.

Chinese restaurateurs are nothing if not attuned to the market, and it wasn't long before other restaurants started adding Szechuan, Mandarin, and Hunan dishes to their menus. Some of these were nearly as good as the Dragon's Garden. The Peking and Jade East in New Orleans East, the China Doll on the West Bank, and the Five Happiness in Carrollton were especially good.

Then Andy sold the place. The Dragon's Garden went through a series of owners, and a slow decline set in. It never became bad, but the magic was gone when Katrina closed the place. It reopened after the storm as the China Town Gourmet, but no significant trace of the Dragon's Garden's golden era remained—except for a much-enhanced overall Chinese restaurant community, for which we have Andy Tsai to thank.

Dragon's Garden's Shrimp Toast

Shrimp toast is a wonderful Chinese appetizer that few restaurants do well. It is much simpler to prepare than the finished product would have you believe. It is delicious served with Chinese plum sauce, which can be found at any large supermarket.

**2 cups fresh shrimp, peeled and deveined
2 cups canned water chestnuts, drained
1 egg
1 Tbs. all-purpose flour
6 slices white bread, crusts cut away
Sesame seeds
Vegetable oil for frying**

1. Put the shrimp meat and the water chestnuts into a food processor or blender, and process into a lumpy paste.

2. Scrape contents into a bowl and add the egg and the flour. Stir well.

3. Press down on the pieces of bread to flatten them. With a knife, coat each piece of bread with a mound of the shrimp mixture about 1 inch high. Top with a sparse sprinkling of sesame seeds. Cut each of these into quarters.

4. Deep-fry in vegetable oil at 325 degrees until golden brown. Drain excess oil and allow to cool for 1 minute.

Serves 6.

★★★★
Eddie's
Gentilly: 2119 Law Street
1966-96

The anecdotes people told about Eddie's were as entertaining as the cooking was delicious. Most of the stories were along the lines of one Bill Cosby told on *The Tonight Show* during the Johnny Carson years. One of his friends here offered to take him to what he said was the best soul-food restaurant in New Orleans. Cosby related—in his usual exaggerated way—the ordeal of getting to Eddie's. To even get to Law Street, you had to go underneath an overpass next to some railroad tracks, alongside a deep drainage canal. Then you had to navigate around potholes that could swallow an automobile and leave nothing showing. When Cosby's party got to the restaurant's address, they weren't sure whether they'd arrived. Eddie's didn't have a sign on its building.

Cosby stopped overstating when he started in on how good the fried chicken, gumbo, and fried seafood were. Eddie's food really was worth all this trouble and then some.

Eddie Baquet cooked for many years around town before he opened his own place in Gentilly. He didn't seem to be all that interested in spreading his fame or even pulling in business from anywhere other than the neighborhood. That was true of most neighborhood cafes of the time, but especially of those in the primarily African-American areas. Even Richard Collin—who blew the cover off most of the great soul-food restaurants around town—didn't find Eddie's until seven years into writing his column.

Eddie was all about fine details in his cooking. Visiting my radio show in 1990, he went on for about a half-hour on his technique for making Creole gumbo. That variation is common in soul-food restaurants but not often tasted elsewhere. Eddie made his Creole gumbo with both seafood and sausage, both okra and filé. The amazing thing about his dissertation on the dish was that he never let on exactly what went into the pot. Secret recipe, he said.

Eddie's fried chicken and seafood were everything one could want from those classic dishes: hot, crisp, greaseless, amply served. The robust red beans and rice came with the potent hot sausage from Vaucresson's. Poor-boy sandwiches were the equals of anybody's. If you were lucky, you could finish up with bread pudding. (They often ran out.)

The premises—a converted frame house—were much nicer inside than the rest of Law Street. It was as much a bar as a restaurant, with two large dining rooms, almost always full, especially on the days when the fried chicken buffet went up.

After Eddie Baquet died in the early 1990s, his son Wayne took over Eddie's and kept it going for a few more years. He also opened a second, much nicer, easier-to-find restaurant called Zachary's in the Carrollton section. Wayne shut down both Eddie's and Zachary's in the late 1990s, but not long after he brought his father's recipes back to life at two restaurants called Li'l Dizzy's. Wayne Baquet also had a brief stint in the mezzanine at Krauss Department Store on Canal Street. Both Li'l Dizzy's and Zachary's were good soul-food vendors, but neither has the magic that was Eddie's, a strong contender for Best Creole Neighborhood Restaurant of All Time.

★★★★

Elmwood Plantation
Old Jefferson: 5400 River Road
1946-77

Few lost New Orleans restaurants engender memories as fond as does the Elmwood Plantation. Atmospherically, it offered everything the New Orleans soul could desire: a bona fide crumbling ruin with a history going back to Louis XIV, who granted the large tract of land in French colonial times. The main house was built in 1782; that made it the oldest plantation house in the Mississippi Valley. There was no missing its antiquity. The walls were strikingly thick (they had to be, to hold the place up), and the live oaks that surrounded it were of startling size.

The main house of Elmwood Plantation, along the historic River Road, was built in the mid-eighteenth century. The restaurant was open opened in 1946 and lasted more than thirty years. (Photo © Kevin R. Roberts)

The cover of this Elmwood Plantation menu shows the many graceful oaks surrounding the restaurant. (From the collection of Billy Gruber)

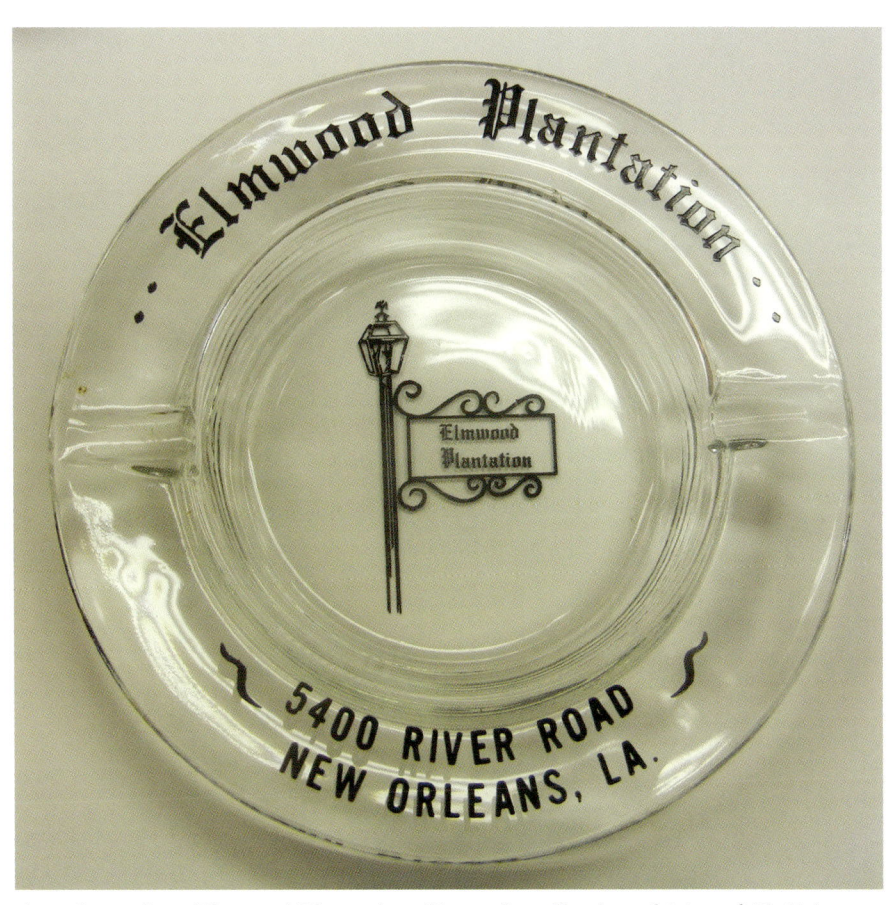

An ashtray from Elmwood Plantation. (From the collection of Edward Piglia)

Elmwood Plantation was one of the most architecturally important structures in the New Orleans area in the post-World War II era. Houses all around the area—notably along the Lake Pontchartrain lakefront—copied its design. Ironically, what they imitated was the unconventional look Elmwood took on after the first of its two disastrous fires. The damage was mostly on the second floor, which was completely removed. They just lowered the roof.

As interesting as its premises were, the Elmwood's fame derived equally from the food served there. The kitchen was terrific. And it was terrific with a very simple menu, one derived to a great extent from Mosca's. The chef during most of the restaurant's lifetime was Nick Mosca, who left his family's restaurant, Mosca's, in Waggaman when he was a young man and went back to work for his parents' old employers, the Marcello family, the owners of Elmwood Plantation.

Chef Nick's menu was equal parts Creole, Italian, and Creole-Italian. It was a magical combination, because while the food was clearly in the realm of fine dining, it was easy for even the occasional restaurant diner to get his head around it all.

So you started with shrimp remoulade, or shrimp Chandeleur (way oversized fried ones), or shrimp Mosca, still bigger ones baked with garlic, olive oil, and rosemary in the shells, like barbecue shrimp but different. Or you began with oysters Mosca, baked with a wetter version of the garlicky, herbal breadcrumb topping you got at Mosca's, or with the great chicken-andouille gumbo (a relative rarity in those days) or turtle soup.

Hold it. No. You didn't start with any of that. What you started with was a cocktail and a significant wait for your table in the bar. You did that regardless of whether you reserved or not and regardless of what time you showed up (unless, of course, you were a high-powered Jefferson Parish figure or a friend of the Marcello family). The Elmwood was always busy, and the time spent hanging with friends or notable strangers in the bar was part of the evening.

But now you're at the table, and you have ordered. There's a strong chance that you went for the filet mignon. It would come out in a straightforward manner, no sauce, with a roasted skinless potato alongside. It was one of the best steaks in town and stood high off the plate.

If you were given to more ambitious eating, you would have had some kind of bird. They had plenty for you to choose from. The roast chicken Elmwood was the signature entree and everything a chicken could be: crisp at the skin, tender inside, never dry, and seasoned well, with the flavor of rosemary dominant. You might have had chicken cacciatore or chicken grandee (roasted in pieces with garlic and rosemary).

Or you had a squab, or a Cornish hen, or a pair of quail. They came out with yams and wild rice, and they were perfection.

They served fish, of course, but that never seemed to me to have the brilliance of the rest of the menu, unless they started throwing crabmeat around, which the waiters liked to do.

Ah, the waiters. They were all African-Americans, with so much style that many of them continued to draw regular customers long after the Elmwood closed and they were posted elsewhere around town.

One of the finest treats the Elmwood offered came at the end of the meal. It was the check. As delicious and generous as this restaurant's food was, it could have charged 50 percent more than it did. The place was always a bargain, amazingly so at lunch. I have a dinner menu here from 1977 that shows you could have an appetizer, soup, salad, and non-steak entree for $12—dinner!

Elmwood Plantation's end came with that second fire. It burned the place to the ground, never to rise again. Plans to rebuild it have been floated, but essentially it would be a new building. Meanwhile, the property has been subdivided, and hardly anything is left.

But it's a wonderful memory. I found out just how wonderful when my annual April Fool restaurant review reported that the Elmwood had reopened, with the same food and prices. The barrage of calls and e-mails I received from hopeful diners ran into the hundreds, even though I intentionally made the story very hard to believe. But with an icon like that, people want very hard to believe.

Elmwood Plantation's Chicken Grandee

Nick Mosca, the chef at Elmwood Plantation for many years, was a master of chicken dishes. They seemed simple but were magically delicious. Chicken Grandee was the best of them.

1 whole chicken, about 3 lb., or 3 chicken breasts
1-2 Tbs. Italian seasoning
1 qt. water
2 lb. small white potatoes
1 lb. Italian sausage
⅓ cup olive oil
1 red or yellow bell pepper, seeds removed, cut into ½-inch dice
6-8 large garlic cloves, peeled and crushed
2 Tbs. lemon juice
1 Tbs. rosemary
2 tsp. oregano
2 tsp. salt
2 tsp. black pepper
Fresh chopped parsley

Preheat the oven to 400 degrees.

1. Cut the chicken up into pieces about a third the size that the Colonel uses. Remove small bones, but it's okay to leave the big ones. Season the pieces with salt and Italian seasoning.

2. Bring water to a light boil. Peel the potatoes and cut them into half-moon-shaped slices about a quarter of an inch thick. Drop them into the boiling water for about 2 minutes. Drain and set aside.

3. Prick the skins of the sausages a few times with a kitchen fork. In a large, heavy skillet over medium-high heat, cook the sausages until browned and firm. (They don't need to be cooked all the way through but nearly so.) Remove the sausage, and pour off excess fat from the skillet. When the sausage has cooled enough to handle, slice into coins about a quarter-inch thick.

4. Add 2 Tbs. olive oil to the skillet. Raise the heat to high and heat until the surface begins to ripple. Add the bell peppers and garlic and cook until brown around the edges. Remove with a slotted spoon and set aside.

5. Add the chicken pieces to the skillet and brown on all sides. They don't need to be fully cooked. Sprinkle the lemon juice over the chicken and set aside.

6. Add the remaining olive oil to the skillet and brown the potatoes lightly over high heat, turning once.

7. Put the sliced sausage, peppers, garlic, chicken, and potatoes into a

roasting pan, sprinkling the rosemary, oregano, salt, and black pepper as you go and distributing all the ingredients evenly.

8. Put the pan in the oven and roast for 15-20 minutes, uncovered. When the biggest pieces of chicken are cooked all the way through, it's ready. Garnish with fresh chopped parsley.

Serves 4.

★★★
El Ranchito
Downtown: 1811 Elysian Fields Avenue
1960s-81

In the months following Hurricane Katrina, some small Mexican cafes opened in (among other places) the vicinity of North Claiborne at Elysian Fields. Their main clientele was the large number of Mexican workers who came to town to help us clean up the mess. This caught the attention of those of us who are always on the lookout for close-to-the-source ethnic food.

Mr. and Mrs. Bernardo Villafuerte Hernandez were the proprietors of El Ranchito. Mrs. Hernandez, known as "Mamita," was the cook. Among the many highlights on the menu were mole poblano, guacamole, and tamales. (Courtesy of the Hernandez/Jolet families)

A number of these venturers had the same encomium when they called on the air to tell me what they found. "The place was exactly like El Ranchito used to be!" they said, with great excitement. "Remember El Ranchito?"

Of course I remember it. So does everyone who liked Mexican food in the 1960s and early 1970s, when there were few Mexican restaurants in the area. (Manuel's Hot Tamales didn't count.)

El Ranchito was not much like any of the post-K taquerias shops. But I can see the likeness. El Ranchito was a converted house set back from Elysian Fields, using the former yard as a parking lot, dwarfed by the enormous Jaeger's Seafood Restaurant a half-block away. Only a green neon sign saying *"El Ranchito"* in script marked it as a restaurant.

The single dining room was stark and too bright. It was presided over by a waitress who, well, let's say she took up more than her share of the available space. She never passed a table or chair without brushing it. If I remember right, her name was Bobbie.

Bobbie's other outstanding quality was that she knew what was going on in the kitchen every night and would tell you what would be a good idea to order and what wouldn't be. If you wanted to go counter to her suggestions, she'd argue the point. In fact, she was doing you a favor, and when she left the restaurant it never was quite as good.

The actual food was the work of Rosa "Mamita" Hernandez. For some time in the 1950s, she made hot tamales, which her husband sold from the corner of Canal and Broad streets. Somewhere along the way, they took the concept upscale and opened El Ranchito.

Mamita was a first-generation Mexican American and an older one at that. Born in 1902, she lived to be 105, spending most of her life in New Orleans. However, her food was quite different from what's being served in the taquerias opened by more recent immigrants.

The first thing you noticed was that the guacamole—ordered by everybody—was unique. It had the texture of mashed potatoes and the color of a newly opened leaf. It came out in a beige, melamine bowl, with a slice of cooked carrot on top and a grating of cheese.

After that, most people got tacos, cheese enchiladas, tamales, and combo plates. But this place had on its menu something that has remained rare in New Orleans to this day: the bitter chocolate-based sauce called mole poblano. You could get it on chicken or on cheese-and-onion enchiladas. It was great, but only a few people ordered it.

Also good here was the chili. It was made with chopped meat—I think it may have been pork, not beef—and although it wasn't spicy, it carried a big flavor in ways not familiar to most gringo palates. Mamita made all this stuff herself, from scratch.

One of the hallmarks of dining at El Ranchito was that you didn't leave the place feeling inflated. The portions were modest and prices even more so. Maybe that's why it left the scene, when Mexican places such as Dos Gringos came along with their mountain ranges of food on big sizzling platters. Mamita was not that showy.

★★
The Enraged Chicken
Lower Garden District: 1115 St. Mary Street
1976-80

The Enraged Chicken was as quirky as its name. One night, the menu would be Mexican. The next, Chinese. After that Italian, Creole, and Spanish. Maybe. You not only had to take what cuisine you found, but accept the set menu with no choices.

But if you were caught up in the phenomenon that had built up around The Enraged Chicken, you knew that it was essential to stop in at the end of the week to pick up the following week's menu. That would tell you exactly what would be served each night. So, instead of picking the dish you wanted, you chose the day of the week with the best-sounding food.

You also knew that behind this apparent madness was something entirely rational. Two brothers named Schaeffer operated The Enraged Chicken as a school for cooks, servers, and restaurant managers. Each night, the students would move from one position to the next. The chef of the day would decide what kind of food was to be served and what dishes. Keeping a lid on the kitchen was Chef Gary Darling, then in the early years of his career. (He's now one of the owners of Zea.)

And the customers would fill the two small rooms of a converted neighborhood bar for lunch and dinner, Monday through Friday. They would pay with cash. If you made a reservation and didn't show up, you'd be put on the "you-know-what list" (they really called it that), and you couldn't get a reservation anymore. The Enraged Chicken had its customers well trained.

I ate there four or five times. Some nights, the place was brilliant, and the prices were low enough that it was easy to understand why people were so worked up about the place. Other nights, it was just okay, maybe even disappointing. The service gaffes were the biggest problem. Most of the students were inexperienced in serving gourmet customers. A few seemed never to have dined in a restaurant before.

But most customers turned a blind eye to the shortcomings and enjoyed the hipness of the place. But like all things hip, The Enraged Chicken's day in the sun ended. When it stopped being hard to get a reservation, and especially when there were empty tables at every meal, the novelty wore off. People stopped coming. And that was that.

The idea was a good one, however, when applied twenty years later by nonprofit operations such as Café Reconcile and Café Hope, which do more or less the same thing but with at-risk young people learning the restaurant trade and a straightforward, predictable menu.

★★★
España
Old Jefferson: 2705 Jefferson Highway
1960s-70s

España was thirty years ahead of its time. Here's a lightly edited version of a review I wrote about it in 1977 that captured the place better than anything I could write now.

I had dinner at España a couple of years ago, really loved the food, and resolved never to return. The place was a dump.

A thrice-restored wreckage, España's building was best known as the Cotton Club, a members-only swimming pool, behind peeling, mildewed stucco walls. When the restaurant came, the pool went, but the walls stayed the same. Behind a closed door are owner Antonio Lopez's living quarters.

It was not an inviting ambience, not even on the occasional nights when name flamenco acts were on tap. (One of the regular performers was Teresa Torkanowsky, former wife of Werner Torkanowsky, conductor of the New Orleans Philharmonic.)

However, friends tell me that this facility is a big step up from the original location of España, just off Earhart Boulevard on South Broad Street.

Lately, they've fixed the place up a little. The dining rooms are plain but clean, with stacks of colorful plates atop sideboards. But there's a long way to go.

Fortunately, one can get around all these quirks. All you need is a love of (or a curiosity about) offbeat cooking. Here are all the Spanish dishes you may have heard of all your life but never eaten.

The menu warns that all dishes are made from fresh ingredients and take at least a half-hour to cook. It's fortunate that there are a number of first courses that take more than the typical appetizer time to eat. The most appealing is a plate of cool sliced ham, salami, cheeses, pickles, tomatoes, olives, fat white anchovies, and chunks of tuna. This requires at least two big eaters to finish. The Spanish salad features some of the same ingredients, sans salami but plus peas. The greens are crisp, the dressing tart, herbal, and pleasantly oily.

By this time, the dishes worth crossing town for will be nearly ready. The most interesting is arroz con calamares: rice with squid. If you've never tried squid, come here to take the plunge. The little mollusks are cut up and have their nice rubbery texture and marine taste, with a slightly gritty, primal juice that scatters through the firm rice, peas, and pimientos for some satisfying, sturdy food. It comes in a big earthenware dish that holds enough to serve two people.

Moving from fish and rice to meat and potatoes, we find, under the name carne asada, an interesting combination of beef tenderloin (can they always use that?) stewed lightly with discs of potatoes and peppers. The meat has a rich flavor with a touch of something mysterious. Is it liver? Maybe it's just well aged—really well.

Arroz con pollo—rice with chicken—is no less filling but

considerably less of an adventure. The rice is cut by a sufficiency of chunky, warm, fatty chicken. Paella, the Spanish jambalaya, is a mishmash of flavors, dominated by the seafood component, and excessively fishy.

Bacalao, the salted, dried codfish found everywhere in Europe but especially in Spain and Portugal, is here for those who like their fish even stronger. It comes three ways, again in the earthenware dishes. The serving with garbanzo beans is best, because when you get tired of picking at the bony fish you can eat the round beans.

The selection of Spanish dishes is enough to address all the appetites you might bring to this table. But the España has another oddity: it serves just as large a menu of Italian food. The Italian food is more popular, of course. This speaks more for the taste of the public than that of the food. While the Italian food is safer, the Spanish choices hit higher peaks. But what strange menu partners!

The best Italian dish at España is manicotti, stuffed with ricotta and topped with a crimson, smooth, sweet tomato sauce to make a high-contrast duo that reminds me a little of Pickapeppa sauce atop cream cheese.

The veal is tasty, but all the combinations (there must be a dozen) are salty, especially the braciolone, with its much more intriguing interior than the rolled veal wrapper. Cheese, garlic, bread, and meat are in there, and it's good.

A high point comes at the end of the meal: the best flan I've ever tasted, with an uncommonly smooth texture that feels good in the mouth. The flavor, even with the heavy caramel, is elemental egg and vanilla. Fine coffees are available. The bar touts its sangria, but it looks better than it tastes.

In the years following this review, España continued to improve its food and surroundings. But New Orleans apparently wasn't ready for Spanish food, and it closed. Only now are we warming up to what ought to be a natural affinity for Spanish food. After all, Spanish is part of our Creole culture.

★★★
Etienne's Cuisine Francais
Uptown: 7638 Maple Street
1963-72
Metairie: 3100 19th Street
1972-85

In the twenty years after World War II, New Orleans was a boomtown. It tried to be like other growing American cities and succeeded rather too well. Ancient, funky aspects of the city were deemphasized. Mardi Gras was restrained. The city's epithet was "America's Most Interesting City," which was, clearly, America's Most Boring Civic Slogan.

In the 1950s and 1960s, the leading restaurants of the town

Etienne's
Cuisine Francaise

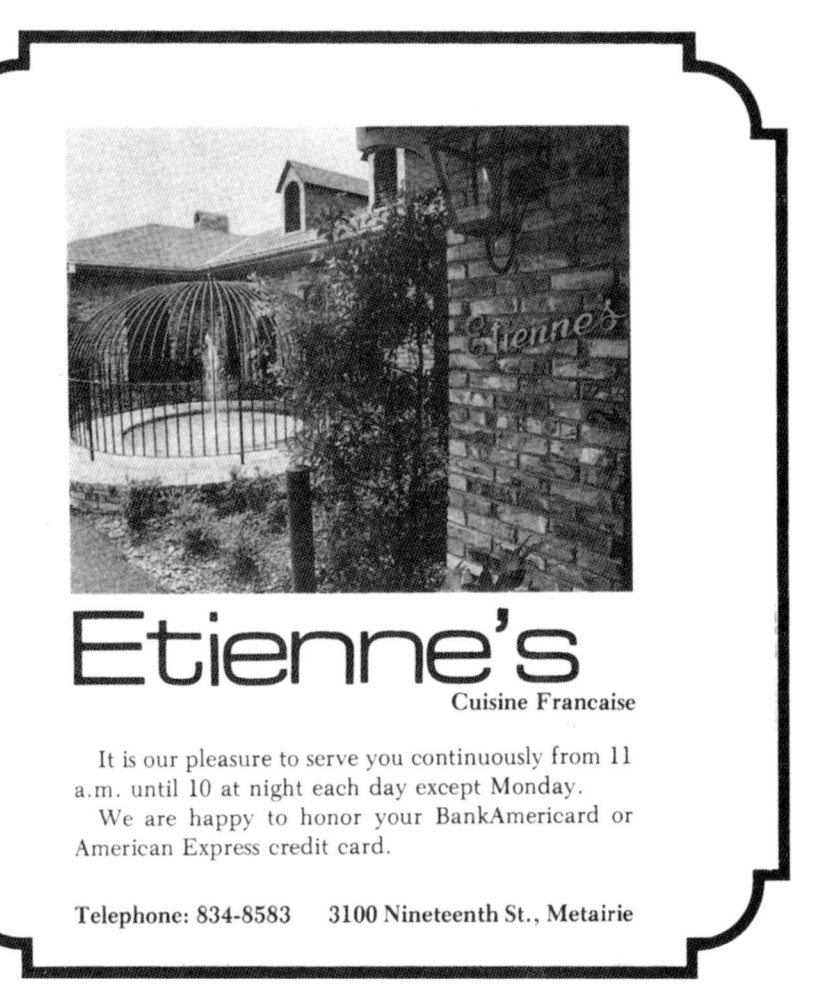

It is our pleasure to serve you continuously from 11 a.m. until 10 at night each day except Monday.

We are happy to honor your BankAmericard or American Express credit card.

Telephone: 834-8583   3100 Nineteenth St., Metairie

Etienne's, owned by Etienne DeFelice, served classic French and New Orleans Creole dishes. Sauces were a standout. After DeFelice retired, Andrea's opened in the same Metairie location in 1986. (Courtesy of New Orleans Magazine*)*

purveyed a provincial French style. What province? New Orleans, of course. These restaurants ranged from serious to pretentious, as if the mere utterance of the words "French cuisine" was enough to inspire reverence. The dining rooms resembled some hybrid of Galatoire's, Antoine's, and Arnaud's: gilded, mirrored, and filled with chandeliers (unless they had ceiling fans).

The menus of such places were practically interchangeable. Oysters Rockefeller and Bienville, shrimp remoulade and crabmeat ravigote, and turtle soup and seafood gumbo began the meal. Trout amandine or meunière, redfish with hollandaise, steak marchand de vin, and chicken Clemenceau continued it. Crawfish was rare (yes, really).

Etienne DeFelice was a Cajun, and most of his waiters were, too. But Cajuns speak French, so they fit right into the French Provincial style of the 1960s and 1970s. Etienne's was the apotheosis of such places, both before it moved from Uptown to Metairie and after. If you asked a fan of Etienne's what he liked about the place, you'd invariably hear, "They make such wonderful sauces!" Sauces ran around and over almost everything: cream sauces, hollandaise-based sauces, brown sauces with mushrooms and wine, sauces, sauces, sauces. The standard side dish—creamed spinach—was itself nearly a sauce.

Despite a somewhat uppity attitude, Etienne's was welcoming and affordable. Dinner at Etienne's could be had for right around five dollars in the middle 1970s—including the salad, soup, entree, dessert, and coffee. Even after the double-digit inflation of the late 1970s, that dinner was still only about nine dollars. If you paid a dollar and a half extra, you could get shrimp remoulade, too.

That was a good way to start. It was one of the better remoulades, with a sharp sauce made in the red-orange style, with palpable chips of savory vegetables and firm shrimp. (Shrimp for this dish were much smaller than they are now, and I think they had the right idea back then.)

The standard entrees were well made: trout meunière with the opaque brown sauce like the one at Arnaud's, the fish broiled instead of fried; redfish with capers, mushrooms, and a massive flow of hollandaise; chicken Rochambeau with béarnaise and red wine sauces; tournedos of beef with a thick brown sauce with mushrooms, completely obscuring the actual beef from view when it arrived. A famous specialty at Etienne's was its liver and onions with bacon, and indeed it was delicious.

Etienne's was the first restaurant where I noticed waiters routinely offering to top almost any entree with crabmeat. They pitched this as a special deal that they'd worked out with the chef, just for you. The practice is all but unavoidable in restaurants now, but it was uncommon then.

The dessert to get was crepes suzette—almost extinct in these parts now. They flamed them at the table with orange liqueur and brandy and served them grandly for all of a dollar fifty.

Etienne's cooking was rarely brilliant. But it was good enough, and the rich sauciness of all of it had its own appeal. The restaurant continued to do reasonably well into the 1980s, although most of its clientele was on the older side. Suburban Creole restaurants such as Sal & Sam's and the Red Onion, with their freewheeling, more casual style, had stolen the younger customers.

Etienne's moved to Metairie in 1972, relocating from its pretty but small dining rooms on Maple Street. The new restaurant was thoroughly suburban in style: low ceilings, a fountain in front, just enough gilding to give off a rich atmosphere.

In the 1980s, Etienne DeFelice was getting on in years, but he rebuffed potential buyers of his restaurant—until he met Agnello De Angelis. He owned hotels on the Italian resort island of Capri and had two sons and a nephew who wanted to open an Italian restaurant called Andrea's here. The two older men had a meeting of minds, and within a few weeks Andrea's opened in the former Etienne's. That was 1986. It was the passing not only of a restaurant but an entire genre of New Orleans dining. We haven't seen its like since.

★★★
Flamingos
Lee Circle Area: 1625 St. Charles Avenue
1977-81

A review I wrote of Flamingos in 1979 called it "a screaming queen theme restaurant." I wouldn't have said that if Paul Doll—who owned it with his partner, Tom Struve—hadn't used the same line to describe what was going on in his utterly unique cafe.

The outrageousness of every aspect of Flamingos was so attention grabbing that it's hard to recall anything else about it. (Fortunately, I have extensive notes.)

Flamingos on St. Charles Avenue was filled with eclectic décor and lots and lots of plastic flamingos. Fried eggplant sticks was a favorite appetizer. (From the collection of Peggy Scott Laborde)

The dining rooms were formerly the parlors of a mansion quite similar in style to the one next door, where the genteel, quiet Corinne Dunbar's was still operating. In contrast, Flamingos' rooms were painted in the most garish, saturated shades of pink, green, and lavender, with feathers, balloons, and fabrics.

And in every size, color, and corner were plastic lawn flamingos.

Flamingos' menu was a sixteen-page magazine. A long paragraph riddled with jokes and double entendres explained each dish. It also dished at length on the entire staff of the restaurant and their various supposed proclivities. All of this was so shameless and funny that you felt bad about laughing at it—but you couldn't help yourself.

The food actually was not all that far out. However, most of it was rare around New Orleans. The specialty of the restaurant was—well, quiches, which is a joke right there. These were extraordinarily good, tall and light, filled with a wide range of cheese, vegetables, and other ingredients.

The second major department was omelettes. They were better than most—not the dry kind the Camellia Grill fooled us into thinking were good, but beautiful, fluffy, moist, unscorched omelettes with interesting fillings.

Flamingos also took a stand on cold soups, which should be popular in New Orleans but aren't. The chilled cucumber and sour cream soup was a signature. But the gazpacho was good too, as were the hot soups. They made a fine turtle soup and a flawless black bean soup.

Salads were the final area of concentration. They were enormous, served in oversized scallop shells, and dressed with offbeat sauces with a lot of richness and tang.

You could make a meal of Flamingos' appetizers. The fried eggplant sticks, sent out by the giant-sized basketful, were terrific. The Greek-style spinach pie and stuffed grape leaves were good, too. The rest of the menu included the standard number of fish, chicken, and meat dishes. When the kitchen and service staff were on, all of it was wonderfully good.

However, Flamingos was not always on. Some days, everybody in the place seemed to be in a bitchy mood. That happens in all restaurants, but here the moods seemed not only to be tolerated but encouraged. The owners had their bad days, too. If you ever ate at Flamingos on an off day, you might never come back.

The novelty had to wear off, and it did. Straight people no longer found it funny. Gay customers had seen it all before. I also got the idea that the owners themselves were tired of running a restaurant. One day, it just closed.

Paul Doll and Tom Struve both died in 2001. Their restaurant didn't last, but their previous project remains a major part of the city's cultural scene. Paul and Tom were the founding managers of WWNO,

Matches from Flamingos. (From the collection of Richard Morelock)

the classical and jazz public radio station at the University of New Orleans. They set the standards for WWNO at a time when there were few such radio stations around the country. I worked at WWNO before and after it went on the air and knew them well. They were highly creative in every project they undertook.

★★★★
G&E Courtyard Grill
French Quarter: 1113 Decatur Street
1990-93

It was only around for a few years, but the G&E introduced a lot of New Orleans diners to the pleasures of Tuscan Italian food—something so little known around New Orleans at the time that it made a lasting impression.

The G&E occupied a narrow French Quarter building built in the late 1700s by the Ursuline nuns. Its front room was finished in travertine stone left over from the building of One Shell Square. It was illuminated by fixtures that looked reclaimed from a church. A passageway past the kitchen led to a small courtyard with an open grill and rotisserie, with spare but pretty gardens (growing fresh herbs as well as flowers) along the brick walls. Tables were set out there, too.

Chef Michael Uddo of G&E Courtyard Grill. One of the restaurant's specialties was oyster Rockefeller soup. (Photo by George Long)

The G&E was named for Giuseppe and Elaynora Uddo, who in the early 1900s founded a New Orleans Italian food emporium that evolved into Progresso Foods. Their great-grandson Michael Uddo was a chef who had already made a name for himself at Bouligny, one of the first of the Creole bistros of the early 1980s. Michael opened the G&E with the idea of blending Italian country cooking with current New Orleans styles. The premises were perfect for that sort of thing, and the place was an immediate hit.

Michael's twin brother, Mark—also a chef, although his most recent job was as maitre d' at Andrea's—joined the business after its success became apparent. The two of them ran a tight, consistent, innovative trattoria. Chickens and ducks were always on the rotisserie, tuna puttanesca and other fish on the grill, and oysters in the oven with prosciutto and cornbread. Michael made oyster Rockefeller soup popular (he may even have invented it). There were spicy cheese ravioli, penne with Italian lamb sausage, and dozens of other ideas from Michael's fertile imagination. Mark, a good wine guy, built a list of offbeat bottles that went perfectly with the food.

It was all terrific. Then the lease ran out. The new rent was so much higher that Michael didn't think he could make a profit from the small restaurant, and he closed it.

Michael and Mark have each surfaced again and again in the years since. But the magic of the G&E was never recaptured. New Orleans had not had such a restaurant before and hasn't had one since. You'd have to go to Tuscany to find its like.

G&E Courtyard Grill's Pasta Puttanesca

The name is an embarrassing Italian joke. Puttanesca *means "in the style of the prostitute." That notwithstanding, this was one of the many Tuscan-style dishes that the Uddo brothers introduced at their short-lived but superb trattoria. It's the best Italian dish I know involving fresh tuna.*

1 lb. yellowfin tuna
¼ cup extra-virgin olive oil
½ tsp. Italian seasoning
½ tsp. salt (preferably sea salt)
1 cup chopped tomatoes
½ cup pitted calamata olives
12 sprigs fresh parsley, leaves only, finely chopped
12 leaves fresh basil, finely chopped
4 anchovies (preferably white anchovies), finely chopped
2 Tbs. capers
½ tsp. crushed red pepper
1 lb. penne pasta, cooked al dente

1. Brush the tuna with some olive oil and season it with a little Italian seasoning. Grill it or cook in a hot skillet to the medium-rare stage (still red in the center). Cut into 1-inch cubes.

2. Heat the ¼ cup olive oil in a skillet until it ripples. Add all the other ingredients except the tuna and pasta. Sauté until everything is heated through, then add the tuna.

3. Turn off the heat. Add the pasta to the pan and toss everything around to distribute the sauce ingredients.

Serves 4.

★★★★
Genghis Khan
Mid-City: 4053 Tulane Avenue
1975-2004

Owners of restaurants come to the business from many kinds of past lives. I can think of only one whose immediately previous job was as first-chair violinist for a first-class symphony orchestra.

That man is Henry Lee, and that career shift wasn't the only unusual part of his story as a restaurateur. He opened the first Korean restaurant New Orleans ever had. It was also the only one here for decades.

Recalling Genghis Khan creates a memory conflict between two equally distinctive and enjoyable aspects of the place. Which was better: the food or the music? Both were first class.

I just flipped a coin and the cooking won. Korean food is obviously East Asian, but it's just as clearly different from Chinese, Japanese, or any other cuisine from that part of the world. It's unusual in that it includes many spicy dishes, which are not often seen in countries as far north as Korea.

Genghis Khan cooked a wide range of Korean specialties. But its best-remembered dish was a whole fried drumfish, brought to the table with the head, tail, fins, and everything else in place. That such a thing could become a house specialty in the 1970s—when diners were much more squeamish about trying something so primal—attests to the infectious enthusiasm of Henry Lee. How could you not go along with a tuxedo-clad, smiling guy who, between helping to deliver trays of food to tables, would pick up his violin and play a few classical pieces for you?

See, Henry Lee never gave up music. He continued with the symphony, and as of this writing (when he is in his seventies) he still performs around the country. He also leads a local Korean children's chorus. Sometimes he even shows up in restaurants he likes and plays.

Back to the menu. You'd start with kimchee, the pickled, peppery, crunchy vegetable national dish of Korea. Genghis Khan made it with cabbage most of the time, but other crisp vegetables got in there too. The favorite hot starter was fried mandu—beef-and-stuff-stuffed dumplings. Or kim, made by wrapping sheets of dried seaweed around a spoonful of fried rice. Or fried calamari, or tempura shrimp.

By this time in the meal, another performer would sit down at the

For many years the Genghis Khan was the only Korean restaurant in New Orleans. (From the collection of Edward Piglia)

piano and serenade the dining room for awhile, with a few duets with Henry Lee sprinkled in for contrast. Or it might be a guitarist or a flautist or some other deft local musician.

Then, if the whole fish wasn't dominating the table, you'd have bulgogi, another Korean standard. Henry always talked about installing a charcoal grill in the restaurant, to properly char the marinated beef at the center of this dish. Fire codes made that dream impossible, but Henry never stopped talking about it.

Or your table might have made a meal out of the chongol hot pot. This was a nearly-clear broth (it resembled Vietnamese pho) riddled with seafood and vegetables, served in a special utensil that looked a little like a tube pan for cakes. A fire burned in the middle, keeping the soup surrounding it like a moat nearly boiling hot. You were invited to add some of the homemade pepper sauce, too, to heat it in the other sense.

And now you'd hear voices raised in song. Operatic tenors and sopranos and baritones and altos (but rarely basses, I always noticed) would perform a few recognizable pieces from the repertoire. Diners with trained voices would sometimes join in. By that point, the marvelously urbane energy of the restaurant, usually full to capacity, reached a crescendo never seen in any other restaurant before or since. Even the wine lovers were ecstatic; Henry Lee always maintained an extraordinarily well stocked cellar.

All this magic was in mind-boggling contrast to the premises. The neighborhood around the corner of Tulane and Carrollton avenues was very much on the way down in the Genghis Khan years. Maison Blanche closed its store across the street, and the once-classy Fontainebleau Motor Hotel was turned into a storage facility. The restaurant's own building never was much to look at inside or out.

In 2002, Henry Lee did something about that. A downtown hotel in the former Sears building on Baronne and Common was looking for an operator to take over its restaurant. It was a highly visible, large space. And it was only a block from the Orpheum Theater, the home of the Louisiana Philharmonic Orchestra, with which Henry Lee still played. It seemed like a natural. And for awhile, it was a grand stage for Henry Lee, his food, and his music.

But the hotel expected the new Genghis Khan to serve breakfast, lunch, and dinner seven days a week. That was challenging when the hotel was full. But it was impossible to do without losing a lot of money when the place was empty. Henry Lee tried to renegotiate the deal with the hotel's owners but ended up in court and broke. He couldn't go back to the old place, because he'd leased it to someone else. Katrina's flood made that a finality. The glorious history of Genghis Khan ended after almost thirty years.

Henry Lee moved to Houston after the storm, but he still comes to town. His musicians are scattered all over the place. Many of them wound up at Café Giovanni, where opera singers have always been part of the program. A couple of other Korean restaurants managed to open.

But there will never be another Genghis Khan.

★★★
Gin's Mee Hong
French Quarter: 739 Conti Street (off Bourbon Street)
1940s-87

In the early 1900s, there was a major Chinese commercial district along Bourbon Street from Bienville to St. Peter. Remnants of that lingered into the 1970s, when Bourbon Street had more Chinese restaurants than the whole French Quarter has now. The best remembered of those was Gin's Mee Hong. The menu explained that "mee hong" meant "good taste." The place was well named.

But as usual, what most people remember about Gin's was a service quirk. If you wanted a drink stronger than tea, you'd order it from a waiter who came in off the street from the Old Absinthe House next door. He was an older man, thin and short, wearing the standard waiter uniform of white shirt, black bow tie, and black pants. He'd take cocktail orders from the whole room and exit via the front door. After a few too many minutes, he'd return with a tray of beverages. There was no connection between Gin's and the Old Absinthe House; the explanation of why Gin's wouldn't or couldn't serve its own drinks is unknown.

Gin's dining room was narrow and simply decorated, but there were white tablecloths and lots of china. The Chinese mustard and sweet-and-sour sauce were served in a tiny rectangular, two-compartment dish; it was difficult to obtain more sauce for your fat egg rolls, which you would almost certainly order.

Gin's food came mostly from the era when Cantonese food reigned over all Chinese menus. There were no hot and sour soup, moo shu anything, pot stickers, or General Tso's chicken. The closest thing to a spicy dish was the very good ginger beef, which had quite a bite from the ginger but no red pepper.

What you ate here was moo goo gai pan—chicken with vegetables in a mild, light sauce—or its slightly more exotic version, tung goo gai pan, with its black Chinese mushrooms. Everything came out in those stainless-steel pedestal serving dishes for easy sharing, even though the portions were something like half what a typical Chinese restaurant serves these days.

Gin's was my introduction to Chinese food, in 1971. At that time, Mr. Gin himself was still on duty. Even taking into account the distorted perspective of my age (I was twenty), he seemed incredibly ancient, and his Asian aspect made him seem like an old Chinese philosopher. He was just about the last of his generation, one that dominated the business of that part of Bourbon Street for decades.

I don't know exactly why Gin's closed, but my guess would be that when tourists took over the Quarter, they didn't see the point of eating in a Chinese restaurant in a town with so many other local options (which is a good point). There had also been an explosion in the number of other Chinese restaurants around town (there were over a hundred), and the food served by many of the new places was

A BITE OF HISTORY

Gluck's Restaurant
124 Royal Street

Located in the historic 1830s Merchants Exchange building in the French Quarter, Gluck's (1930s-61) featured what longtime Times-Picayune *restaurant critic Gene Bourg regarded as "very good basic food." Upperline Restaurant proprietor JoAnn Clevenger recalls, "It was full of people bustling around and they had these doors right in front and it's interesting, even their menu opened up like little doors on the front. The doors were kind of a very big deal. The other thing about Gluck's is that Tennessee Williams actually worked there as a waiter and later in one of his plays there's a character named Mrs. Gluck." Among the featured traditional New Orleans seafood dishes was redfish courtbouillon. (From the collection of Peggy Scott Laborde)*

Gluck's was open twenty-four hours a day. (From the collection of Reno Daret III)

Interior of Gluck's Restaurant. The restaurant was located in the first block of Royal Street where the Holiday Inn French Quarter is today. (Courtesy of Joseph Fein III and Jerome Fein)

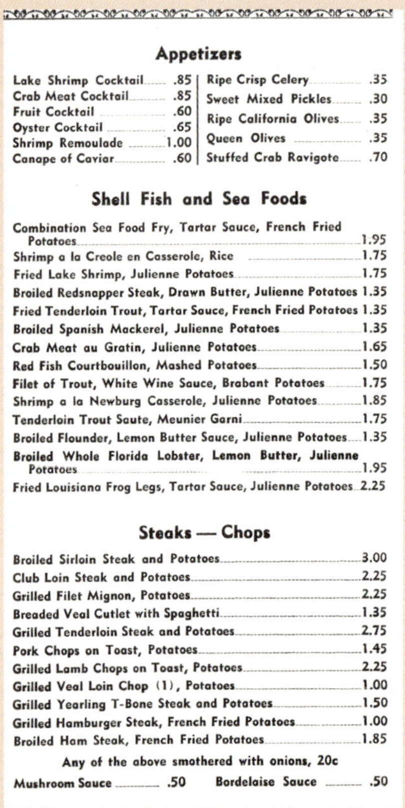

This Gluck's menu gives a hint of the variety of dishes the restaurant offered. (From the collection of Peggy Scott Laborde)

—Peggy Scott Laborde

much more exciting than Gin's old style. But nobody who went there as a regular part of their dining schedule holds it in anything less than high regard.

★★

Home Plate Inn
Mid-City: 4033 Tulane Avenue
1906-2005

New Orleans never was as rabid about baseball as it is about football. But baseball has enough fans that we've almost always had a minor-league team here. The New Orleans Pelicans played here from 1887 to 1959. Their glory days were 1915 through 1957, when they played at Pelican Stadium, on the corner of Tulane and South Carrollton avenues. People filled streetcars to get there and afterwards would hang around in any of a number of neighborhood bars and restaurants nearby.

One of those was so well liked that it persisted for decades after Pelican Stadium was torn down and the Pelicans became extinct. It had a baseball theme, yet. The Home Plate Inn literally was as close to Pelican Stadium's home plate as it was possible to be—right across the street.

Through its long history, only two families owned the Home Plate: the Gatipons and the Lehrmanns. A lot of what we know about the Lehrmann years comes from Phil Johnson, the longtime news director of WWL-TV and a big fan of the Home Plate Inn. In a piece entitled "What I Love About New Orleans" (who would write that but Phil Johnson?), he noted that not only did the Home Plate serve great New Orleans food, but in the old days it ran a betting book on the side. This made it even more solidly a part of the culture. It was as much a bar as a restaurant—a common configuration, particularly before 1965.

The Home Plate's roast-beef poor boy was a bit pepperier and garlickier than most, had just the right amount of gravy, and was very generous. If you sat down to a plate of red beans or hot tamales, you'd leave happy. (I once got both together and found an unlikely but great new flavor synthesis.)

The eternal topic of conversation at the Home Plate was what a shame it was that they tore the stadium down. The volume of that remorse rose even higher when the Fontainebleau Motor Hotel that the stadium was torn down to make room for closed and became a storage facility.

The water was very deep in the Home Plate Inn after Katrina. Matt Lehrmann didn't reopen. Some other owners came in using the Home Plate name as a suffix to "La Finca." But it's not the same. Thus one of the two or three greatest restaurant names in New Orleans dining history fades into a book like this.

The Hummingbird Grill was open twenty-four hours a day. (Photo by Douglas Barden)

★★★
Hummingbird Grill
Arts District: 804 St. Charles Avenue
1946-2001

The Hummingbird Grill would probably be a wildly successful restaurant if it were still open. It was a twenty-four-hour diner—one of the few in New Orleans. And it was unarguably a dive. A little harder to grasp was that it was a hotel restaurant. The Hummingbird Hotel never won any stars for its accommodations.

But the Hummingbird Grill did get stars from critics and fans, of which it had many. They came from a broader a socioeconomic spectrum than was seen by any other restaurant. People who would spend their last dollar, then had to find a place to sleep that night, were at the Hummer's counter. But so were men and women in formal wear, en route home from an underfed, oversloshed, high-society party.

The late-nighters came not only because the place was open but because the food was good. More than a few times, the Hummingbird Grill was compared favorably with the much more genteel Camellia Grill at the other end of the St. Charles streetcar line. The menus were quite similar. And the coin deciding which had the better hamburger is still in the air.

The Hummingbird Grill got rolling in the flush times following

---

A BITE OF HISTORY

Houlihan's Old Place
315 Bourbon Street

Opened in 1973, Houlihan's Old Place on Bourbon Street was ahead of its time with its eclectic décor. The second of then only two restaurants belonging to a Kansas City, Missouri-owned chain, it didn't have that cookie cutter feel at the time. The New Orleans restaurant closed in 1997, but many patrons still fondly recall the ten-cent oysters, French onion soup, and sangria. (Photo by George Long)

Houlihan's menu. (Menu collection gift of Richard and Rima Collin courtesy of The Historic New Orleans Collection)

—Peggy Scott Laborde

A BITE OF HISTORY

House of Lee
3131 Veterans Boulevard

House of Lee was one of the most popular Chinese restaurants in Jefferson Parish. (Courtesy of Davis Lee.)

House of Lee (1959-95) was one of the first Chinese restaurants in Metairie. Serving Cantonese and American food, the enormous restaurant was shaped like a pagoda and located near the corner of Veterans and Causeway Boulevard. It was run by Lee Bing and his family. He and his wife had eight children; one was Harry Lee, who went on to become sheriff of Jefferson Parish. Before Harry Lee went to law school, he managed his family's restaurant for a brief time.

Swizzle stick from House of Lee. (From the collection of Edward Piglia)

—Peggy Scott Laborde

---

116 LOST RESTAURANTS OF NEW ORLEANS

Menu board at the Hummingbird. (From the collection of Kevin Kelly)

World War II. Although it and the hotel were in one of the Thirteen Sisters buildings on Julia Street—a century earlier as fine a place to live as could be found in New Orleans—the neighborhood by then was thoroughly industrial. I remember, for example, the Active Linotype Service was around the corner, melting lead to make hot metal type for printers. These blue-collar people worked around the clock and wanted food that was ample, inexpensive, hearty, and (because this is New Orleans) delicious.

You could not have found a plate of red beans and rice much better than was served at the Hummingbird Grill. Not only were the beans and sausage hot and savory, but they came with a big cube of dark-crusted cornbread, baked on the premises every day. The cornbread was a draw unto itself.

And that was only one of five or six daily platters in the offing. Some were better than others, but you wouldn't be embarrassed to be seen eating any of it. They used ingredients of at least decent quality, and whoever was in the kitchen was almost as gifted as the guy who lettered the sign on the sidewalk.

Little-known fact: a surprising percentage of sign painters are very familiar with Skid Row. A lot of cooks turn up there, too, or did, in the days when the homeless population of New Orleans was centered on the corner of Camp and Julia, a block away. I know, because I lived near there for a few years in the late 1970s, when the pioneers of what would become the Arts District started moving in.

Those who could not be dragged into the Hummingbird Grill had problems with the neighborhood. Those who did like the place pointed out that the lunch counter was always full of uniformed New Orleans policemen on their meal breaks. Only an idiot would try to start a rumble there.

There was always a daily plate special at the Hummingbird. (From the collection of Kevin Kelly)

The Hummingbird was famous for its breakfasts, which I found less impressive than their lunch and dinner food. It's the only restaurant where I ever saw milk toast on the menu. That's the very poor man's bread pudding: toasted bread soaking in sweetened milk. I asked the waiter what it was like. He shook his head. "It's what you can hold down if you have a bad hangover." Yes, yes.

The Hummingbird Hotel and Grill closed at the end of 2001, as investors saw the building as an ideal place to advance the burgeoning redevelopment of that part of St. Charles Avenue. The property changed hands a few times and it's now being developed for commercial use. Meanwhile, the owner of the Camellia Grill bought the rights to the name and even opened a Hummingbird Grill—in suburban Elmwood, of all places. It didn't last long. How could it have? There weren't enough grease deposits.

★

Jim's Fried Chicken
Carrollton: 3100 South Carrollton Avenue
1940s-90s

Everybody remembers Jim's Place for fried chicken, including a lot of people who never ate there. Here's why: a big red neon sign saying *Jim's Fried Chicken* hung outside its big restaurant on the corner of South Carrollton and Earhart. That intersection is traversed by a large percentage of New Orleans people, many of whom cross it twice a day.

After years of seeing that sign—especially on the way home from school or work, when your appetite was primed—how could you not think of Jim's whenever fried chicken came to mind? Popeyes later used this same gambit. The sign on its very first location on opening day yelled *Popeyes Famous Fried Chicken.*

Jim's was open twenty-four hours. That brought in a lot of people who otherwise might not have tried the place. The heyday of Jim's was in the 1950s and 1960s, before the fast-food places destroyed fried chicken's image as a gourmet dish.

For all its fame, Jim's was never one of the great places to eat fried chicken in New Orleans. But it comes up so often on my radio show that I had to include it in this book. I call it the Wistful Palate Effect. The longer it's been since you experienced something, the better it seems.

On the other hand, Jim's wasn't bad. The crust was in fact one of the better ones. I think it was made with cracker meal. It wasn't seasoned especially well (I wonder how palates used to Popeyes would like it), and sometimes it was a touch soggy.

What I know for a fact is that it was fried to order—a mark of quality in fried chicken. After getting off work at the Time Saver one 1971 midnight, a coworker and I couldn't agree about where to have a late-night supper. I went to Ye Olde College Inn, and he went to Jim's, a block away. I ordered, ate, read the newspaper, paid, and left. My friend's car was in front of Jim's, so I pulled in. He was still waiting for the chicken. Fried chicken takes time.

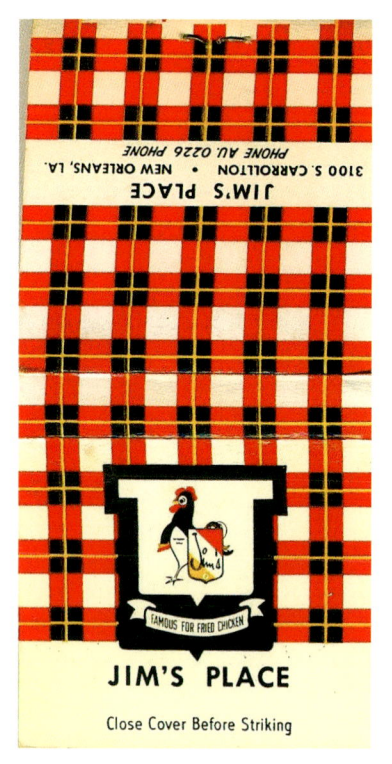

Jim's Place, also known as Jim's Fried Chicken, was owned by the LaRocca family. (From the collection of Edward Piglia)

Matches from Jim's Place. (From the collection of Edward Piglia)

Jim's big old original restaurant closed in the late 1970s. It was torn down and replaced with—ironically—a Popeyes. The family reopened in a small space on Airline Highway in Kenner, with the big red sign hanging in front. Jim's continued to cook the same fried chicken into the 1990s—a member of the family appeared on my radio show in 1991. Then one day I saw it was gone. The sign has made its way to Jim's Feed Store on LA 41 in Pearl River.

★★★★
Jonathan
French Quarter: 714 North Rampart Street
1976-86

Jonathan was among the most promising new restaurants in the mid-1970s, a time when the big-deal dining scene was stagnant and marked more by the whimsical Anything Goes than by anything serious.

It was also a time when a tourism boom in the French Quarter seemed imminent, which, in fact, it was.

Architect Jack Cosner and restaurateur Jim Maxcy (who owned restaurants both here and in New York) partnered to renovate a building into an Art Deco masterpiece. Jonathan was featured in more architectural magazines than food-and-travel ones. The three floors were filled with Deco pieces, some custom made, some from the 1920s. Paintings and drawings by the Deco master Erté covered the walls. Wherever possible, windows were round. Three of them in the entrance foyer had aquariums inside the walls. Early jazz and big band music played throughout the dining rooms. In the bathrooms, comedies and dramas from the golden age of radio entertained. The place was fantastic.

Jonathan, with its lavish Art Deco interior, was an architectural gem on North Rampart Street on the edge of the French Quarter. (Courtesy of New Orleans Magazine*)*

According to longtime friend and colleague JoAnn Clevenger, Tom Cowman, chef of Jonathan, was "a sophisticate who was very down home and jolly at the same time." (Photo © Mitchel Osborne MMX)

JONATHAN — A RESTAURANT

• TODAY •

• HORS D'OEUVRES •

NEW ORLEANS CEVICHE	3.25	MUSHROOMS PAPRIKASH	2.50
SEAFOOD QUICHE NIÇOISE	3.25	AVOCADO VINAIGRETTE	2.75
MELON WITH SMOKED IRISH SALMON	4.75		

• POTAGES •

REDFISH CHOWDER	2.00	ICED CREAM OF BROCCOLI	2.25

• ENTREES •

SAUTÉ OR BROILED REDFISH OR TROUT	8.50
SAUTÉ SOFT SHELL CRABS • REMOULADE	9.25
SWEETBREADS AND OYSTERS EN BROCHETTE	8.75
MALAY CHICKEN CURRY • CONDIMENTS	7.75
TENDERLOIN OF PORK NORMANDY	8.25
ROAST LEG OF LAMB • DILL MUSTARD SAUCE • WHEAT PILAF	9.50

• SALADES •

WATERCRESS, MUSHROOM AND BACON	2.75
TOMATO, FRESH BASIL AND MOZZARELLA	2.75
MIXED GREEN SALAD • CHOICE OF DRESSING	1.90

• DESSERTS •

BARBADOS RUM TRIFLE	2.25	FRESH FRUIT CRÊPE	2.25
ALMOND AMARETTO CAKE	1.75	PEAR, PEACH, PLUM SORBETS	1.75
CHEF'S VANILLA, PEACH, CHOCOLATE, GRAND MARNIER, BANANA, PINEAPPLE • RUM ICE CREAMS			1.75

• CLOSED ON SUNDAYS •

714 NORTH RAMPART • NEW ORLEANS 70116 • (504) 586-1930

This Jonathan menu shows off the creativity of Chef Tom Cowman. (Courtesy of JoAnn Clevenger)

Jonathan opened with an enhanced version of the menu from Maxcy's other New Orleans eatery, the Coffee Pot. That wasn't quite glitzy enough for the place or the crowd, though, and soon a chef was brought in to add sophistication. This was Tom Cowman, who after a long career in advertising switched to cooking. He had just closed his restaurant in New York and was available.

Cowman was perfect for Jonathan. Not only was his food polished and offbeat, but he was highly literate and steeped in the arts. His style fit right in with a dressy restaurant across from the new Theatre of the Performing Arts, whose patrons found Jonathan the ideal place to dine before the opera.

Chef Tom cooked American food in the still-new tradition of James Beard. Jonathan's menu when he arrived included oysters Rockefeller and Bienville, gumbo, and trout amandine—all but required by law of upscale restaurants then. He replaced the oyster classics with his

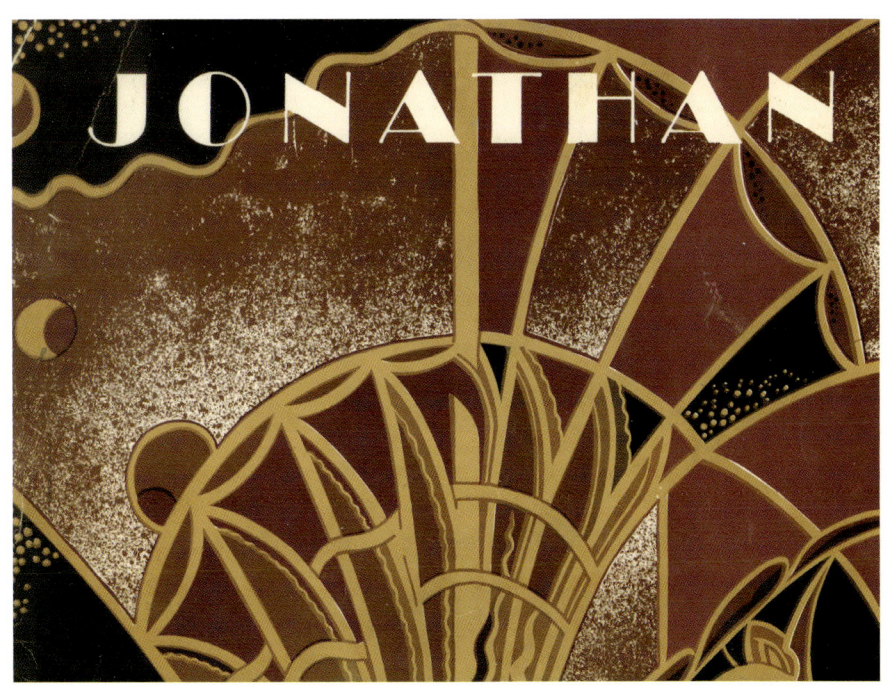

The cover of this Jonathan menu gives a hint of the Art Deco glamour of the dining establishment. (Courtesy of JoAnn Clevenger)

own assortment of four different and new baked oyster dishes, all wonderful. He made a signature dish out of his cold trout mousse with dill aioli—the likes of which nobody else was serving around town. He served lots of cold soups, notably vichyssoise in flavors other than potato and leek.

Chef Tom's most impressive achievement was in making a veal liver dish into a hit. Simple idea: he served it with the same kind of orange sauce common on roast duck. It was spectacular. At a time when few restaurants made desserts more ambitious than bread pudding, he baked his own unique cakes and tarts.

But the owners of Jonathan had guessed wrong about one important matter. They expected that the opening of Armstrong Park would pull French Quarter tourists and development towards North Rampart Street. But the Jax Brewery development along the riverfront proved to have stronger gravity. Everything moved that way. Armstrong Park was, to put it mildly, a disappointment. North Rampart Street dried up and began being perceived as dangerous—the kiss of death for a restaurant wooing local diners.

Those of us who loved Jonathan began saying good-bye to it. My last great meal there was my thirty-fourth birthday party. I asked Chef Tom to just cut loose, and he did. Ten courses of dishes whose flavors ranged from Paris to San Francisco to Oaxaca to New Orleans; some great wines from the overstocked cellar—it was everything Jonathan could be but wouldn't be for much longer.

The next time I saw Tom Cowman, he was at Lenfant's, of all places. (He would wind up at the Upperline, where he found a kindred spirit in JoAnn Clevenger.) The Art Deco artwork was sold at auction. An Italian restaurant tried to reopen in the Jonathan space a couple of years later. It failed, and there's been nothing like Jonathan since.

JOANN CLEVENGER REMEMBERS TOM COWMAN

Tom Cowman was an extraordinary person. He was witty, generous to a fault. Actually he spent all of his extra money on presents for other people. One of his greatest thrills was to go through the Tiffany's catalog planning Christmas presents for his friends.

He loved to cook. He didn't plan to be a chef when he started out. He was in the advertising business in New York. He got sidetracked into cooking because he loved it so much and I think part of why he loved it was to make people happy. Tom would have the most wonderful glee in his voice when somebody adored a dish and he would peek behind the door to see the response when he was serving someone a new dish for the first time. He knew so much about food. He was a sophisticate who was very down home and jolly at the same time.

He was also a great teacher. Chef Tom was so sweet and so kind to the people that worked with him in the kitchen. He didn't interact in the dining room too much but he was also a great teacher of the waiters. He wanted all the people who were responsible for bringing food to the guests to actually know more about the food.

His "Liver à l'Orange" dish was an accidental discovery. When Chef Tom was at Jonathan, he had a "Duck à l'Orange" on the menu. One day he was sautéing liver and something went wrong and it fell into the orange sauce and

Jonathan's Red Pepper Vichyssoise

Classic vichyssoise is a cold leek-and-potato soup. But Chef Tom Cowman used to do variations with watercress, bell peppers, and other colorful infusions when he was at Jonathan and, later, the Upperline.

2 lb. white potatoes
½ red bell pepper
1 leek, white part only, well washed
1 qt. vegetable stock
⅓ cup finely chopped ham
1 pt. half-and-half
2 oz. sour cream
Snipped chives for garnish

1. Prepare the vegetables carefully. Leave no peel or spots on the potatoes, seeds or membranes in the pepper, or dirt in the leek. Cube the potatoes and chop the pepper and leek.

2. Bring the stock to a light boil and cook the vegetables with the ham until the potatoes are soft—about 25 minutes.

3. Pour the pot contents into a food processor and puree. Then push the puree through a strainer or a food mill.

4. Microwave the half-and-half on high for 2½ minutes. Stir it into the soup. Whisk in the sour cream, then refrigerate the soup. Serve chilled, garnished with chives.

Serves 4 to 6.

★★★

Kolb's
CBD: 125 St. Charles Avenue
1899-1995

It's hard to believe that Kolb's is not still around. It commanded an extremely prominent location for almost a century and was the first name anyone thought of when German food was so much as mentioned. Its premises were so distinctive that no small number of people went there just to be there.

Kolb's was founded just before the turn of the last century by Conrad Kolb. Its home was a fine three-story, galleried brick building built in 1846 as the headquarters and townhouse of Daniel Pratt, a manufacturer of cotton gins. The restaurant became so popular that it expanded into the former Louisiana Jockey Club next door, in a similarly venerable brick structure. Through the years, ownership changed; while German food was of course ever present, the menu also featured local dishes.

of course Chef hated for anything to go to waste so he ate it himself and he adored it. It's a miracle kind of dish because it's not something you would think work but it was delightful.

The interior décor of Kolb's recalled nineteenth-century Bavaria. (Photo © Mitchel Osborne MMX)

KOLB'S

Gebratene Ente. Milk-fed Long Island Duckling, crisp roasted to taste-tantalizing perfection. Flanked with Fruit Dressing, Burgundied Red Cabbage and Boiled Potatoes _____ 2.25

Wiener Schnitzel. A tender cutlet of Choice Veal, dipped in egg batter and bread crumbs and sauteed to a well done perfection — An outstanding dish from Old Vienna! _____ 2.75

Huhn im Topf, mit Gemuese und Nudeln. One-half of a tender young milk-fed Chicken boiled in a rich chicken broth with Vegetables and German Noodles 2.50

Schnitzel a la Kolb. A selected Schnitzel, with Imported Cheese and Ham folded in and served with our special white wine sauce, a "house specialty" _____ 3.25

Chateaubriand Marchand de Vin, for Two _____ 12.50
(Service for two or more only — 45 minutes requested)
A Choice Tenderloin of Beef with Marchand de Vin Sauce served with an assortment of Garden Vegetables, a Masterpiece of the Culinary Arts.

Roast Prime Rib of Beef au jus. A standing Rib Roast of the finest aged Prime Beef, roasted as succulently rare or tenderly well done as may please the most discriminating palate _____ 4.65
Extra Cut _____ 5.50

Kolb's featured German dishes as well as New Orleans-style cuisine. (Menu collection gift of Richard and Rima Collin courtesy of The Historic New Orleans Collection)

A stein from Kolb's. (From the collection of Peggy Scott Laborde)

No location in New Orleans could have been better for a restaurant in those times. Kolb's was just off Canal Street, the center of all commerce in New Orleans. It was a half-block from the St. Charles Hotel, the leading hostelry in the city at that time. In the early 1900s, the French Quarter was in a state of decay, and even though it held many great restaurants, the main action had moved to the business district, on and just off Canal Street.

German food was experiencing a wave of popularity. Many Germans lived in and around New Orleans—maps of what are now the River Parishes, upstream of the city, called the area "The German Coast."

And like all restaurants here, as years went on, the menu took on a local flavor, both from the ingredients and the Creole tastes of the patronage.

Kolb's remained busy for most of its history, even surviving the anti-German sentiments that ran through American minds during two world wars. It could be that people didn't think it was really German, since it had been part of the city for so long, and they knew the owners and staff so well.

Kolb's was certainly not ashamed of its German heritage. The dining rooms were thoroughly Teutonic, with dark wood paneling, an immense collection of beer steins hanging on the wall, and all manner of German insignias except (of course) swastikas.

The most memorable part of the décor was Ludwig and his ceiling fans. The original dining room of Kolb's featured a marvelous leather-belt-driven ceiling-fan system, running about a dozen fans. It had come from one of the exhibition halls of the Cotton Centennial Exposition of 1884, held in what is now Audubon Park. Later, a wooden man dressed in German garb was added to it. A name plate called him Ludwig, and he appeared to be hand-cranking the whole array. (It actually was propelled by an electric motor mounted in the floor above.) One of the further curiosities of the ceiling-fan system was that one fan turned the opposite direction from all the rest.

When I finally got to Kolb's, in the mid-1970s, it was in decline. Part of this had to do with the revival of the French Quarter and the decline of Canal Street as a shopping district. German food was, by then, very much out of vogue across America, except in cities where that was all they had (Milwaukee, for example). Kolb's was essentially the only German restaurant left.

Worse, the German food was not all that good. Keep a certain menu going long enough, with not enough customers eating it regularly, and the pressure falls too low to keep the bubble inflated.

And by this time, most people who went to Kolb's ate not the German food but the Creole cooking. During a couple of years during which my office was two blocks away, I ate there once or twice a month and remember eating turtle soup, barbecue shrimp, baked oysters with crabmeat and hollandaise, roast chicken, and bread pudding.

All of this was actually pretty good. Occasionally, I'd have Vienna

A leather-belt-driven ceiling-fan system was a highlight of the décor at Kolb's, and it all started with this Bavarian gent named Ludwig. (Photo © Mitchel Osborne MMX)

schnitzel (as they called wiener schnitzel). Kolb's signature schnitzel (probably the only restaurant here that could be said to have such a thing) was called Kaiser schnitzel; you'd look at it and call it panéed meat with shrimp etouffee on top.

One wonderful oddity passed through Kolb's for a brief time. Chef Warren Leruth had an idea to make a sausage from pickled pork, the classic seasoning meat for red beans. He liked it but couldn't figure out what to do with it at his restaurant. So he gave the recipe to Bill Martin, who ran Kolb's in the mid-1970s. They served it with red beans, with a runny mustard dipping sauce on the side. It was terrific. Then one night, I came in for dinner wanting to try it again, and it was gone, never to be seen again.

During all the years I dined at Kolb's, and long before that, a maitre d' named Angelo ran the front door. He knew everyone, and everyone knew him. I remember him as a very old guy who seemed to have a permanent scowl, but old-timers say he was a nice fellow.

The day I went to Kolb's for lunch and saw that Angelo was gone was when I knew the restaurant's days were numbered. With all the offices moving out of the CBD, all the new restaurants in the area, and the continuing suspicion of what had become to most people a very unfamiliar cuisine, Kolb's no longer had a lunch crowd. Dinner business was very slack. New management tried to revive interest with a long list of new schnitzels with unusual sauces. But it was too little, too late.

And the place was run down. Dick Brennan, Sr., told me that his family had investigated the possibility of buying Kolb's, but after looking at what was needed in the renovation, they decided against it.

A few years after Kolb's closed, a group formed to reopen it as a restaurant—but not Kolb's. It was to be the Jockey Club again, they said, and made a big deal about the great location (balconies over St. Charles Avenue, where all the Mardi Gras parades pass!). But nothing came of it.

And the big KOLB'S sign still hangs there. Inside, the steins are gone, the fan system is packed away somewhere, and the old restaurant sleeps.

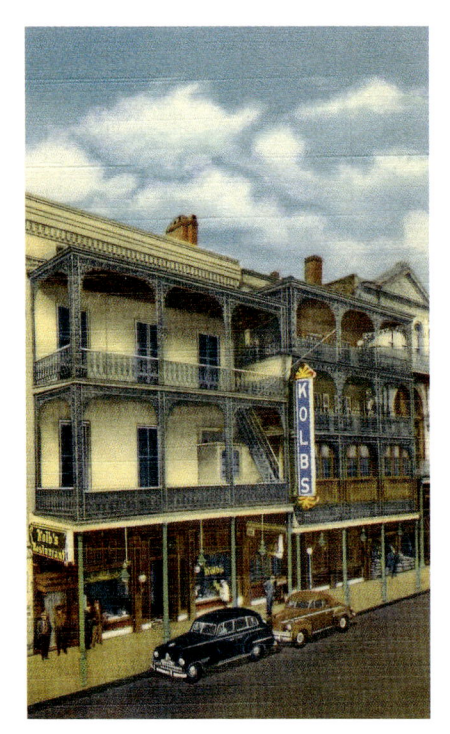

This postcard from the 1930s showed that Kolb's didn't change very much through the years. (Courtesy of The Historic New Orleans Collection)

★★★★
La Cuisine
Lakeview: 225 West Harrison Avenue
1965-2005

This restaurant proved that everything sounds more delicious in French. Its name in English would be "The Kitchen." It's like the difference between *saucissons* and hot dogs.

But La Cuisine had little Frenchness beyond having a Cajun in the kitchen and dining room. Lete Boulion—Mr. Lee to most of his customers—managed La Cuisine off and on for most of its history. Mr. Lee was the oldest of the old pros, already thirty-five years on the job when he opened La Cuisine. He was eighty-six when he retired in 1999, probably the oldest active restaurateur in New Orleans.

La Cuisine was a dining highlight of the Lakeview neighborhood. (Photo © Kevin R. Roberts)

In the restaurant's prime years, Joe Martin was also involved. Like Mr. Lee, he managed a number of New Orleans restaurants over the years. The men were both in command of two bits of knowledge, neither of which is well enough known to restaurant people. They knew what people like and what people are impressed by. And that's what they gave their customers, always, without ever going beyond.

Most of the menu at La Cuisine was familiar Creole-French cooking. But Mr. Lee and Mr. Joe knew that people liked a little Italian food, too. So there was Italian food. They understood that any restaurant can serve steaks and brisket and red beans but not many knew how to cook or serve fish beyond just frying it. So there was a lot of broiled, saucy, and stuffed seafood.

The seafood and Italian food and steaks and even beans had a little bit more going on than average. That impressed people, so much that by the 1970s, La Cuisine was a packed house with people waiting at the bar and even more standing in line outside, lunch and dinner, every day. All these people knew Mr. Lee and Mr. Joe, who would tell them what great big trout they saw in the kitchen tonight—and to tell the waiter that Mr. Lee said to put some crabmeat on top of that fish. That was kind of new in the 1970s. It impressed people.

What came out of all this after a few years was a cooking style I call Suburban Creole. It's sufficiently reminiscent of the food at Antoine's and Galatoire's to seem special but not as expensive, complicated, or fancy. And the potatoes and green beans and salad were free. People liked that. Suburban Creole was to spread to most of the upscale restaurants that opened in Metairie in the 1970s.

But it all started at La Cuisine. Business declined over the years, mainly as a result of the aging of their regular customers. The food remained good to the end, even as the ownership moved from father to daughter to husband. The latter took one look at the mess created by the ten feet of Katrina flood water and walked away. The building—owned by Tony Angello, whose restaurant a block away quickly reopened—was torn down. How do you say "empty lot" in French?

La Cuisine's Joe's Hot Shrimp

Joe Saladino, who owned La Cuisine in the 1990s, added this to the menu and had a hit with it. Its goodness owes much to the quality of the shrimp we have in New Orleans. Make a million of these: once people start eating them, they won't be able to stop.

24 large (16-21 count) shrimp, peeled and deveined
8 oz. mozzarella cheese
12 slices bacon, cooked until browned but not crisp
2 jalapeno peppers, chopped

1. Wash the shrimp and pat them dry. Butterfly the shrimp, leaving the tail section intact.

2. Cut the cheese into pieces a little smaller than the shrimp. Cut each piece of bacon in half.

3. Fill the center of each shrimp with about ¼ tsp. chopped jalapeno. Place a piece of cheese in the center. Wrap each shrimp with a piece of bacon, and secure with a toothpick.

4. Place the shrimp on a baking pan or pizza pan and broil until they turn pink. Turn the shrimp and return to the broiler until the cheese begins to melt. Serve immediately.

Makes 24.

La Cuisine's Oysters Deanna

After Bienville and Rockefeller, this garlic-and-breadcrumby concoction is the most popular in the pantheon of local oyster dishes. Every Italian restaurant has its own version, the most famous of which is oysters Mosca. This version uses a bit more olive oil and red pepper and comes out the oven bubbling. It may be the most irresistible dish I know. It's named for Deanna Saladino, the owner of La Cuisine in the 1990s.

⅓ cup extra-virgin olive oil
24 large oysters, partially drained
½ tsp. crushed red pepper
2 Tbs. finely chopped garlic
1 Tbs. lemon juice
2 Tbs. chopped Italian parsley
2 cups breadcrumbs
⅔ cup grated Parmesan cheese
1 Tbs. Italian seasoning

Preheat the oven to 400 degrees.

1. Pour a little of the olive oil in the bottom of a baking dish of almost any size, from a small au gratin dish to a pie plate. Arrange the oysters with about a half-inch between them in the dish.

2. Sprinkle the oysters with the crushed red pepper, garlic, lemon juice, and parsley. Combine the breadcrumbs, Parmesan cheese, and Italian seasoning. Cover the oysters with the blend.

3. Put the dish in the oven, uncovered, for 10 to 15 minutes (depending on the size of the dish) until the sauce is bubbling and the breadcrumbs on top brown.

Serves 6.

★★★
Lakeview Seafood
New Orleans East: 7400 Hayne Boulevard
Late 1950s–mid-1980s

Long before tract development began in New Orleans East, residences and businesses filled one side of Hayne Boulevard. On the other side was Lake Pontchartrain. Over those waters, fishing camps on stilts lined the shore from Lakefront Airport all the way to the old community of Little Woods. If you didn't own a camp, you could rent one, and my family did for a week or two every summer in the 1950s and 1960s.

Some nights, we walked across the tracks and Hayne Boulevard to one of the many casual seafood restaurants. The famous names were Gee & Lil's, the Edgewater Grocery, Bourda's, and (past the end of the road, accessible only by foot) Henderson's.

The best of these, however, was Lakeview Seafood. It was a misnomer, having no view of the lake or an address in the Lakeview section of town. But as inconvenient as its location was, people drove there from all over town for a unique specialty: the seafood boat.

Charlie Smith, the owner, was a former Marine baker. He baked his own loaves of white bread, not French bread. He'd cut them from end to end, hollow out the bottoms, brush the insides with butter, and fill them with fried shrimp, fish, and/or oysters. They were big enough to feed two hungry people. I'm not positive whether Charlie originated the idea—at one time you could get a seafood boat from any of a number of restaurants. But his were the best and the most famous.

Lakeview Seafood also boiled shrimp and crabs, fried seafood platters, simmered gumbo, and made regular poor boys. You never went there in a hurry, because they cooked everything to order. And if the place were full, you'd notice that people were in even less a hurry to leave than they were to eat. It was a change of scenery from the camp across the street for most customers.

Lakeview Seafood was a dumpy place in the tradition of Uglesich's. The floor sagged here and there, and the exterior always needed a paint job. It felt more like a bar than a restaurant and indeed often did have more than a few guys standing up at the rail having a cold one.

A review by Richard Collin sent many new customers to the place, as happened a lot in the 1970s. Many of them didn't know Little Woods existed, let alone anything about its hypercasual, edge-of-town culture. A friend told me that he was in the place one afternoon when the pay phone rang. Charlie answered it:

"Lakeview Seafood. [Pause.] Yeah, we're open. [Pause.] Yeah, we got fried seafood. [Pause.] Yeah, we got boiled seafood. [Pause.] What? [Pause.] Dress code? Cap, you can come here in your drawers if you want!"

Probably that would have been noticed. But bathing suits weren't. We would swim in the lake back then.

Lakeview Seafood's Oyster Boat

The bread—which is what makes a boat a boat—is usually available from supermarkets with in-house bakeries, or you can bake the loaves yourself. Cutting the hollow is easier if you freeze the loaf first, but that's not necessary. You can also make this great oversized sandwich with shrimp, catfish, or even small soft-shell crabs.

1 loaf unsliced white bread
1 stick butter, softened
2 Tbs. fresh chopped garlic
1 Tbs. chopped flat-leaf parsley
½ tsp. lemon juice
Peanut oil for frying
½ cup Fish-Fri (corn flour)
½ cup yellow cornmeal
1 Tbs. salt-free Creole seasoning
1 Tbs. salt
4 dozen medium oysters

Preheat the oven to 300 degrees.

1. Slice off the top half of the bread. Make a vertical cut about 2 inches deep around the top of the lower half of the loaf, about a half-inch from the sides. Push the part of the bread inside the cut down to make a pocket in the center.

2. In a saucepan, heat 1 Tbs. butter with the garlic and parsley. Cook until fragrant, then add the lemon juice and remove from the heat. Stir this into the remainder of the softened butter.

3. Coat the inside of the loaf and the top half of the loaf with the garlic butter. Toast the bread in the oven until the inside of the bread just starts to turn brown.

4. Pour peanut oil into a heavy pot or skillet, preferably cast iron. The oil should be 1 inch deep. Heat over medium-high heat to 375 degrees.

5. Combine the corn flour, cornmeal, Creole seasoning, and salt in a large bowl and mix with a fork. Coat 6 oysters at a time by putting them, good and wet, into the bowl and tossing them in the mix.

6. Fry the oysters, a dozen at a time, until golden brown and crisp. Drain on paper towels. Load them into the pocket of the toasted loaf. When all the oysters are inside, place the top of the loaf over the oysters, and serve with lemon wedges, hot sauce, and French fries.

Makes 1 oyster boat—enough for 2 people.

Matches from La Louisiane. (From the collection of Peggy Scott Laborde)

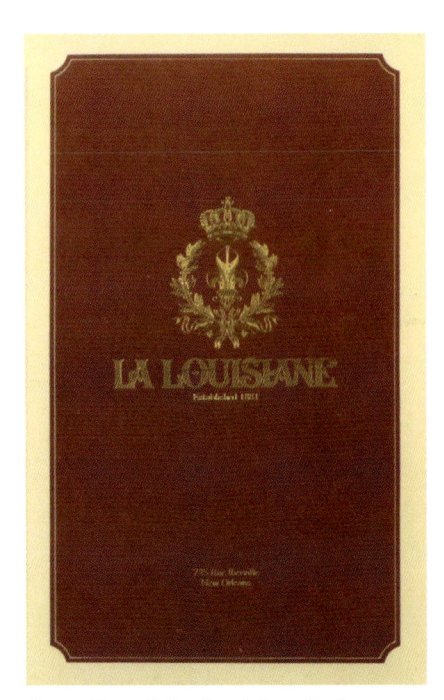

Even though La Louisiane had a series of different owners, it remained a well-respected fine dining restaurant. (Menu collection gift of Richard and Rima Collin courtesy of The Historic New Orleans Collection)

"Diamond Jim" Moran's passions were diamonds and fine food. He loved wearing diamond-studded tiepins and belt buckles. (Courtesy of The Historic New Orleans Collection)

★★★

La Louisiane
French Quarter: 725 Iberville Street
1881-2005

No major restaurant in New Orleans has had as checkered a history as La Louisiane. Its high points were very high indeed. But times came when its customers wondered how such a beautiful, historic establishment could be allowed to become so mediocre.

La Louisiane was founded in 1881 by a partnership involving no less than Antoine Alciatore, the founder of the restaurant that bears his first name. In its first incarnation, La Louisiane was one of the city's most formal and expensive restaurants. It occupied a townhouse, built in the prosperous year of 1837 with such style that its inhabitants had clearly been well heeled. Its windows were made of beveled, leaded glass. The chandeliers were built in France by Baccarat.

The food was very French. Scoop Kennedy's 1946 book *Dining in New Orleans* notes that La Louisiane was famous for its bouillabaisse and may even have been the first New Orleans restaurant to make that a specialty. (Logical: Antoine Alciatore was from Marseilles, also the home of bouillabaisse.)

The time between the world wars was not good for La Louisiane. Its premises and kitchen were tired, and business drifted away to new hotspots—particularly Arnaud's. After the Second World War, new investors came in with a renovation. But the French Quarter was changing, and La Louisiane lost its main dining room when the building it was in was torn down for the parking garage now behind Mr. B's.

It was around this time that the La Louisiane most people remember came to be. Jimmy Brocato made a few nickels in the 1930s setting up slot machines around town. He changed his name to Jim Moran, took over La Louisiane, and dubbed it Moran's La Louisiane. There he got his nickname—"Diamond Jim"—by wearing an immodest number of diamonds on his person. He impressed special customers by serving some of them a gigantic meatball studded with a diamond. He had quite a few special customers, including celebrities and a few shadier figures.

La Louisiane was on a roll when Diamond Jim died in 1958. His sons Jimmy and Tony picked up where he left off and improved the restaurant consistently. Both were knowledgeable about Italian food and developed more than a few house specialties. Not many diamonds went out on meatballs anymore, but those meatballs were distinctive on their own merits. They were at least twice as large as normal meatballs, but they were so light in texture that they may have weighed less. They came out on a bed of angel-hair pasta asciutta, whose red sauce was both light and spicy with red pepper.

But the dish that everybody talked about was the fettuccine. Jimmy Moran, dressed up in a fine suit, made it himself while standing next to the table that ordered it. He did this all night at seemingly every table. Pasta with a cream sauce was new to most New Orleanians, even those of Italian extraction. That fact, combined with the undeniable deliciousness of Jimmy Moran's version of fettuccine Alfredo, created a legend that would outlive not only both Moran brothers but three restaurants where they tossed their magical fettuccine. Many of their cooks—notably the brothers Sal and Joe Impastato—went on to open their own restaurants. Moran's way with fettuccine was always on their menus.

Moran's (sometimes people left off the "La Louisiane") had crabmeat-stuffed, hollandaise-covered mushrooms that were mind-bendingly good. The fish was always first class. Regular customers would find dishes they hadn't ordered arriving at the table. Sometimes they were charged for these, but nobody complained, because they knew that freebies would come, too.

Jimmy Moran built a second restaurant in a new building at the French Market in 1975. For awhile he ran both places, but the new Moran's Riverside (about which more elsewhere) was such a stunning place that all the regulars went over there.

One of "Diamond Jim" Moran's specialties was diamond-studded meatballs. (Menu collection gift of Richard and Rima Collin courtesy of The Historic New Orleans Collection)

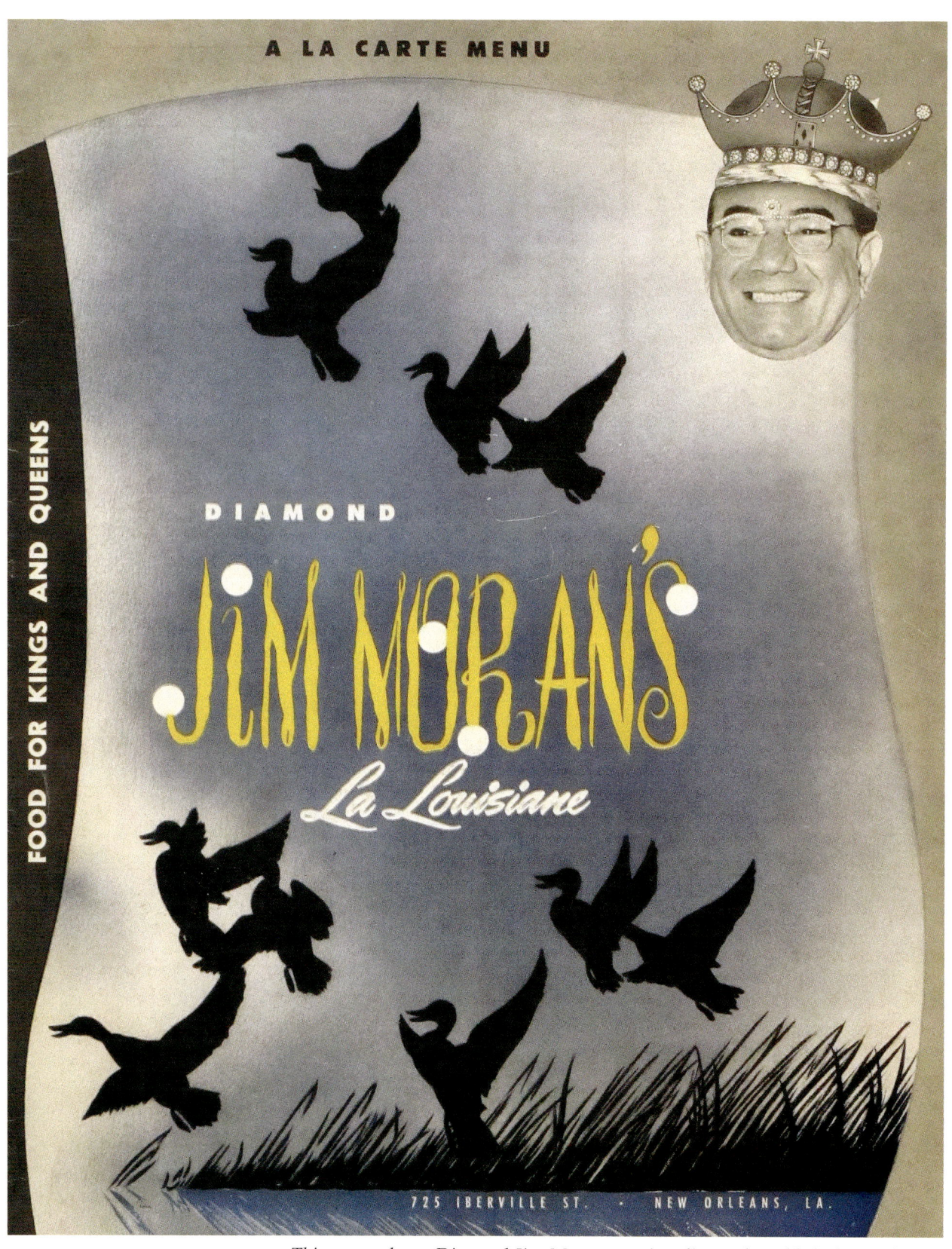

This menu shows Diamond Jim Moran wearing diamond-studded glasses. (Menu collection gift of Richard and Rima Collin courtesy of The Historic New Orleans Collection)

Taking over La Louisiane after Moran left was Joe Marcello, who with his brother Carlos operated the recently incinerated Elmwood Plantation and newly renovated Broussard's. The Marcellos turned La Louisiane into Elmwood Plantation in Exile. Many of the cooks and waiters from that legendary restaurant moved to La Louisiane, and yet another golden age began—with a different, mostly Creole style of cooking. In the 1980s, the Marcellos bought and sold their restaurants every couple of years, while the Elmwood guys and their boss, Nick Mosca, kept moving around.

La Louisiane changed hands so many times in the late 1980s and 1990s that it was hard to keep track. It didn't help that none of the revivals was especially good. Jim Chehardy, who'd had a big success in Metairie and suddenly closed, was there for awhile. So was hotelier Mark Smith, the owner of Louis XVI. The historic restaurant closed for long stretches of time. When it came back after the hurricane, it lost its identity to a Brazilian steakhouse that lasted only a couple of years.

At this writing, La Louisiane is closed and in limbo. It would make an ambitious restaurateur a great—if expensive—venue. Lots of pedestrian traffic passes by, and many other great restaurants are near.

La Louisiane's Trout LaFreniere

This dish was created by the late Nick Mosca, formerly chef of Elmwood Plantation and La Louisiane. It is deceptively simple to prepare; it looks and tastes like a much more complicated dish.

4 6-to-8-oz. speckled trout fillets
¼ cup lemon juice
Salt
Pepper
1 Tbs. smallest possible capers
1½ cups seasoned Italian breadcrumbs
1 cup lump crabmeat
1 cup peeled medium shrimp
½ cup white wine

Preheat the oven to 400 degrees for 15 minutes.

1. Place the trout fillets in a buttered skillet with an ovenproof handle or on a metal baking pan, and spoon lemon juice on top of them. Sprinkle with salt, pepper, and capers, then about half of the breadcrumbs.

2. Distribute the crab lumps and shrimp uniformly over the breadcrumb layer, and pour the white wine gently over it. Top with the remainder of the breadcrumbs, and put the trout in the hot oven for 15 minutes. Check it after 10 minutes to make sure fish is not overcooking; it should not be falling apart when jabbed with a fork.

Serves 4.

La Riviera chef Goffredo Fraccaro's signature dish was crabmeat ravioli. (From the collection of Phil Johnson)

★★★★
La Riviera
Metairie: 4427 Shores Drive
1972-2005

For most of their first century in New Orleans, Italian restaurants were almost all homegrown operations: Mamma cooking, Papa running the dining room, and the bambinos doing everything when they got old enough. The wait staff just fell into the business. The food was likely to be lusty and wonderful. But the service and surroundings weren't up to what the French restaurants were doing.

Then Chef Goffredo Fraccaro came to town. Born in Genoa in 1926, he worked in restaurants until he was old enough to go to sea. For decades, he cooked on ships. Sometimes the ship called at New Orleans, and he liked the place. He cooked in Baton Rouge for a few years, then moved to New Orleans in 1969 to open the city's first big-deal Italian restaurant. Even the name was grandiose: Il Ristorante Tre Fontane. The restaurant of the three fountains was hidden in the French Quarter on Exchange Alley, where the Pelican Club is now.

It was too soon. Most New Orleanians with a taste for Italian food only wanted the rustic, inexpensive style and couldn't get their heads around a ten-buck Italian dinner, regardless of its goodness. The tourists were not in New Orleans for Italian food. After three years, the Tre Fontane partnership ended. Goffredo then opened in Metairie, a block off Clearview Parkway at West Esplanade, in an area only beginning to be developed.

He toned down his menu but only a little. He had his friend Phil Johnson from WWL-TV write some copy for the menu to make the point that each part of Italy had a different style of cooking, none of which was much like New Orleans Italian food.

Nobody paid much attention to all that and instead ordered spaghetti and meatballs, then veal Parmigiana, then fried calamari (the best ever in New Orleans, served in massive, golden-brown piles). About twenty years later, he had people eating veal saltimbocca, osso buco, trout with anchovy sauce, and all the other stuff he couldn't sell them back at Tre Fontane. Ironically, he even served it on the same beautiful plates he brought with him from the French Quarter and kept using for thirty years.

Along the way, Goffredo entered and won a crabmeat-cooking competition in San Francisco. The dish was crabmeat ravioli. Hardly anyone in the world had ever heard of such a thing. It became the signature dish at the restaurant: house-made pasta pillows stuffed with crabmeat, Parmigiano-Reggiano cheese, and cream, served in Alfredo sauce. It was spectacular. Not only did everybody eat it when they went to La Riviera, they ate it everywhere else, as restaurants rushed to copy the new classic.

Metairie people came to love not just Goffredo's food but the man himself. Getting a hug from him was unavoidable. He didn't come out into the dining room a lot, but he gave a warm welcome to any customer who infiltrated the kitchen to say hello. He'd almost always hand you something to pop into your mouth right out of a bubbling pan on the stove.

Goffredo's two best friends were Chris Kerageorgiou and Warren Leruth, the owners of La Provence and LeRuth's respectively. The three great chefs looked a lot alike, and when they got together they'd cut up, shout, and laugh at one another. They were the founders of the Chefs' Charity for Children, the oldest and most distinguished of the many culinary fundraisers in New Orleans. Never was there an equal of that troika of cooking talent.

La Riviera originally opened in what looked like an office building on a side street. The small, rectangular dining room's tables were separated from one another by rows of aquariums filled with fish. Looking at the fish, you would also look into the plates of people less than two feet away from yours. In the 1980s, Goffredo built a bigger, much handsomer restaurant across the street. A decade later, he sold La Riviera to his nephew Valentino Rovere. But he kept on working every day, not cutting back for years.

La Riviera was badly flooded by the lake after Katrina. Valentino said he wanted to reopen, but the restaurant became a salon and spa. Goffredo was the last man standing of his chef friends, deep into his eighties, watching the many upscale Italian restaurants follow the trail he pioneered.

★★★★★
Le Chateau
Gretna: 1000 Behrman Highway
1983-86

The best French restaurant to ever open in New Orleans was in a location so unlikely that it wasn't taken seriously until it was too late. Not that it mattered a lot.

Le Chateau was the creation of Denis Rety and his wife, Annick. Both were born in Brittany. Before they came to town, they had an immensely successful restaurant called La Belle Epoque in Bay Harbor Islands, near Miami. What brought them to the West Bank of New Orleans was a major public-relations problem. A customer not satisfied with the way the restaurant handled his complaint created a scene. A man at an adjoining table decided to get involved. He began a public campaign against the chef for alleged anti-Semitic remarks. La Belle Epoque was in a largely Jewish community, and the result was devastating to the restaurant. It had to close, and the Retys left town.

Le Chateau opened and closed without my having heard that story. All I knew was that this middle-aged French chef was running the kind of French restaurant you'd expect to find in Manhattan or perhaps France itself. The degree to which this was true can be measured by how I heard about Le Chateau. It wasn't from the usual network of avid gourmets but from other French-born chefs. They were knocked out by this guy. When they asked him how he made such perfect puff pastry in house, or demi-glace, or soufflés of everything, his answer usually was to hold his arms in front of him and say, "I make it with my own hands!" Which was a fact.

The menu was a catalog of Escoffier-style French classics and included a lot of foodstuffs that were very exotic in New Orleans—mussels, for example, which nobody cooked here in 1983; sweetbreads in a vol-au-vent whose pastry was so good that you ate all of it instead of using it only as a container; pheasant Souvaroff, the rich-tasting bird stuffed with handmade foie gras mousse. That remains a candidate for the Best Dish of My Life So Far.

Le Chateau didn't look like much on the outside, but the dining room was bright and handsome. Silver trolleys rolled up to your table so Annick Rety—whose skills in the dining room were flawless—could finish the preparation before your eyes. She boned out whole Dover sole, carved chateaubriands or ducks, flamed crepes suzette.

But the best thing she and her husband did was serve hot dessert soufflés. Nowhere have I had better. They were big and airy, with a variety of sauces made to order to match the main flavor.

Chef Denis brought an amazing wine collection with him to New Orleans. He had a few pages of very old Bordeaux, including an 1887 Chateau Lafite and 1900 Chateau Latour. When Denis came to the end of his short New Orleans run, he invited me and a few other regular customers to open those two and a few others. I still have the handblown 1887 bottle on a shelf in my office.

The reason Chef Denis shut down his magnificent restaurant was that he won his lawsuit against his defamer. The first judgment was $33 million. On appeal, it wound up being reduced to $5 million, but that was enough for him to be able to end his exile and spend the rest of his life raising horses. His son-in-law, who had cooked with him for some time, took over Le Chateau, but that didn't last long. The locals couldn't exactly figure out how a French restaurant could get by without trout amandine and oysters Bienville.

You can't find a restaurant like Le Chateau even in New York anymore.

★★★

Lenfant's
Lakeview: 5236 Canal Boulevard
1940-88

Lenfant's had three lives, each different from the others. Louis Lenfant and his family opened the restaurant just before World War II and established it as what in New Orleans speak would have been called a "modren" place. It had a unique look, with curved corners not just inside but outside, too. Neon tubes wrapped around the facade. Historian Ned Hemard calls the look "Streamline Moderne," noting the resemblance of Lenfant's to the rides at Pontchartrain Beach.

The restaurant's logo—also in neon—was another distinctive icon. It was a lobster dressed in a tuxedo, standing upright with a napkin

This photo from the 1980s shows Lenfant's unique Art Deco architecture. It was a mainstay in the Lakeview neighborhood for more than forty years. (Photo by Frank Methe)

over one claw and holding a waiter's tray. The fact that Lenfant's didn't often serve lobster never seemed to be questioned. Perhaps it was a crawfish. That would have made more sense, since Lenfant's was famous for its crawfish bisque.

But of all the memories of Lenfant's, the one that lives on most pervasively is its parking lot. It was bigger than it needed to be. And it was adjacent to one of the many cemeteries in the neighborhood. No lights in a cemetery, no prying eyes—for many years, Lenfant's was the place you went on a date to get a little dinner and then make out. Although the memory is fading now, for a very long time after Lenfant's stopped serving in its parking lot, the immediate response to the mention of its name would inevitably concern romantic moments in that shell-covered expanse.

I am among many Orleanians who have a second association with Lenfant's. It's where you went after a funeral or right before All Saints' Day, when your family went to the cemetery to dress up the tomb of loved ones.

Lenfant's menu was enormous and almost laughably cheap. A copy of a specials sheet I had until Katrina stole it listed about twenty entrees, complete with salad or soup and vegetables, for less than a

Lenfant's longtime logo on its menu and sign was a lobster dressed as a waiter. The restaurant was a real landmark in the Lakeview neighborhood. (Menu collection gift of Richard and Rima Collin courtesy of The Historic New Orleans Collection)

dollar fifty. Most of it was home-style cookery, with a clear influence of the just-past depression. Although a lot of this was good enough, it was clear that Lenfant's wasn't trying to serve the best food in town. Nobody ever accused the place of that.

After the war, Lenfant's became a very popular venue for private parties—everything from wedding receptions to Rotary Club meetings. It seemed to me that they were more involved with those than with a la carte business in the 1960s and 1970s.

Special Today

OUR SEAFOODS ARE STRICTLY FRESH CAUGHT DAILY

SEAFOOD
OYSTERS — SHRIMP — FISH — CRABS

SHRIMP LENFANT
(REMOULADE)
1.50

Fried Shrimp In Pants
1.75

CHEF'S SEAFOOD PLATTER DeLUXE
FRIED
Oysters - Red Fish - Shrimp
Trout - Stuffed Crab
3.00

STUFFED CRAB
With Lots of Crabmeat Dressing
1.10

Fried Stuffed Shrimp
2.25

BROILED Florida Lobster
Stuffed with Crabmeat
4.75

SOFT SHELL CRAB
French Fried Potatoes
1.85
Stuffed With Crabmeat Dressing
2.25

Crayfish Bisque
In Season
.95

Fresh Caught GULF FLOUNDER
Stuffed with Crabmeat
2.75
and up
BROILED WITH BUTTER
1.75

Fried Jumbo Louisiana Frog
In Season
2.50

Fried Bayou Cook OYSTERS
½ Dozen 1.00
Dozen 1.75
Stuffed
½ Dozen 1.50
Dozen 2.50

Deep Sea New England SCALLOPS
2.25

Seafood Salad Platter
Shrimp, Egg Salad
Tuna Fish
1.85

RED FISH Steak Almondine
1.75

All Seafoods Served with Chef's Tossed Salad and French Fried Potatoes

Tenderloin of Speckled Trout
1.75
TROUT MEUNIERE
2.00

LENFANT'S SPECIALS

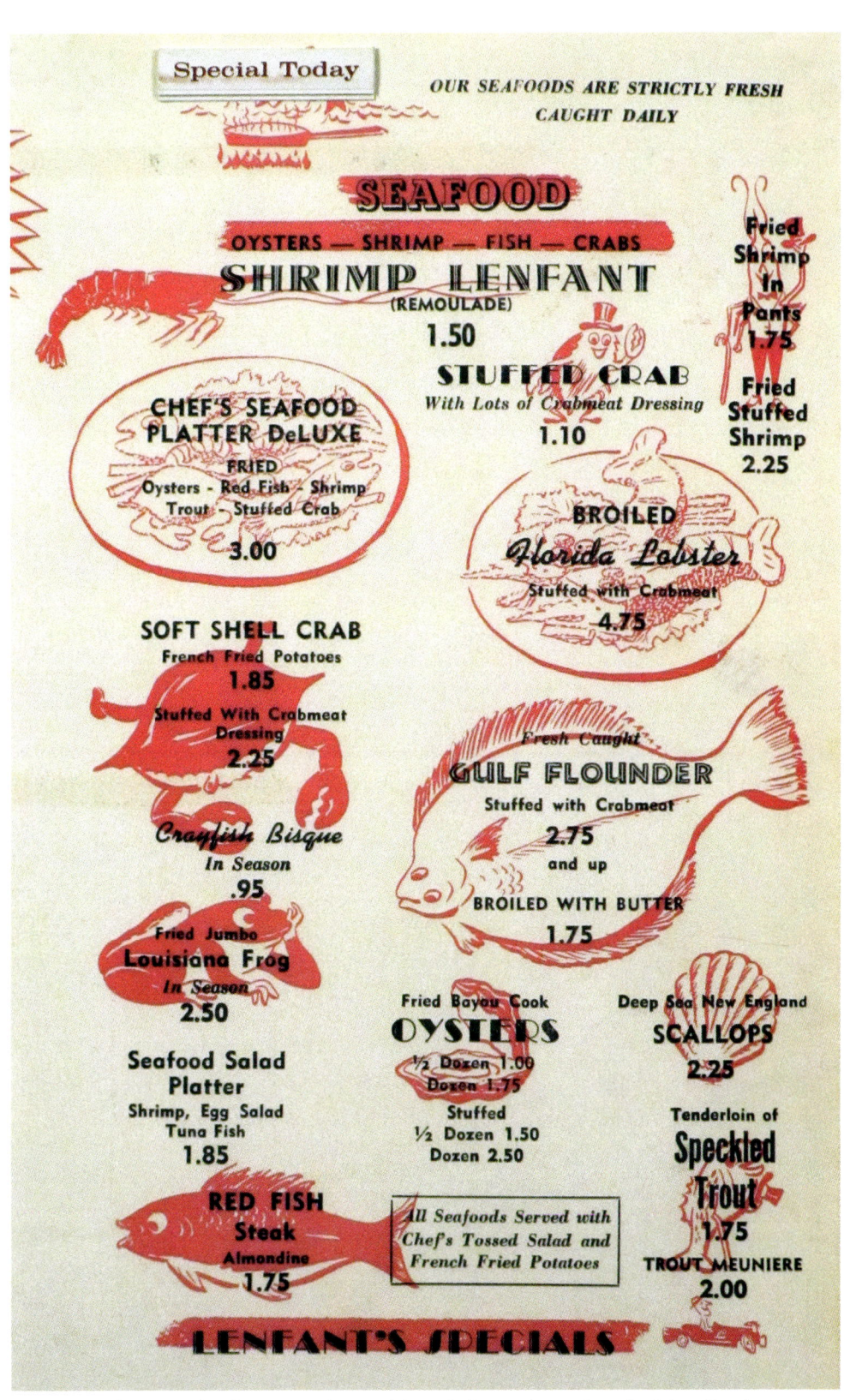

This page from Lenfant's menu gives a hint of the variety of seafood it offered. Lenfant's was known for its seafood dishes, including "Fried Shrimp in Pants," fried shrimp with the tail left on. (Menu collection gift of Richard and Rima Collin courtesy of The Historic New Orleans Collection)

Louis Lenfant retired in 1975 and sold Lenfant's to Joe Fein, Sr., the owner of the Court of Two Sisters. Fein—someone else who wasn't going for multiple stars in guidebooks—modernized the menu but kept Lenfant's going as before, continuing the emphasis on catering.

That phase didn't last long. In 1982, Fein closed the restaurant, and it sat empty for a few years. Then it was Joe Marcello's turn. The former owner of the burned-down Elmwood Plantation saw Lenfant's as a prime spot for a revival. In 1986, he renovated the building thoroughly, keeping a streamlined look while modernizing it quite a bit. What came out of the work was a striking restaurant. Marcello moved in with an adaptation of the Elmwood's old menu and with a seriously good chef: Tom Cowman, who was looking for a gig after Jonathan closed.

Chef Tom and Joe Marcello were not a logical team, sort of like Leonard Bernstein and Louis Prima. Joe knew what he wanted on the menu, and Chef Tom cooked it. But Joe questioned a lot of Chef Tom's flights of fancy. One that the chef got away with was serving popovers at the table as soon as guests sat down. The popovers, looking like oversize muffins, eggy and hollow in the middle, were hot and buttery and wonderful.

The Marcello edition of Lenfant's was the all-time culinary peak for the restaurant, but it got caught in a tangle that would choke it to death. The city wanted to rebuild the busy intersection of Canal Street, Canal Boulevard, and City Park Avenue, for drainage and other issues. Lenfant's was inside the work area. Having all the access streets torn up was bad, but Joe Marcello just gritted his teeth and prepared to ride it out. Then a workman pulled up unmistakably human bones. Not a big surprise—this part of town had been used as a cemetery for a very long time. But it brought work to a halt for months.

That was too much for Lenfant's, and in 1988 it shut down. After languishing for a few years, the great old streamlined building was torn down to make room for a funeral home. The parking lot came in handy for that, with a very different mood from that of the old days.

★★★★★
LeRuth's
Gretna: 636 Franklin Street
1966-91

So many superlatives apply to Chef Warren Leruth and his namesake restaurant that it's hard to know where to start. But this should work: LeRuth's was the most delicious New Orleans restaurant of all time.

Leruth (he capitalized the R in the restaurant's name but not his own) began cooking in the military, as a baker. He kept his baker's habits all his life. LeRuth's always baked its own French bread, at a time when nobody else did that.

His baker's sensibilities carried over into all his recipes. While most cooks of savory dishes approximate ingredients and cooking times, bakers must measure and time everything exactly. Leruth added ingredients by weight—a degree of exactitude I've never seen since in any restaurant. It did wonders for the consistent flavor of the restaurant's food.

LeRuth's milieu was inauspicious. It was an ordinary raised Victorian single house in a middle-class Gretna neighborhood that was on its way down. To get there from the East Bank, you had to drive past the notorious Fischer housing project. Despite that, LeRuth's in its prime years (which was most of them) was always full. Getting a reservation required calling weeks in advance.

Some of that success had to do with lucky timing. When LeRuth's opened in 1966, most of the grand restaurants of New Orleans were coasting on menus that were essentially interchangeable. Nobody was doing anything new.

LeRuth's was ready when a new dynamic entered the restaurant community. In the summer of 1970, Richard Collin published *The New Orleans Underground Gourmet,* the first rated restaurant guide in the city's history. Its influence on the dining habits of New Orleanians was incalculable. And the *Underground Gourmet* said in no uncertain terms that LeRuth's was the best restaurant in town.

LeRuth's food lived up to the accolade. It was based on two sources: restaurants in France that Leruth admired and Galatoire's. Dinner was a five-course table d'hôte repast. These were not tasting portions. When you went to LeRuth's, you needed to be ready for a big, lengthy meal.

The famous appetizer was crabmeat St. Francis, a baked ramekin of crabmeat with a rich, peppery sauce. (It was so good that when Leruth closed the restaurant, he said his greatest regret was that he wouldn't be able to eat crabmeat St. Francis anytime he wanted.) They also made good baked oysters, shrimp remoulade, escargots Bourguignonne, and a couple of other items.

Leruth invented oyster-artichoke soup. He called it potage LeRuth, and it was always on the menu. It was one of only two dishes there that would be widely copied by other restaurants, and it is now such a universal classic that it's hard to imagine a time when it wasn't around. Leruth's version had no cream, just a good oyster stock with recently added oysters, chunky artichokes, and herbs.

An interesting measure of how far we've come is that potage LeRuth always was made with canned artichokes and dried herbs. Such ingredients would be unthinkable in a deluxe restaurant now.

Matches from LeRuth's, located in an old Victorian shotgun home in Gretna, practically underneath the Mississippi River bridge. (From the collection of Richard Morelock)

LeRuth's Restaurant was renowned for such memorable dishes as crabmeat St. Francis and oyster-artichoke soup. (From the collection of Phil Johnson)

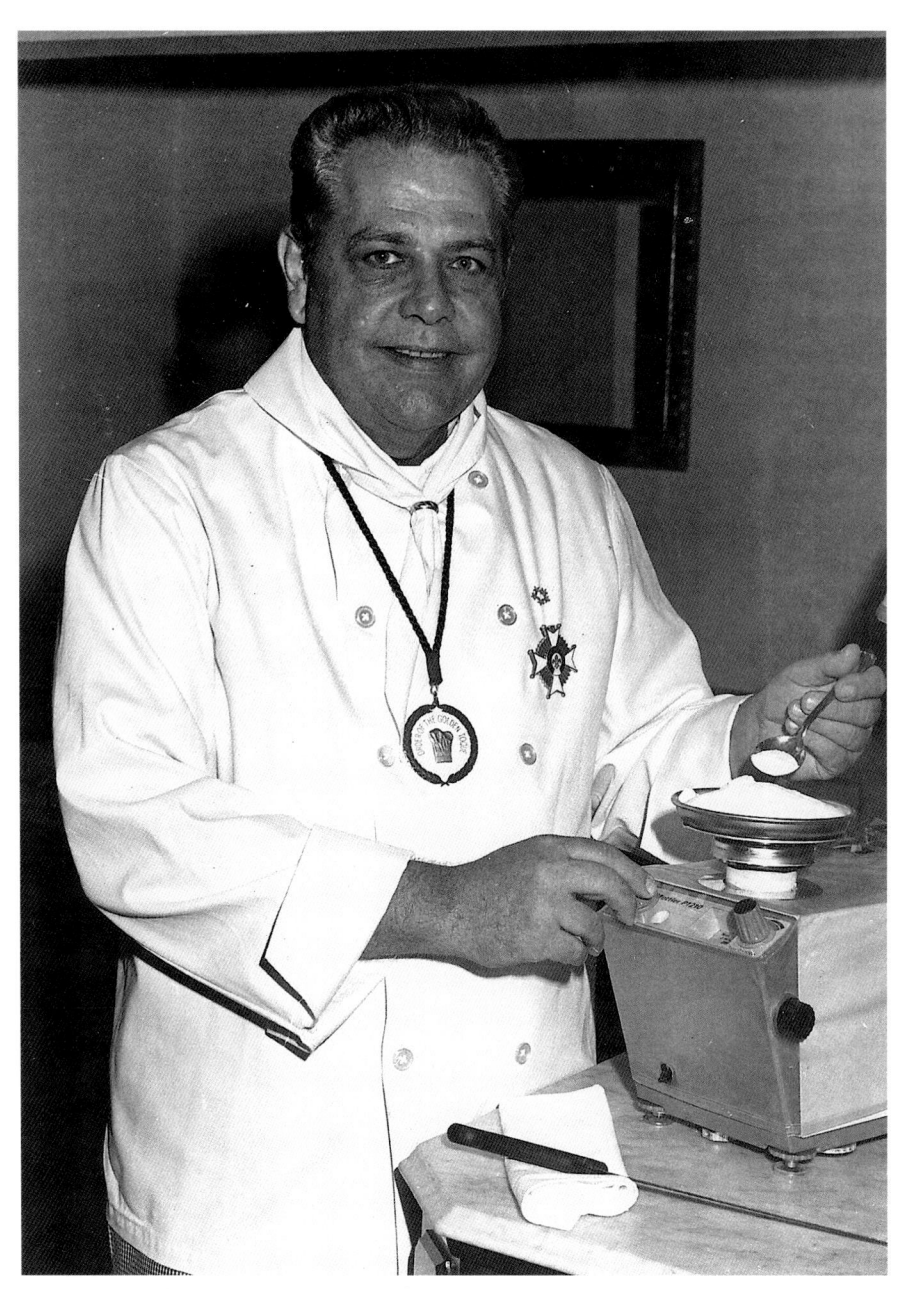

Warren Leruth was considered one of New Orleans' most creative chefs. In addition to running a topnotch restaurant, he created Green Goddess dressing for the Seven Seas food brand and developed the red beans and biscuits recipes for Popeye's Fried Chicken and Biscuits. (From the collection of Phil Johnson)

Next came a salad with avocado dressing. That was a derivative of the Green Goddess dressing Leruth had developed for the Seven Seas label, and it was as wonderful as it was unique.

The second LeRuth's dish to be adopted by many other restaurants was a big fried soft-shell crab topped with crabmeat and brown butter. I can remember what Richard Collin said about it without checking: "It defies description and approaches apotheosis." Crab on crab? But why not?

That was great, but to my palate the most memorable entree was

Canard Ferme Frères LeRuth. (All the dish names at LeRuth's were in French.) This was a rustic French and Cajun fusion dish, a half-duck roasted just right, served atop a smoky stuffing of oysters, herbs, and sausage—a sort of advanced dirty rice—and topped with a peppercorn sauce.

In contrast to all this Frenchness was the chef's steak. It was almost certainly the best steak being served anywhere in New Orleans, a twenty-four-ounce prime aged sirloin strip, roasted to crustiness and bulging with juiciness, served in sizzling butter. The chef really did like that, and when someone ordered it his face beamed. "When an order comes in for that, I keep my eye on it personally," Leruth told me. If you got the chef's steak, the only other thing you got was a salad. The chef wanted you to give your entire appetite over to that steak.

Other great dishes included a magnificent stuffed trout, tiny frog legs with butter and garlic, rack of lamb with fried parsley, and sweetbreads meunière. Leruth claimed to be the first chef in town to use Plume de Veau baby white veal, and every night he made up a new dish for it. Chef Frank Brigtsen, who knew Leruth well, keeps that tradition alive at his restaurant.

If there was one thing to complain about at LeRuth's, it was that every entree came out with the same two side dishes. Pommes dauphines (rich nuggets of mashed potatoes bound with a little

Chef Warren Leruth in the kitchen at LeRuth's. He was one of the founders of the revered St. Michael's Special School Chefs' Charity for Children fundraiser. (From the collection of Phil Johnson)

egg and cream, then fried) and bananas au four (underripe, starchy bananas baked till soft) were on every plate. The issue didn't come up often, because few customers dined at LeRuth's frequently.

That wasn't because of the expense. LeRuth's was a bargain, really, considering the extent of the dinner. It was just that hard to get a reservation.

And besides, Leruth did not like complainers. Even mild criticisms were not suffered gladly. Letters expressing displeasure got a scathing reply, written by an anonymous customer (I think I know who), the import of which was that clearly the complainer must be a moron to find fault with LeRuth's.

The response could be worse. LeRuth's had a strategy for real troublemakers. The chef stepped up to the table as four waiters moved to each corner of it. On a signal, each one grabbed his corner of the tablecloth and lifted it, with all the plates, wine bottles, water glasses, food, flowers, and everything falling into the center of what was now a large, leaking sack. "I've picked up your check," said the chef. "Get out of my restaurant!" The usual response from the rest of the room was applause.

The wait staff could be asked to do something as outrageous as that because they were totally beholden to the chef. Most of the waiters were the kind you'd find at Galatoire's—from which, in fact, a few of them had come. Gilbert LaFleur and Homer Fontenot were most noteworthy among those. Gilbert ultimately became LeRuth's maitre d'.

Leruth demanded precision from his staff. He lined up the waiters daily to inspect fingernails, shoe shines, and oral hygiene. When one of them objected to this military-like inspection, Leruth told him, "Look. I'm giving you 15 percent of my gross. You want that, you do it my way!"

The dessert menu was simple. A centerpiece of LeRuth's offerings was his French vanilla ice cream, made with over 25 percent milk fat. It was incredibly rich, far more so than any of the premium brands out there now. Leruth made it himself, to the point of manufacturing his own vanilla. (He created four variations of vanilla extract, later selling the formula to Ron Sciortino, who still sells it under his Ronald Reginald's brand. It's the best vanilla out there.)

My favorite of LeRuth's desserts was the macaroon bread pudding. He made that with coconut, his Melipone (Mexican-style) vanilla, and enough eggs to make it incomparably light. A big pan of it sat on a sideboard in the dining room; it was served at room temperature, without a sauce, and was still the best bread pudding in town.

The wine cellar—which was actually in the attic—was not equaled locally for a long time. At its peak, it held over thirty thousand bottles, including some very great ones. It did not start that way, however. In the restaurant's early years, Leruth struck up a lifelong friendship with David Martin, the founder of Martin Wine Cellar. A few times a week, Leruth asked to have a few bottles of an assortment of wines that interested him delivered to the restaurant.

"I kept sending my driver way over there with those little deliveries," Dave Martin said. "I was just about to tell him, 'Warren, I like you a lot, but I can't keep doing this.' Then he called me and said, 'I found the wine I want. Send me 200 cases.' From then on, he was one of my best customers."

That wine was a Puligny-Montrachet, which, along with an Aloxe-Corton, became the house wines of the restaurant (at under $10 a bottle!). But the wine I remember best at LeRuth's was Chateau Latour 1970, which was served with roast-beef poor boys one Monday evening in the summer of 1975. The occasion was the publication of *The New Orleans Cookbook*, which Richard Collin wrote with his wife, Rima. "The best food in the world and the best wine in the world!" said Collin at the party.

The Latour flowed like water that night. I don't know, but I suspect that Leruth underwrote that. Because as much of an ogre as the earlier stories may make him appear, he was a genuinely likeable man, a lover of living well, laughing most of the time, and often startlingly generous. He cofounded the Chefs' Charity for Children, the first local event in which chefs got together to cook and raise money for a worthy cause, still a sellout every year. When Dave Martin remodeled his deli at Martin Wine Cellar, Leruth sent over a new professional stove of the kind he thought the place ought to have. Martin hardly needed a donation, but to Leruth a friend was a friend.

LeRuth's rolled merrily along into the 1980s, installing along the way the first requirement of a deposit for a reservation ever seen in New Orleans. Leruth's sons Lee and Larry, who'd worked in the kitchen throughout their childhood, joined their father in the kitchen full time.

Leruth renovated the restaurant in the 1980s, greatly upgrading creature comforts. He replaced the old workhorse china with beautiful bone china and heavy, unique silverware. He bought a substantial collection of art, including an original Picasso. Nice new chairs came in, and with them, something new: pillows for the ladies' feet. (Sometimes when the waiters reached down to position these, the ladies reacted with alarm.) The menu grew a little bit, too, the new dishes seeming to have been there all along.

Then he opened a second restaurant. LeRuth's Other Place was in a renovated house across the side street from LeRuth's. It had an Italian tilt, using the best ingredients (it was the first restaurant I remember making a point of serving Parmigiano-Reggiano

Chef Warren Leruth in his wine "cellar." (From the collection of Phil Johnson)

and Pecorino Romano cheeses). The food was very good, the prices modest, and the service informal, and with all the traffic that LeRuth's generated, Leruth figured he could make a bundle here on his overflow alone.

He figured wrong. LeRuth's Other Place went nowhere. Or maybe the story was that it was already nowhere and stayed there. You had to have a really good reason to go to that part of Gretna, and the Other Place wasn't reason enough. It closed within a year.

Meanwhile, the center of gravity in the New Orleans restaurant business had shifted. The Uptown gourmet bistros were pulling a lot of business away from LeRuth's and other outlying restaurants. Then came a sudden shrinkage in the local oil industry. That hit the West Bank hard, and within a few years most of the great restaurants there had closed.

And the old man wanted to move on to other projects. He was heavily involved with Al Copeland's restaurants (he created the biscuits and red beans and rice, among other dishes) for Popeyes, and he had consulting gigs all over the place. He sold his restaurant to his sons Lee and Larry. Both were excellent chefs who had apprenticed all their lives to the master. And LeRuth's recipes were so exact that it wasn't hard to keep the quality level up. LeRuth's continued to do very well. Lee told me in 1985 that LeRuth's was putting $1 million a year profit into his pocket. That was serious money for a freestanding restaurant in a secondary location back then.

But the brothers had personal problems. Larry dropped out for awhile. Lee opened a second restaurant, Torey's, in the French Quarter (where Bayona is now). He told me it was going to be a restaurant with purely his own creations. None of his dad's food was on the menu. This mystified diners. Torey's did not do well, and Lee's frustration with that took him to the breaking point. One evening, a diner asked to talk to him. The diner wanted to compliment the chef, but Lee had had a rough day and thought it was another complainer. After giving the man a piece of his mind, Lee stormed out of the restaurant and went home.

What happened there is called an accident by the Leruth family. Lee Leruth, alone in the house, was killed by a bullet from his own gun. He was still in his twenties.

Warren Leruth took over the restaurant again. He brought in a chef de cuisine and got the place back up to speed, even though Leruth wasn't always on site. The customers and wait staff were much relieved.

But the momentum was gone. LeRuth's lasted only two more years. Then Leruth sold everything but the name at an auction: wine, china, artwork, everything. A lot of that is still circulating in local restaurants and private cellars.

Leruth kept on working. I saw him once a year at Manresa Retreat House until he died in 2005. He was the same smiling, optimistic, brilliant guy, with a million projects and even more opinions. I loved hearing his insights. My favorite: at one of the silent Manresa breakfasts, he passed me a little note under the table. "Too much baking soda in the biscuits!" it said. Things like that were obvious to his astonishingly keen palate and encyclopedic knowledge of cooking.

One project that all his fans wished he would undertake was never done. Leruth wrote two small cookbooks, neither of which had much of the restaurant's food in it. But he never wrote a book of his serious recipes, the ones that made LeRuth's great. Larry Leruth still has the recipes. Maybe someday he'll put them into a LeRuth's cookbook at last.

In its relatively short history, LeRuth's left behind many memories of a golden chapter in the annals New Orleans dining. It was the first serious chef-owned restaurant in New Orleans and set the standard for all the ones that would follow.

LeRuth's Crabmeat St. Francis

This was one of the best and most popular dishes created by Chef Warren Leruth at his spectacular restaurant. He told me once that the thing he missed most about not having LeRuth's open anymore was that he couldn't grab and eat an order of this dish at moment's notice.

Sauce:
2 Tbs. butter
2 green onions, sliced
½ medium onion, coarsely chopped
2 inner ribs celery, bottom 2 inches only, coarsely chopped
1 bay leaf
½ tsp. dried thyme leaves
¼ tsp. celery seed
¼ tsp. white pepper
Pinch cayenne
¾ tsp. salt
¼ tsp. Accent
½ cup evaporated milk
3 Tbs. flour

½ cup breadcrumbs
3 Tbs. grated Parmesan cheese
½ tsp. spicy paprika
1 lb. lump crabmeat
2 Tbs. butter, melted

1. To make the sauce, heat the butter in a saucepan until it bubbles. Add the remaining sauce ingredients except the milk and flour, and sauté until the vegetables are well browned and sticking a little bit to the pan. Remove from heat and set aside for 15 minutes.

2. After 15 minutes, add the milk and ¾ cup water to the saucepan. Bring to a boil, stirring lightly.

3. While the boil is coming up, whisk the flour into 3 oz. water. After

the pan comes to a boil, stir the flour-water mixture slowly into the other ingredients. Simmer for 3 minutes, until the sauce is thick.

4. Spoon the sauce into a pan and refrigerate until it thickens, or overnight.

5. To complete the dish, preheat the oven to 425 degrees. Mix the breadcrumbs, Parmesan cheese, and paprika.

6. Divide the crabmeat among 4 to 6 scallop shells or small au gratin dishes. Top each with about ¼ cup of the chilled sauce. Sprinkle each with a heaping Tbs. of the breadcrumb mixture. Bake until the crumbs brown and the sides of the dishes begin to bubble—20-25 minutes.

7. Remove from the oven and top each with 1 tsp. melted butter. Serve very hot.

Serves 4 to 6.

★★★
L'Escale
French Quarter: 730 Bienville Street (St. Louis Hotel)
1982-83

My favorite cover of my *New Orleans Menu* publication was the one on the May 1982 edition. "This Is What a French Fry Looks Like at L'Escale," says the headline. Below was a strange object that looked as if it came from an M. C. Escher drawing. Inside a cube with windows on all sides was a ball that looked too big to have gotten inside.

It was an accurate portrait of L'Escale's fries. They'd give you two of them with your entree.

"Extravagance Unchained," read the headline on the review. That was accurate, too. L'Escale was without question the most extravagant restaurant ever opened in New Orleans. That can be confirmed just by referring to the cost of dining there.

When it first opened, you had two choices for your dinner. You could have the $75 prix fixe. Or you could have the $95 version. Both were what we would call a chef's tasting menu now. (Such a thing didn't exist in New Orleans then.) The $95 version included an extra (but very grand) appetizer. That's without tax, tip, or wines. In 2011 dollars, the $95 dinner would cost $177. There is nothing comparable to that around New Orleans today.

What was Mark Smith thinking? He was the owner of the hotel, along with a few others in the French Quarter. He had opened Louis XVI, which since 1970 had set the standard for full-tilt dining. He had pretty good luck with Louis XVI and thought the market would support another step or two up the ladder.

To this end, he brought Chef Jean Louis Montestrucq to town. Montestrucq held the highest formal honors it was possible for a chef to have. Mark Smith told him to let 'er rip, sky's the limit. The space—formerly a lovely little French restaurant called Le Petit—was renovated into a sleek, mirrored room with the most subtle use of neon lighting I've ever seen. (The room is still intact and has been the home of Louis XVI since 1986.)

The china and silverware were the best available. The servers were arrayed in white tie and tails—and white gloves.

Let's recall the $95 dinner, shall we? It began with Les Voyages Nordiques: an ice floe with an igloo, sleeping polar bear, and penguin carved in ice. Between it all were smoked and marinated fish—salmon, caviar, and oysters. Not oysters like at Acme across the street, mind you, but belons flown in from France.

Now Les Symphonies Brettone: lobster, scallops, poached mussels, all cold. Then escargots, brought out in a little skillet made of pastry. Nice! Soupe des pecheurs: lobster, oysters, crawfish. Delicious, but not quite as elegant as the clear consommé with a dash of Cognac.

Fish course: nothing from around here. Turbot, with a sauce made with expensive Champagne, as if that could be discerned.

Palate-refreshing time. A sorbet of raspberries, and "l'alcool blanc": eau de vie, or French white lightning.

Then it was time for steak in a shirt (the fabric was spinach). Or pheasant for two. Or quail poached in—Chateau d'Yquem? How was that possible? It was. There was the bottle to prove it.

Salads next, in the French style. Then cheese—many kinds, all at cool room temperature, showed off on a silver cart. A different cart presented an array of pastries, all made in house. Coffee was brewed in a French press pot—the first place in town to use one of those.

Patrick Charbonneaux, one of the best maitres d'hôtel I ever met, was accommodating and warm, without a whiff of pomposity. I heard the chef had the market cornered on that. But he didn't come out much.

And when he finally did come out, it was to leave the country. Suddenly. Some big problem. By then, the $75/$95 dichotomy died of its own impracticality. It was replaced by an a la carte menu. But it carried a $55 minimum, to keep the standards up. That was a food minimum. The first time a couple spent less than that (but over $150, counting the wine and drinks) and had the $55 minimum applied, the foie gras hit the fan. Their complaint was all over the news. People who otherwise would never have heard about L'Escale called me about this rip-off and laughed.

The minimum was removed. Ads were run in which a couple said how glad they were that their flight to Paris had been cancelled, because now they could go to L'Escale instead.

Nothing would have helped. The local oil industry was being massacred by a steep drop in the price of crude, and expense accounts that supported places such as L'Escale were becoming extinct. The restaurant followed suit.

The L'Escale experience was very impressive. I've never decided whether it was actually good. None of my girlfriends of the time liked it much. Too much food, they said.

★★★★
Maison Pierre
French Quarter: 430 Dauphine Street
1969-85

There was a time when some diners liked to find pretentiousness when they dined out. It seemed that when they went out to an expensive restaurant, they wanted it to be as different as possible from dining either at home or in a modest restaurant. Ornate dining rooms, highly structured menus, sacramental service, and flowery dish configurations all created this effect.

The sons and daughters of these people didn't have this need. Baby Boomers were of the mind that the world should adjust to their tastes, not the other way around. Restaurants specializing in formality began to wane in the mid-1970s. They are almost all gone now.

But while a taste for such places was still around, few New Orleans restaurants could match the pomposity that attended a meal at Maison Pierre. Owner-chef Pierre Lacoste was New Orleans born, but he had relatives in France and spent enough time there to become fascinated by the major restaurants there that were the unchallenged masters of dining ritual.

Lacoste thought a restaurant with French-style service would work here, and in 1969 he opened it. The historic Creole cottage built in 1780 was one of the oldest buildings in the French Quarter. The dining room was overdecorated in the best Belle Epoque style. Every reference in the place was to some vaunted French institution. It was big enough to allow full French service but small enough to be romantic.

The dining room was orchestrated by Pierre's wife—Madame Pierre, as she introduced herself. She was a lovely, welcoming lady who made it clear that you should set aside your petty preferences to allow the magic of Maison Pierre to dictate the details of your dinner. She was so charming that you went along with the program.

The program was in one way ahead of the times. The dinner was what we would now call a *menu degustation*—a long string of many small courses. No other restaurant served that way on such a scale. Maison Pierre was the first restaurant where I was ever served an amuse-bouche, intermezzo, or post-dessert bon-bon.

It was also the first place in which the waiter presented the cork from the wine bottle for me to inspect. ("Sniff it, to make sure it's not rotten," he said.) And it was the first where I saw the use of many different shapes of wineglasses for different kinds of wine. All this was new to me not because I was inexperienced but because no other restaurants bothered with these touches. You certainly didn't see them at Antoine's or Galatoire's.

I was just the customer Maison Pierre was looking for when I got there in 1974. Although I am a member of the generation that would later run places like this out of business, I was two years into my career as a restaurant critic and thought I needed some pretentiousness injections.

I dug all the French gourmet stuff, all the folderol. The nine courses began with oysters Bienville—so, not a huge leap into the future. Then came a clear consommé, then a fish I'd never heard of before called rouget (probably just redfish).

I remember the entree most vividly. It was prime rib, but "Ah!" said Madame Pierre. "The chef, he cooks it on one side only, so the juices and aroma rise to the top. Surely you will like it medium rare. I will add fresh horseradish." That really was as good as advertised.

Then came dessert, cheese, and the surprise bon-bon at the end—a chocolate truffle. It was the most expensive dinner of my life to that time: $78 for two. I was delighted by the whole thing. My date seemed undecided as to whether to be impressed with or laugh at all the fillips of service.

For the next few years, Maison Pierre was where you went if you wanted to really show off what a gourmet you were. Then Paul Prudhomme led us in a completely different direction, and the Bistro Revolution began, with the full support of the Baby Boomers.

Lacoste toned down the menu, but that just killed the magic without adding anything. I remember the last time I went there, the fish of the day was catfish. It closed not long after.

The former Maison Pierre became the short-lived Torey's, the second restaurant of Lee Leruth, who with his brother was then running his father's five-star West Bank restaurant. Then Susan Spicer and Regina Keever moved in to start Bayona—a better restaurant than Maison Pierre ever was, without very much ceremony at all.

★★★

Martin's Poor Boy Restaurant
French Quarter: Ursulines Street at Decatur Street
Marigny: 1940 St. Claude Avenue (originally 2000)
(1919-75)

★★

Martin Brothers Restaurant
New Orleans East: 5838 Chef Menteur Highway
1950s-80s

Martin's has a well-documented distinction: it invented the poor-boy sandwich. The story has been known for a long time, but the coming of the annual Po-Boy Festival in 2007 triggered a great deal of research and scholarship on the subject. It unearthed convincing evidence that, indeed, Clovis and Bennie Martin started making the iconic New Orleans sandwich during the controversial 1929 New Orleans Transit Strike, when most of the streetcar conductors and motormen went on the picket line.

The idea was to provide the "poor boys" out on the picket lines with a big, filling sandwich containing only scraps of meat for a low price. It originally cost a nickel, but the Martin brothers dispensed a lot of them for free.

Martin Brothers Restaurant began as a French Market stall selling coffee, doughnuts, and lunches. The food it served—the poor-boy

---

A BITE OF HISTORY

Marco Polo
Gretna (349 Whitney Avenue)

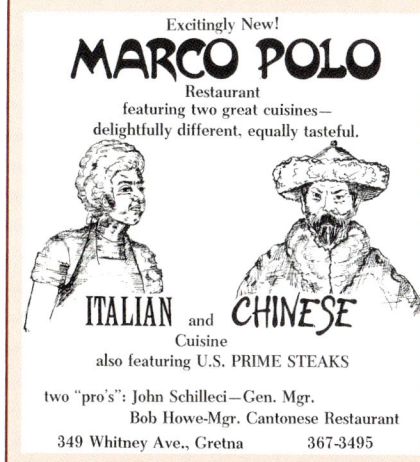

Excitingly New!
MARCO POLO
Restaurant
featuring two great cuisines—
delightfully different, equally tasteful.

ITALIAN and CHINESE
Cuisine
also featuring U.S. PRIME STEAKS

two "pro's": John Schilleci—Gen. Mgr.
Bob Howe-Mgr. Cantonese Restaurant
349 Whitney Ave., Gretna   367-3495

The restaurant's name reflected its choice of serving Italian and Chinese food. Italian explorer Marco Polo spent many years in the Far East. (Courtesy of New Orleans Magazine*)*

In these days when chefs cross all national culinary lines with ease, it's hard to grasp just how far out this restaurant's concept was in the 1970s. As Marco Polo did, the place brought East and West together in a menu that featured both Chinese and Italian food.

Martin's invented the poor-boy sandwich. (Courtesy of Shelley Martin)

sandwiches in particular—made the place so popular that in 1931 the brothers moved to the corner of St. Claude Avenue and Touro Street. Some years later it moved across Touro, so it could have a parking lot. During all the years it was at that intersection, Martin's hardly ever closed, serving its full menu around the clock, seven days a week, until shortly before the end of its history in 1975.

The story of the poor boy has one more player: John Gendusa. He owned a French-bread bakery two blocks up Touro from St. Claude. Martin's sold so many of its poor boys that it had a production problem. The standard French bread in the 1930s was a double-ended torpedo, with a wide, thick middle and tapering ends. Gendusa created a loaf of uniform width for its entire three-foot length. It has all but replaced the old shape.

While Martin's kept a reputation for the best poor boys in town until it closed, the sandwich spread from one neighborhood cafe and bar to another, until it was the universal New Orleans sandwich.

The deliciousness of Martin's sandwiches could not be explained by the quality of the raw materials. Picky people would not have wanted to open the thing up and look at the beef. The gravy was the tastemaker. That, and one other thing that few of Martin's imitators picked up on: after the cook assembled the sandwich completely, he put the whole thing into a hot oven for a couple of minutes. This toasted the bread on the outside and set loose that irresistible aroma of hot bread. To this day, only a minority of poor-boy makers understands what a difference that makes.

The price of the sandwich lived up to its name. In the 1970s, a roast-beef poor boy at Martin's was fifty cents. A potato poor boy—made with fresh-cut French fries, roast-beef gravy, and the usual dressing of lettuce, tomato, and mayonnaise—was all of forty cents. The lowball item was a BLT poor boy for thirty-five cents.

The rest of the menu was good too. Fifty cents would get you red beans and rice, with hot sausage for a further investment of a quarter. The sausage was grilled to order and plopped on top of the beans with a good bit of the rendered sausage grease. I never had a better plate of beans than that one. In my college days, I had many plates of the stuff at two in the morning.

Also on the menu were pork chops, veal chops, hamburger steaks, fried seafood, fried chicken, and everything else you could imagine on the menu of a restaurant that served working people for decades. All of it was at least pretty good; the fried stuff was tremendous, perhaps because of the presence of the hand-cut fries they routinely served here. A lady in the neighborhood made a yellow layer cake with chocolate icing that you always ordered the minute you sat down, in case it was the last one in the house.

Some real characters stepped into Martin's from the streets, especially late at night. Some of them showed up to work. Martin's staff was a highly miscellaneous crew, most of them with their own amusing or maddening quirks.

The Martin brothers split in the 1950s. Bennie kept the Poor Boy Restaurant. Brother Clovis went on to open several other eateries around town. The most famous of these was Martin Brothers Restaurant on Chef Menteur Highway, just on the other side of the Industrial Canal drawbridge. A much bigger place with a lengthier menu, Martin Brothers was also open twenty-four hours a day. Poorboy sandwiches, of course, loomed large among the choices.

Martin Brothers on Chef was a busy restaurant. It was on US 90, the main east-west route in and out of town, and anyone heading that way at least thought about stopping. It was especially busy in the wee hours. Martin Brothers had its healthy volume shot out from under it when the I-10 highrise bridge replaced US 90. It closed in the early 1980s.

The original Martin's Poor Boy Restaurant shut down in 1975. The neighborhood had declined a good deal in the last five years, and after a couple of violent incidents in the restaurant, the family decided to bring that important chapter of New Orleans eating to a close. But their famous sandwich continues its illustrious career.

★★★★
Marti's
French Quarter: 1041 Dumaine Street
(corner of
North Rampart Street)
1971-88

"When I opened Marti's, there were no restaurants serving real Creole food."

Marti Shambra was fond of making big claims like that—and moving on to another one before you could calculate the veracity of what he just said. You never quite caught up with him.

The matter of his opening Marti's is one example. Actually, he had a partner who was at least as involved in the opening as he was. That

Playwright Tennessee Williams was a regular customer at Marti's. (Photo © Mitchel Osborne MMX)

was Dr. Larry Hill, who would later open another groundbreaking restaurant in Cafe Sbisa.

But never mind. His saying that only Marti's served real Creole food just needed to be translated. What he meant was that no other restaurant with style served panéed veal, or red beans and rice, or raw oysters in the bar.

The unofficial slogan of Marti's (given not by Marti, but by his customers) was that it was the Sardi's of New Orleans. For more than ten years, it was the place where people stopped for a light pre-theatre meal or lighter after-opera meal. It stayed open late—till one in the morning or later. At all open hours, you would see familiar and sometimes famous faces. Tennessee Williams, who had an apartment across the street, had a table in the corner of the bar on most nights when he was in town.

Four years into Marti's history, Marti got the idea to push the restaurant upscale. Gone were the poor boys and home-cooked daily specials, replaced by oysters en brochette, steak au poivre, and stuffed capon—at significantly higher prices, of course.

The howl this set off among the customers would not be equaled until Galatoire's got rid of block ice thirty years later. It had particular

The tables along the back wall at Marti's were elevated above those in the rest of the dining room—a touch common in the 1940s and 1950s but usually renovated away later. The mural depicts the entrance to City Park at the end of Dumaine Street. It originally was in the DeSoto Hotel and moved to Marti's along with another mural of the Peristyle in the park. (Photo by Tom Fitzmorris)

resonance in the arts and gay communities, both of which were important constituents of Marti's clientele.

It didn't matter. Marti stood behind his chef, Henry Robinson, who was very obviously a practitioner of Creole cooking. He was quite good at it, actually, and his cooking in combination with Marti's filigree was good enough to shut everybody up—although it took a couple of years.

The truth was that if you didn't take seriously too much of Marti Shambra's bluster, you probably liked the restaurant. The food was always good, and although the menu would look very traditional now, it really was different from what any other restaurant was serving.

Strangely, the dish for which the restaurant was best known was its spinach salad. There wasn't anything spectacular about it. But it was the first spinach salad served anywhere in New Orleans. Marti claimed to have invented it.

And the premises were unique and cool. It took over the old Gentilich's, for fifty years a twenty-four-hour restaurant. (Until the 1970s, such places were scattered all over the city.) Gentilich's had been well designed in a somewhat Art Deco way, with a tile floor, big

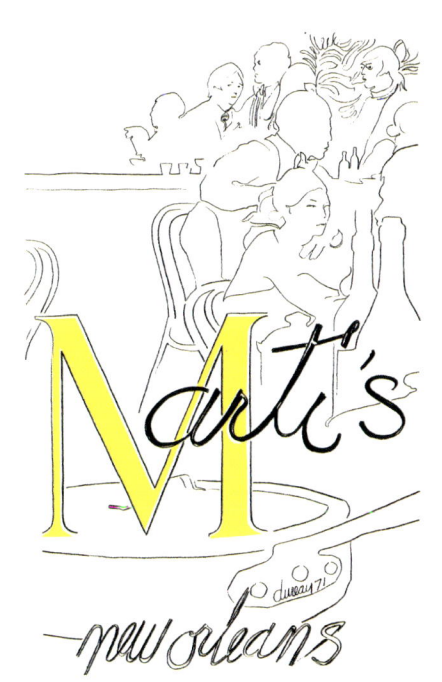

A drawing by noted New Orleans artist George Dureau graced Marti's menu. (Menu collection gift of Richard and Rima Collin courtesy of The Historic New Orleans Collection)

windows, and antique bar. When Marti's was under construction, Larry Hill found two wonderful murals of City Park scenes, claimed from the defunct DeSoto Hotel.

Every few years, Marti would make a big change in the menu and style, just to remain fashionable. Each iteration of this was less successful than the one before. The restaurant seemed to be primed to do well from the new Theatre of the Performing Arts and Louis Armstrong Park—right across the street from Marti's. But neither attraction came close to meeting expectations. French Quarter development moved to the Mississippi River, and North Rampart Street began a decline from which it is only beginning to recover.

Marti Shambra's health deteriorated, and he closed the restaurant in 1988. It sat empty for a couple of years, until Chef John Neal took it over and opened Peristyle there in 1991. That was a five-star restaurant under two owners, then became Tom Wolfe's, which closed after Katrina.

★★★

Masson's Restaurant Français
West End: 7200 Pontchartrain Boulevard
1945-92

The original name was Masson's Beach House, but when the gourmet bug first swarmed in the air in New Orleans, Ernie and Albert Masson figured they could join in. They had traveled in Europe a bit and had a chef who was easily capable of producing what they called "provincial French cuisine."

Masson's was a big, rambling restaurant that looked elegant through the 1960s and 1970s. That was when, year after year, it won the Holiday Restaurant Award, the equivalent at the time of today's DiRoNa and James Beard awards. And it wanted to make sure that you knew it: the certificates covered the better part of the wall separating the main dining room from the bar.

I wish I still had a copy of Masson's menu from those days. There was none better to illustrate how far we've come. It was corny even in the 1970s (hopelessly so in the 1980s), but nobody (not even the Massons, I believe) knew this.

Nobody cared either. Because actually, Masson's food was fairly good. It was now what a French chef would have put out. But we didn't have many of those in Masson's heyday, so who knew?

This is not to say that Masson's had a hack for a chef. Robert Finley, who led the brigade for decades, was one of those old-school Creole chefs who knew it all. He taught a lot of it to chefs who are still working today.

Most of the menu was assembled into table d'hôte dinners of four courses, which even as late as 1995 (not long before the place closed) were only about fifteen dollars complete. You started with a basket of peppery, hot breadsticks, a pleasant and unusual welcome.

The three kinds of baked oysters were always good: Rockefeller,

A banquet dining room at Masson's. (Courtesy of Debbie Masson)

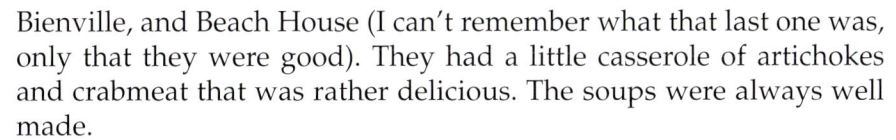

Exterior of Masson's. Almond torte was the restaurant's signature dessert. (Courtesy of Debbie Masson)

Matches from Masson's. This restaurant was one of the few fine-dining establishments near the Lake Pontchartrain lakefront in the 1950s and 1960s. (From the collection of Peggy Scott Laborde)

Bienville, and Beach House (I can't remember what that last one was, only that they were good). They had a little casserole of artichokes and crabmeat that was rather delicious. The soups were always well made.

My first pick for an entree would be the fine rack of lamb, marinated and roasted to a juicy turn, eight chops wide. When's the last time you were served a full rack of lamb? They sent it out with a natural jus and mint jelly, the latter of which you'd ignore if you knew anything.

As good as that was, the better part of the menu at Masson's was seafood. They had the entire range, starting with fried platters that were only slightly fancier than the ones being slammed down around the corner in West End Park. But they had a lot of complicated dishes, too. Shrimp Robert, a major specialty, took the idea of shrimp Creole up two or three notches. A clever dish called surf and surf (you read that right) paired a broiled tropical lobster tail with a shrimp, oyster, and fish brochette. Broiled fish here was always good, stuffed fish and stuffed shrimp less so.

It was almost a certainty that one would at least consider veal Oscar. Perhaps no dish better captured the imitation-Continental style that ruled upscale restaurants in the 1960s and 1970s. It was sautéed veal medallions topped with crabmeat, flanked with asparagus, and covered with hollandaise sauce. It always sounded better than it was. Each element of the dish fought with the others for supremacy, and none of them won.

On the other hand, on more than one occasion I enjoyed a simple broiled chicken flowed over with béarnaise sauce. We don't see that too often now, but I make it at home often, always with the memory of eating it at Masson's.

For all that, the dish most people recall most vividly from Masson's was a very strange dessert they called almond torte. Many claim to

Albert Masson, Chef Robert Finley, and Vincent Liberto admire a 1978 Pan American Culinary Olympics medal. (Courtesy of Debbie Masson)

have loved it; I never did. A better dessert was the sabayon—a flowing custard flavored with Marsala, I think. And their bread pudding was good. I seem to recall that it had maraschino cherries in it. Or was that the millionaire's pie?

One of the oddities of Masson's is that it was one of only two restaurants here (the other was and is Antoine's) that served sugar not in packets but bowls. But it wasn't normal sugar. They used "party sugar," whose grains were about the size of couscous and came in all the colors of the rainbow.

Masson's went out of business in the early 1990s, then soon after reopened as Debbie Masson's—a new business entirely, her father, Albert, said. (I heard rumblings of discontent about that from a number of suppliers.) The building was greatly in need of renovation, its floors sagging here and there. The food remained reasonably good, but the magic was gone. *Holiday Magazine* was gone, too—let alone its awards, which kept on coming every year for Masson's to the very end. An era had closed, and Masson's—a paragon of the old ways—did too.

Masson's Shrimp Robert

Save this recipe for when extra-pretty shrimp are available. An interesting and colorful variation is to use red, green, and yellow bell peppers instead of all green. The dish is the creation and namesake of Masson's longtime chef, Robert Finley. I copied it from a calendar they sent to their customers every year.

24 medium shrimp, peeled
½ stick butter
1 medium white onion, sliced julienne
1 ripe tomato, peeled, seeded, and cut into eighths
1 Tbs. chopped garlic
1 medium bell pepper, sliced julienne
1 tsp. green peppercorns
Salt to taste
Dash Tabasco
1½ cups cooked rice or pasta

1. Sauté shrimp in the butter until they turn pink. Remove shrimp from pan and set aside.

2. In the same butter, sauté the vegetables until they just begin to soften.

3. Add green peppercorns, salt, and Tabasco.

4. Return shrimp to pan; toss lightly with vegetables. Serve pan contents, including butter, over cooked rice or pasta.

Serves 4.

Masson's Almond Torte

The memory of Masson's at West End is fading, but some of its famous dishes live on. In particular, I'm often asked about a rather strange dessert for which they were famous. It was essentially a log of butter cream, frozen and sliced. A similar dessert was served at Christian's, covered with chocolate sauce and referred to as the "Skip" (after a waiter who devised it). Here it is for those who like it. I am not one of you.

2 sticks unsalted butter, softened
1 cup light brown sugar
1 egg
5 Tbs. flour
1 tsp. almond extract
½ cup toasted almonds, chopped fine
½ cup pecans, chopped fine

1. With an electric mixer in a mixer bowl, cream the butter at medium-high speed until very pale in color. Add the sugar gradually, and keep mixing until there's no grittiness.

2. Add the egg and flour, and blend on medium-low speed. Add almond extract, and mix until it disappears.

3. With a wooden spoon, mix in nuts, and roll into a cylinder. Wrap in aluminum foil and freeze for 3 hours.

4. Slice into discs about a half-inch thick. Serve 2 per person.

Serves 6 to 8.

★★★
Maylie's
CBD: 1009 Poydras Street
1876-1983

Maylie's was a relic restaurant for decades before it closed. It was one of many eateries located in or near the big public markets around town. (Tujague's was the most famous of these and the only survivor in the species.) The market merchants began their days well before dawn and knocked off around one in the afternoon. They had their big meal of the day then and went home.

Maylie's was immediately adjacent to the Poydras Market, which stood in the wide neutral ground on its namesake street. Its customers bought tickets for dinner and then waited for the big bell to ring, calling them to long communal tables where the table d'hôte dinner was served in big platters, family style.

"A Unique Place to Dine"
Maylie's Restaurant
French Table D'Hote
Established 1876
A distinctive New Orleans dining place famous for 64 years for its French Style "Boulli" (Boiled Beef)
Lunch—11 A. M.-2:30 P. M.
Dinner—5-9 P. M.
Poydras Cor. Dryades Street
Telephone MAgnolia 9469

An ad promoting a Maylie's specialty, boiled beef. (From the collection of Peggy Scott Laborde)

The main dining room of Maylie's in the 1980s. (Courtesy of Ann Maylie Bruce)

An 1880s photo of founders Bernard Maylie and Hypolite Esparbe. Esparbe's wife was the cook. (Courtesy of Ann Maylie Bruce)

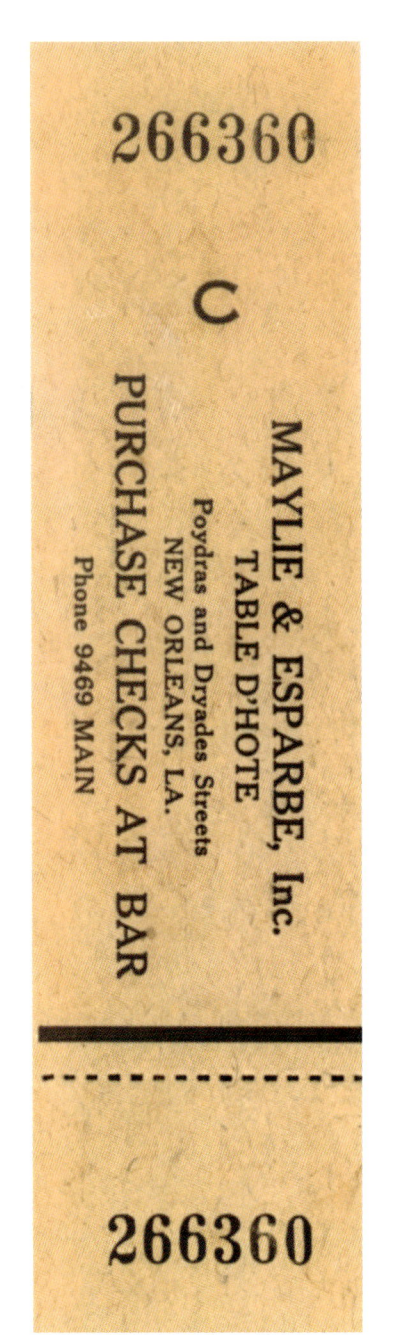

This postcard shows one of the dining rooms at Maylie's, known as the Stag Room. (Courtesy of Anne Maylie Bruce)

When the Poydras Market was right across the street, hungry market workers would purchase tickets for their meals. (From the collection of Peggy Scott Laborde)

Maylie's bar in 1959. From left, Johnny Hoffman, proprietor Anna May Deano Maylie, Clement Dazet, and proprietor Willie Maylie. (Courtesy of Ann Maylie Bruce)

A Maylie's menu with a recipe for the Roffignac, the dining establishment's signature drink. (Courtesy of The Historic New Orleans Collection)

A glass water carafe from Maylie's. (From the collection of Peggy Scott Laborde)

By the time I got to Maylie's, in the early 1970s, the market was long gone. So was the restaurant's main building, a victim of street widening in the late 1950s. What remained was a two-story frame building with the bar, a sixty-seat dining room, and the kitchen on the first floor. The Maylie family lived upstairs. There was the trunk of an ancient wisteria just outside the entrance. The plant was a trademark, twisting its way around the building, covering its upstairs balcony with purple flowers every spring.

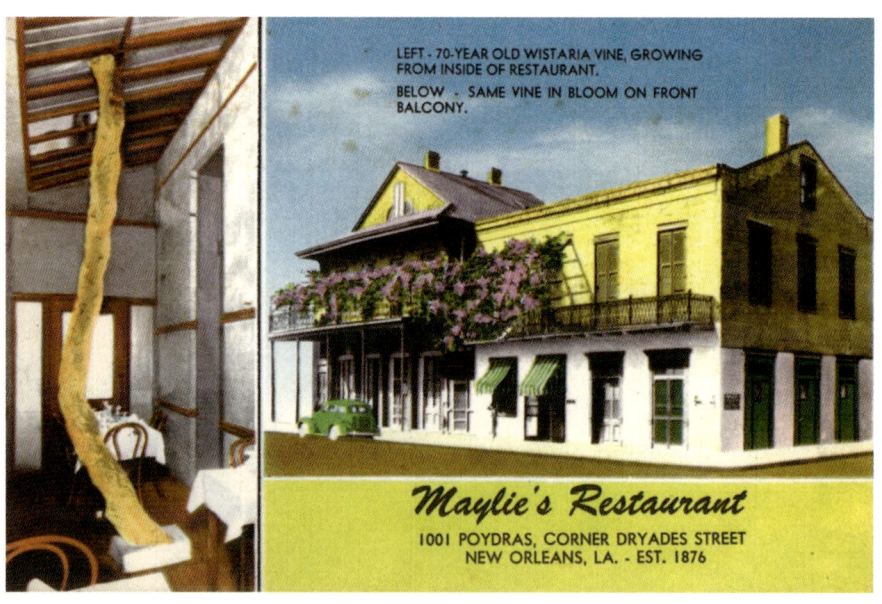

A 1940s-era photo of Maylie's on Poydras Street. A wisteria vine grew from within the restaurant. (Courtesy of The Historic New Orleans Collection)

The loss of its main building was the beginning of the end for Maylie's. In its last decades, it was much diminished in spirit as well as size. Its old customers drifted away or died, and not many new customers took their places. Some nights nobody showed up for dinner at all.

Nevertheless, diners who had a taste for history loved the place. The old table d'hôte dinner remained, although it was now served in conventional restaurant portions. In 1974, its six courses sold for $6.50:

Deviled eggs remoulade
Soup of the day
Salad
Fish course
Boiled beef brisket with potatoes
Bread pudding

The eggs remoulade were wonderful, not only because the eggs and the sauce went together perfectly, but because the sauce was second in goodness only to Arnaud's.

Soup was another specialty at Maylie's. The restaurant made all the Creole classics in a very old style that was much brothier and lighter than is currently the vogue. Here was one of the two or three best turtle soups I ever ate. The seafood gumbo was first class and not afraid of using lots of okra. The vegetable soup was a byproduct of the boiled brisket. That stock makes as fine a vegetable soup as can be imagined.

The fish course in the table d'hôte dinner often was a dish they misleadingly called "redfish vinaigrette." It was poached redfish served chilled, with a sauce that seemed to be a very light, very lemony mayonnaise with a lot of green onions. Not only was this good, but it was nearly the last such dish of its kind to be served hereabouts.

SPECIAL

MAIN COURSE, SALAD, AND DEMI TASSE ONLY	
BOILED BEEF SPECIAL (Soup, Salad, Beef, Potato, Demi Tasse)	1.75
SHRIMP COCKTAIL	1.60
SMALL SHRIMP COCKTAIL	.80
SHRIMP REMOULADE	1.60
SMALL SHRIMP REMOULADE	.80
DEVILED EGGS REMOULADE	.60
SHRIMP SALAD	1.80
SOUP DU JOUR	1.00
TURTLE SOUP OR GUMBO	1.50

DINNERS

REGULAR DINNER: Appetizer, Soup, Fish Course, Main Course, Vegetable Salad, Dessert and Demi Tasse	2.50
BOILED BEEF DINNER: Appetizer, Soup, Fish Course, Boiled Beef, Salad Dessert, and Demi Tasse	3.00
STEAK DINNER	4.75
BROILED POMPANO DINNER	4.50
ROCK CORNISH HEN DINNER	4.00

A section of a Maylie's menu from the 1960s. (Courtesy of The Historic New Orleans Collection)

The boiled beef brisket was the house specialty, but it was just okay—never quite as good as Tujague's. They sliced it about a quarter-inch thick and sent it out with ketchup and horseradish on the side to make into a sauce.

Maylie's cooked many other entrees, ranging from steaks to fried seafood to broiled chicken. At lunch, they ran one or two good, very inexpensive specials every day. Some of these were so old-fashioned it was hard to believe they were still making them (tripe stew, for example).

The bread pudding, when it came right out of the oven, was one of the best I ever remember eating. Most of the time, it was a day or two or three old and less good for it. It showed up with an eggy, yellow sauce, the likes of which I never saw before or since—but it was good, too.

Maylie's food was wildly inconsistent. Sometimes it was so far past fresh that it's amazing they had the gall to sell it. But sell it they did, even to their best customers.

As in most old New Orleans restaurants, Maylie's kitchen was staffed by black cooks who had been there for decades. Willie Maylie, the owner and son of the founder, was also back there a lot, in his white shirt and bowtie. He was quite knowledgeable about Creole-French food. He knew from firsthand experience what the local cuisine was like fifty years earlier. His wife, Anna May, ran the dining room, sitting at one table in the corner smoking cigarettes and drinking cocktails through lunch and dinner. She was something of a socialite and knew everybody in town.

Maylie's closed in 1983. It sat there crumbling for fifteen years. Then Smith and Wollensky, the New York steakhouse chain, bought the place and performed a first-class restoration in 1998. They installed as their chef Robert Bruce, the grandson of Willie and Anna May Maylie, who had a good career with the Brennans at the Palace Cafe and elsewhere. Hurricane Katrina closed Smith and Wollensky, and the old Maylie's building once again went into suspended animation. At this writing, it is being renovated into a sports bar and restaurant.

Willie Maylie, longtime proprietor of Maylie's, on the day the restaurant closed, New Year's Eve 1983. (Photo by Peggy Scott Laborde)

A BITE OF HISTORY

Meal-A-Minit
1239 St. Charles Avenue
1000 Canal Street
(at University Place)
1717 Canal Street
222 Loyola Avenue
113 University Place
(The Half Shell)
1801 Airline Highway

Meal-A-Minit was one of the earliest restaurant establishments to use an open kitchen concept that allowed for quicker service. Meal-A-Minit had a large menu that included KC sirloin steaks, shrimp in shorts (with tails on), smoked Virginia ham steaks and a sandwich called The Night Hawk, a triple decker with melted cheese on top. The chain was owned by William Joseph Gruber, Sr., and operated from 1935 to the 1960s

The first Meal-A-Minit stood at 1239 St. Charles Avenue, near the corner of Clio Street. This photo was taken in 1935. (Courtesy of Billy Gruber)

The Meal-A-Minit at the corner of Canal Street and University Place featured a distinctive bulb light sign. (Courtesy of Billy Gruber)

—Peggy Scott Laborde

Maylie's Turtle Soup

New Orleans-style turtle soup is as unique to our cuisine as gumbo. Unlike the clear turtle soup eaten in most other places, Creole turtle soup is thick and almost a stew. The hardest part of any turtle soup recipes is finding turtle meat; if you can't, using veal shoulder turns out a very credible mock turtle soup. It is traditional to serve turtle soup with sherry at the table, but I've never liked the alcoholic taste and aroma of that. I add the sherry into the recipe early to get the flavor but not the bitter alcohol.

3 lb. turtle meat, veal shoulder, or combination, including any bones
3 bay leaves
3 whole cloves
Peel of 1 lemon, sliced
1 Tbs. salt
½ tsp. black peppercorns
2 sticks butter
⅔ cup flour
2 ribs celery, chopped
2 medium onions, chopped
1 small green bell pepper, chopped
2 cloves garlic, finely chopped
½ tsp. thyme
½ tsp. marjoram
1 cup dry sherry
2 Tbs. Worcestershire
1 cup tomato puree
1 tsp. black pepper
1 Tbs. Louisiana hot sauce
2 hard-boiled eggs, chopped
1 bunch flat-leaf parsley, leaves only, chopped

1. Simmer the turtle meat and/or veal with bones in 1 gal. water, along with the bay leaves, cloves, lemon peel, salt, and black peppercorns. Keep the simmer going very slowly for about 2 hours.

2. Strain the stock, reserving the liquid and meat. If you don't have at least 3 qt. stock, add water or veal stock to get up to that quantity. Chop the meat into small shreds and set aside.

3. Make a medium-dark roux (the color of a well-used penny) with the butter and flour. When the roux is the right color, add the celery, onions, bell pepper, and garlic, and cook until the vegetables are soft. Add the thyme, marjoram, sherry, Worcestershire, and tomato puree. Cook for 1 minute, then add the stock.

4. Lower the heat and add the pepper, hot sauce, and meat. Simmer for a half-hour, then add the eggs and parsley and simmer 10 minutes

more. It's ready to serve now, but it gets better if you let it simmer for 1 or 2 more hours.

5. Adjust seasonings with salt and black pepper and serve in heated bowls.

Serves 6 to 8.

★★★★

Moran's Riverside
French Quarter: 914 North Peters Street
(in the French Market, Dutch Alley at Dumaine Street)
1975-91

★★★★

Bella Luna
1991-2005

The restaurant that Jimmy Moran built in the French Market may be the most visually striking ever to open in New Orleans. On the second floor of one of the new buildings added to the Market in the 1970s, the restaurant sported a magnificent view of the Mississippi River. The windows were big and numerous enough that the panorama extended from the bridge all the way to the sharp turn just downstream from the French Quarter.

As integral and as obvious as the Mississippi River is in the geography of New Orleans, few restaurants ever took advantage of it for atmospheric purposes. None of them was as beautiful nor as good as Moran's Riverside and its successor, Bella Luna.

Moran's Riverside began as a subsidiary of Moran's La Louisiane. The beauty of the new place was such a draw that Moran business moved there, along with Jimmy Moran himself. Its menu was a distinctive variation on Sicilian-New Orleans themes. The main action in the dining room was Jimmy's preparation of fettuccine Alfredo right at your table. This was not merely a gimmick but arguably the best fettuccine in town. Moran even made the raw pasta himself, in his Pastificio downstairs.

At the drop of a hat, Jimmy would show off the uniqueness of his operation. This ranged from the kind of olive oil he used to the décor of the ladies' room, which was almost certainly the most beautiful among the freestanding restaurants hereabouts. The private dining room on the upriver end of the restaurant was made to look like a grand palazzo in Venice, with dramatic checkerboard floors in stone tiles and an open mini-piazza.

When Jimmy Moran retired from the restaurant business in 1991 (he would pass away not long afterwards), this distinctive restaurant was taken over by Chef Horst Pfeifer and renamed Bella Luna. As the name suggests, it remained Italian. But although the tableside fettuccine remained as a fixture, the menu was very different from Moran's. Horst—a young native of southern Germany—was a

ERROL LABORDE ON MICHAEL'S MID-CITY GRILL

There was no burger like the Big Bucks Burger. I'm reminded of a classic hamburger that didn't make it back after Hurricane Katrina. It was the specialty item at Michael's Mid-City Grill, located at 4139 Canal Street, at David Street, from the 1990s to 2005. Most of the fare on the menu consisted of sandwiches, grilled chicken dishes, salads, and daily featured items—all at moderate prices—but then there was the Big Bucks Burger.

Its price increased gradually through the years but it started at $100. For your money you would get a burger and baked potato, just like what you could get for $7, but also caviar and a bottle of Dom Perignon champagne. Plus, a photograph would be taken of you and your party. It would be framed and hung on Michael's wall—a Big

Michael Tansel and Fred Sullivan owned Michael's Mid-City Grill, filled with cozy booths and featuring a great jukebox. Sullivan was very adept at creating a Sazerac, and while burgers were a specialty, the other menu items also held their own. Located in Mid-City along the Canal streetcar route, this restaurant was a victim of Hurricane Katrina. (Photo by George Long)

Bucks Burger eater's hall of fame. Gradually the wall was filled with what must have been thousands of dollars worth of pictures. Some were particularly notable. The very first photo was that of Archie Casbarian, at the time the owner of Arnaud's restaurants where the restaurant's namesake once worked. Another photograph was of a man, wearing a bright red shirt, spending his last night with his family before shipping off to federal prison. Ironically the pursuit of big bucks had done him in.

It was whispered that the woman who had ordered a Big Bucks Burger, as pictured in one photograph, did so shortly before committing suicide. Most of the many pictures, however, were of happy occasions: people falling in love, celebrating milestones, or just having a big night.

I will confess that I ordered a Big Bucks Burger several times, though always in jest. "I'll have a dozen Big Bucks to go," I would tell the server before quickly changing my order. In the back of my mind, though, I did sincerely hope to order a Big Bucks one day when, as I told myself, "my ship comes in." Unfortunately for most of that time, that ship, at least in reference to my career, was in uncharted waters and never near homeport.

In 2003 and '04, when part of Canal Street was closed for construction of the streetcar line, Michael's was hit hard.

Katrina was a knockout blow. Today Café Minh, an elegant Vietnamese/Asian fusion restaurant, occupies the space where Michael's once was. The décor is

Bella Luna was located within the historic French Market complex. (Courtesy of Horst and Karen Pfeifer)

Interior of the elegant Bella Luna. (Photo by George Long)

Chef Horst Pfeifer of Bella Luna prepares a pasta dish at table for a patron. (Courtesy of Horst and Karen Pfeifer)

newcomer to New Orleans. But he had a sharp sense of what could get customers excited, and his food did as fine a job of that as the stunning premises did.

Horst's menu encompassed all sorts of flavors. Having come to New Orleans from Dallas, he worked in southwestern flavors at a time when few other restaurants dabbled in that flavor palette. He adopted (and adapted) the Creole cuisine, too, and always had great seafood. When white truffles from Italy began to appear here in the fall, he used them as an irresistible add-on to his fettuccine. (Horst served that to us at the very first convocation of the New Orleans Eat Club, a wine dinner I host for my readers and radio listeners every week.) He developed a garden at the Ursuline Convent two blocks away for raising fresh herbs for the restaurant, long before such urban gardens became popular.

Bella Luna shares the date of its demise with many other extinct restaurants: August 29, 2005, the day Hurricane Katrina visited. Horst—who is such a smiling optimist that sometimes you want to shake him so he'll get real—fully intended to reopen Bella Luna. But the City of New Orleans owned the building (and the whole French Market). And when the first rain fell after the hurricane, it drained right through the roof, spoiling all the repairs Horst and his wife, Karen, had made. The city government was overwhelmed, and it was years before the roof was fixed. By that time, Horst Pfiefer had thrown in the towel and moved on to buy Middendorf's.

Bella Luna sat empty until 2009, when a new Spanish restaurant called Galvez reopened at that address. At this writing, it's the only restaurant in town with a river view.

totally different, but neighbors who remember Michael's can still visualize the line of cozy booths and there is, in my mind, always an echo of the refrain of "Day-O" from Harry Belafonte's "Banana Boat" song that I played many times on the jukebox. Because it's a gourmet restaurant, Café Minh is pricier than Michael's was—but nothing matches the Big Bucks burger in cost. If the chef ever considers Big Bucks spring rolls I'm in . . . at least once my ship arrives.

Thanks to Errol Laborde, who allowed us to reprint his reminiscence from the November 2010 edition of New Orleans Magazine.

A BITE OF HISTORY

Morrison's Cafeterias

Even though this chain had branches citywide, Morrison's Cafeteria's most beloved location was on Gravier Street in the CBD. The décor resembled that of a Spanish hacienda. Movie critic Rex Reed, whose family lived in Baton Rouge, recalls a visit to a Morrison's in New Orleans: "My mother would bring me down here and she would go shopping and deposit me at the RKO Orpheum Theater. And right next door almost was Morrison's Cafeteria, which was a very glamorous place to eat. It had stars in the ceiling and Spanish tiles on the floor. And you dressed to go to Morrison's Cafeteria. I mean, you tell people in the North, 'Well, the best food I ever had was in a cafeteria,' they look at you like you're crazy, but it's not like school-cafeteria time. Morrison's was very special." (Courtesy of The Historic New Orleans Collection)

A creamer from Morrison's Cafeteria. (From the collection of Peggy Scott Laborde)

—Peggy Scott Laborde

★★★
The Red Onion
Metairie: 2700 Edenborn Avenue
1974-89

Fine-dining restaurants were slow to arrive in Metairie. In the 1960s and earlier, if you wanted to dine out in that prosperous, populous suburb, your choices were Elmwood Plantation, Sclafani's, and the House of Lee. From there the pickings dropped to bad chain steakhouses or neighborhood cafes. If those wouldn't do, you went to the French Quarter.

By 1970, however, it was clear that so many people with good disposable incomes lived in Metairie that a real restaurant might make it. The first such ventures met with mixed luck. La Riviera (1972) and Sal & Sam's (1971) did well enough to remain long term (although both are gone now). La Charcuterie (1971) and Christian's (1973) did less well. (The former closed, and the latter moved to Mid-City.)

Then, suddenly, the hits just kept on coming. The Red Onion was the first of those. A partnership of restaurateurs that included Frank Occhipinti (whose first restaurant was in the Quality Inn on Tulane Avenue) and Joe Segreto (he now owns Eleven 79 and has run many restaurants in his long career) built a large new building along the lines of Elmwood Plantation.

It wasn't a great location: in the commercial area between Veterans and I-10. It wasn't on the way to anything else—a fact that still plagues restaurants and businesses in that section.

However, the Red Onion proved enough of a draw that it was always packed. The crowd maxed out at lunch, when not only were all the dining rooms full but the bar, too. The people were the movers and shakers of East Jefferson, which, of course, included no small number of people who could be called cronies.

That brought in even more people, who wanted for various reasons to be in the same place as the powerful. The Red Onion was so busy that after just a few years it added a large dining room and more parking. Even those remained full.

The management, not bound by downtown rules, implemented all sorts of unconventional services. The Red Onion was the first restaurant to stage lunchtime fashion shows, for example (not the lingerie shows that came a decade later in bars, but classy women's wear). At night, they had live music in the lounge, with a pianist who went by the name of Rosario. (He later became one of the Red Onion's owners.)

In the evening, the Red Onion was as elegant as any restaurant in the French Quarter. The dining room was handsomely appointed, spacious, and quiet. The kitchen kept right up with the expectations created by the ambience. The chef was Muse Benjamin, who'd worked a long time at Delmonico before joining Frank Occhipinti at the Quality Inn. Chef Ben, as everybody called him, was an old-school Creole chef who knew it all.

He and Occhipinti assembled a menu that blended Creole-French

The Red Onion was one of Jefferson Parish's early fine-dining restaurants. (Photo by Frank Methe)

restaurant dishes (oysters Rockefeller, turtle soup, trout amandine, rack of lamb) with Creole-Italian classics (oysters Mosca, chicken with artichokes, veal Francesca, barbecue shrimp). This sort of offering would be copied by enough other restaurants that I came up with a name for it: Suburban Creole.

The Red Onion's food was delicious and well served. But what fired its extreme popularity was that the menu prices were significantly lower than what people were accustomed to paying in the French Quarter. That was an important matter. Customers, then as now, have the idea that if a dish is served in a suburban location, it should be cheaper than it would be in town, even if all the ingredients are exactly the same and the restaurant is just as fancy. Occhipinti played to that absurdity (here and in all the other restaurants he ran over the years). His lunches were so cheap that the prices seemed like mistakes.

And again, it made for good eating. And it was at least a little original. They gussied up everything a bit more than we were used to seeing in those days, fleshing out plates with more (and less common) vegetables than one ordinarily saw. They had a great salad made with fresh asparagus and artichokes (both uncommon in restaurants in those days) and a unique, peppery, white house dressing that I've never been able to duplicate.

Other stuff: Prime steaks. Maine lobster (still not common back then). And some really fine veal and seafood dishes that would be called Northern Italian now (nobody made a distinction here then).

The Red Onion had a management shakeup in 1981. Segreto had already moved to Broussard's. Occhipinti was forced out and, within about a year, opened a new restaurant that looked almost exactly like the Red Onion a block away. Chef Ben went with Occhipinti and resumed cooking the Red Onion food, but better than the Red Onion. Occhipinti opened house accounts for those who'd run up unacceptably large balances at the Red Onion.

The Red Onion's new owners held on for a few years. The restaurant's offerings really did not decline tremendously, but its spirit had been ripped out. And there followed that downturn in the oil industry, the explosion of hip bistros Uptown, and a lot more upscale restaurants in Metairie (Augie's, Romanoff's, Chehardy's, and Timothy's, among others). It finally closed in 1989.

In its heyday, however, the Red Onion was not only excellent but a trendsetter. The Suburban Creole legacy lives on in places such as Austin's, Cypress, and the Peppermill.

Muse's Eggplant with Seafood (Eggplant Vatican)

Chef Muse Benjamin was one of the most influential chefs of his time—the 1960s into the 1980s. Restaurants whose food he defined included Delmonico, the Red Onion, and Frank Occhipinti's. The chef prepared this dish in honor of the visit of Pope John Paul II in 1987. It has a few old-fashioned touches, but nobody's saying you couldn't use fresh herbs or leave out the Accent. On the other hand, I thought it would be interesting to give you the recipe as I saw Chef Ben do it.

2 medium, ripe eggplants
2 cups vegetable oil
1 tsp. salt
½ tsp. black pepper
½ cup flour

Stuffing and sauce:
½ cup melted butter
⅓ cup flour
½ cup chopped green onions
2 Tbs. chopped garlic
1 tsp. ground thyme
1½ cups dry white wine
2 cups oyster water
2 cups shrimp stock
2 cups peeled, deveined medium shrimp
4 large mushrooms, sliced
1 cup milk
1 Tbs. hot sauce
1 tsp. salt
1 tsp. Accent
2 cups oysters
½ lb. white crabmeat

1. Peel the eggplants and slice them in half from top to bottom. Scoop out the center of each to form a boat with sides about three-quarters of an inch thick.

2. Heat the vegetable oil to 375 degrees in a large saucepan or Dutch oven. Stir the salt and pepper into the flour, and dust the eggplants generously with the mixture. Fry the eggplant boats in the hot oil, 2 at a time, until golden. Drain on wire racks set on a pan, and keep them warm in a 200-degree oven.

3. In a saucepan, heat the butter until it starts to bubble, then stir in the flour. Make a blond roux, stirring constantly. At the first sign of browning, add the green onions, garlic, and thyme. Cook until the onions are soft.

4. Stir in the wine and bring it to a boil. After 1 minute, add the oyster

water and shrimp stock, and stir in completely. Add the shrimp and mushrooms, and simmer until the mushrooms are tender.

5. Add the milk and bring to a boil. Add hot sauce, salt, and the Accent and stir well. Add the oysters and crabmeat and heat through.

6. Spoon the sauce into the eggplant boats and serve immediately.

Serves 4.

★★★★
Restaurant de La Tour Eiffel
Garden District: 2040 St. Charles Avenue
1986-89

From 1936 until 1981, a major restaurant operated at the 562-foot level of the Eiffel Tower in Paris. Among its customers were Picasso, Bardot, de Gaulle, Chaplin, Hitler, and thousands of honeymooners. During a restoration of the tower, the restaurant was found to be too heavy for the structure. It was removed entirely; the company that did the work was allowed to keep all the pieces in exchange for its fee. Everything was packed in freight containers and stored. A new, smaller restaurant was put in its place.

In 1983, Chef Daniel Bonnot—the founding chef of Louis XVI Restaurant and one of the best French chefs in our city's history—got wind of this. He and Louis XVI's business manager, John Onorio, negotiated the purchase of the restaurant's fixtures for $900,000 and had them shipped to New Orleans. In the meantime, the ground was prepared and plans drawn. Ultimately, it cost $1.7 million—a very large sum for a restaurant in those days.

A bad omen appeared. During the time the parts of the old restaurant were in storage, water got into them, and most of the woodwork was ruined beyond repair. Nevertheless, the project went on. A superstructure designed by local architect Stephen Bingler went up across St. Charles Avenue from the Pontchartrain Hotel. It lofted the restaurant to sixteen feet above ground and in its design suggested the restaurant's old home. Then the work of reassembling the 11,062-piece puzzle began—not without at least a little confusion about what went where.

Restaurant de la Tour Eiffel opened on St. Charles Avenue on the day after Thanksgiving 1986. It was not what anyone expected. It was very French, of course. It was also very good—Daniel Bonnot knew what he was about. But he focused more on country French cooking and a bistro style than the grand French food he had been cooking. This was ahead of its time—that's the only kind of French food you can find here anymore. But in 1986, it puzzled the customers who filled the place.

If you're accustomed to the food at La Crepe Nanou or Café Degas, you have a good idea of what they served at Tour Eiffel: mussels

Restaurant de la Tour Eiffel, on St. Charles Avenue, was constructed from a restaurant that was located within the Eiffel Tower in Paris. (Photo © Mitchel Osborne MMX)

marinière, duck terrine, escargots, onion soup a la Halles, steak au poivre, and duck confit. Chef Daniel reached a little farther than the average French bistro, though, and had crepes with caviar, filet mignon zingara (made with a spicy Gypsy-inspired sauce made with beef tongue, although he never told anyone that), choucroute garni, rack of lamb Nicoise, and occasionally really ethnic French food such as tete de veau.

And he made hot soufflés: savory soufflés, such as the oyster Rockefeller soufflés he'd created at Louis XVI, and even more dessert soufflés. The plan was to keep the place open into the wee hours and serve elaborate desserts and Champagne (it came out in an ice bucket made in the shape of a top hat).

That idea provided me with one of the most memorable evenings of my life. At a party for the New Orleans Opera, a number of young female models from the Mannequins Club were in attendance. The host of the party asked me—since I was single and perceived as sophisticated—to take the girls out for a late snack. I suggested soufflés and Champagne at the Eiffel Tower. So we went: ten beautiful women and me. Chef Daniel sent out thirteen different hot soufflés. I do not expect any aspect of that evening to repeat itself in my lifetime.

One of the most surprising aspects of the Eiffel Tower was that it was very inexpensive. Even the priciest entrees were barely over ten dollars (except, of course, for things like caviar). It seemed too affordable.

And it was. The place was quickly in financial trouble. The food declined, and volume followed—or perhaps it was the other way around. The Eiffel Tower had a problem. As distinctive as the structure was, it was set so far back from the avenue that it was hidden among the high buildings on either side. You could drive in front of it a hundred times and not see it. This remains true, and it is at least partly to blame for the string of other failures at that address. At this writing, it's a very hip restaurant and bar called Eiffel Society.

Restaurant de la Tour Eiffel left Bonnot and Onorio in bad shape financially. Daniel Bonnot had to begin his career all over again, with the grubby but excellent Chez Daniel on Metairie Road. It was a short run for such a distinctive and expensive project. But the Tour Eiffel still sparkles in the minds of everyone who ever dined there, especially in its first year.

Eiffel Tower's Strawberry Soufflé

I love hot soufflés, which are nowhere near as complicated to make as you may have been led to believe. They are, however, every bit as luscious and impressive as they are reputed to be. Just be sure everybody's at the table waiting when they come out of the oven, because they must be eaten immediately. Soufflé dishes are a must for this. Nothing else works well. The dishes should hold about a cup and a half each.

1½ pt. ripe strawberries
8 eggs, separated
1 cup minus 2 Tbs. sugar
2 Tbs. orange juice, strained
1 Tbs. kirshwasser (optional)
Butter
Powdered sugar
⅛ tsp. cream of tartar

Preheat the oven to 425 degrees.

1. Reserve 3 large, good-looking strawberries. Wash and hull the rest. Don't use any that are even slightly less than perfectly ripe. Put them into a food processor and puree.

2. In a mixer bowl, combine the strawberry puree, 4 egg yolks, ½ cup sugar, orange juice, and kirshwasser. Beat until smooth and creamy.

3. Butter the insides of 6 soufflé dishes. (Don't be shy about this: err on the side of too much butter.) Add about 1 tsp. powdered sugar to the soufflé dishes, covering the inside. Shake out the excess.

4. With completely clean, grease-free beaters or a wire whisk, beat the egg whites and the cream of tartar until peaks begin to form. Add the rest of the sugar, and beat until dissolved and the meringue is stiff.

5. Blend about a fourth of the meringue into the strawberry mixture with a rubber spatula. Then blend the strawberry mixture into the meringue, as gently as possible. Don't worry if the blend is not uniform.

6. Divide the mixture among the soufflé dishes. Place all the dishes in a large pan so you can get them in and out quickly. Bake for 8 minutes, then reduce the heat to 400 degrees and bake for 7 minutes. Don't open the oven during the baking process.

7. Slice the reserved strawberries into thin slices. Dust the tops of the soufflés with powdered sugar, then top with a few thin slices of fresh strawberry. Serve immediately.

Serves 6.

★★★★
Restaurant Mandich
Bywater: 3200 St. Claude Avenue
1922-2005

Regular customers of Restaurant Mandich were always amused to hear newcomers call the place a "discovery." That's inevitably what most restaurant writers (including me, in my first review of the place in 1977) called the restaurant. And whenever someone called my radio show about Mandich, I knew he would call it a great restaurant nobody knows about.

But how could a place that was consistently popular for eighty years be considered anybody's special secret?

Here's how: by the time Baby Boomers found out about Mandich, there were few restaurants of its kind left in New Orleans. And its location in the Ninth Ward—not an area with many other restaurants, let alone classy ones with great, carefully cooked food—was unlikely.

In the late 1800s, a wave of Croatian immigrants arrived in the bays and bayous of Plaquemines Parish, where they resumed their lifelong occupations as fishermen and oystermen. Some wound up in New Orleans, where in the 1920s and 1930s they opened a disproportionate number of new restaurants. Among the best known were Gentilich's, Uglesich's, and Zibilich's, plus just as many restaurants whose owners' names ended in the telltale "-ich": Chris Steak House (Matulich),

Bozo's (Vodanovich), and Crescent City Steak House (Vojkovich).

John Mandich opened his restaurant in 1922. His customer base was strong: he was a few blocks away from the busiest part of the port, where a typical day for the shipping-industry moguls began in the predawn hours and ended around one in the afternoon. Then they went out to dinner—not lunch, but dinner. These, plus a fair number of longshoremen, constituted the clientele.

Lloyd English came into the business as a partner a few years later and in 1939 bought out Mandich. It was the depression, and keeping the restaurant going was nothing but work for the Englishes. World War II was good for them—lots of action on the wharves then. By the 1950s, the restaurant was prosperous and a social center for the mostly middle class residents of the neighborhood.

Lloyd English, Jr., came in during the 1950s and took over the management of Mandich from his parents in 1959. He expanded the restaurant to its final size and renovated the dining rooms into as fancy a place as any other neighborhood restaurant in the city. The name *Restaurant Mandich* appeared in neon across the new Mansard roof. Lloyd Jr. persuaded his new bride, Joel, to take over the cooking. She did, and the two of them kept their jobs at Mandich until it closed. Lloyd's station was the bar, where his customers looked forward to having a drink or two before dinner. I never once went to Mandich without seeing Lloyd standing there behind the bar.

The flight to the suburbs had begun, and it wasn't long before Mandich settled into an odd schedule remembered by its regulars as well as they recall the food: lunch Tuesday through Friday, dinner Friday and Saturday only. They still had a lot of management types from the docks coming in for big dinners at lunchtime, but they had poor boys, too.

In his first review in the *States-Item* in 1983, critic Gene Bourg called Mandich a special secret restaurant and "the Galatoire's of the Ninth Ward." That captured the spirit of the place well. The menu seemed to be familiar enough. But everything—from the red bean soup to the fried seafood to the filet mignon—was cooked with more attention to detail than one was accustomed to finding in a moderately priced, casual restaurant like this one.

You started with a soup, unless you didn't know how good Joel made them. The marinated crab claws, fried calamari, shrimp remoulade, and crab cakes were other good starters. But the signature appetizer was the oysters bordelaise, whose sauce was a mildly garlicky version of the brown, buttery New Orleans-style meunière sauce. That dish lingers in memory so strongly that JoAnn Clevenger at the Upperline has a similar dish called oysters St. Claude, with full credit given to Mandich for the idea.

Joel cooked all kinds of New Orleans food, as well as a bit of Italian. But her most distinctive dishes were those denoted as "broiled with a crisp breading." Crisp, buttery breading, she should have said. This was the essence of trout Mandich, the signature dish of the restaurant, made with generous fillets of fresh speckled trout, a wonderful crust, and a flow of lemon butter. It almost seemed panéed but wasn't. It was simple, really, but unique.

Lloyd English, Jr., was the longtime proprietor of Restaurant Mandich. (Photo © Kevin R. Roberts)

Restaurant Mandich's signature appetizer was oysters bordelaise. (Photo © Kevin R. Roberts)

    Joel cooked lots of good specials. The roast duck with sweet-potato sauce was a real original. The tall filet mignon was crusty and juicy. For dessert you had an extraordinary, cinnamony bread pudding.

    Two feet of Katrina flooding brought an end to forty-six years of great food in a delightfully retro restaurant. Joel and Lloyd decided that was the perfect moment to retire. And that was that. They sold the building, and it's now a small grocery store.

★★★
The Riverbend
Riverbend: 734 South Carrollton Avenue (at Maple Street)
1974-87

    The Riverbend appeared when the New Orleans restaurant scene was pregnant. The Baby Boom generation was in its young adulthood and was ready to try restaurants with more going on than hamburgers. But it found that most serious New Orleans restaurants were too serious.

A few years later, the Uptown Creole bistro would be born, and that would change everything. But in the meantime, a few restaurants figured out that if a restaurant served good food and was fun—maybe even frivolous—it would attract a lot of these younger diners.

Peter Uddo was a Baby Boomer himself. He had a food connection: his family owned Uddo & Taormina, the company that evolved into Progresso Foods. He had a restaurant connection, too. He'd married into the Riccobono family, which owned the popular local chain of Buck Forty-Nine Steak Houses. The Buck Forty-Nine concept was running out of gas, particularly in its Uptown and French Quarter locations. And Joe Riccobono wanted to spin off his restaurants to the next generation.

Peter Uddo took over the Buck Forty-Nine on South Carrollton, a block from where the streetcar turned onto St. Charles Avenue. He changed its name to The Riverbend, pulled down the wild-west decor, and replaced it with flowery designs and lots of plants. It was what became known as a "fern restaurant."

He also made the menu over—sort of. Actually, all he did was remove the steak emphasis. The Buck Forty-Nine always had a wide-ranging menu that was more like that of a neighborhood restaurant like Mandina's than a steakhouse's. He kept all of that and added more entree salads and a few other dishes aimed at women.

And then he reworded the menu. Peter's greatest talent may have been his ability to create descriptions of straightforward dishes that made them sound like sheer ambrosia. I recall that his paragraph (it was no less than that, for every dish) about soft-shell crabs told of how rare they were ("these softies are hard to find!"), with the suggestion that anyone who was lucky enough to be there on the day when the crabs were available was in for the dinner of his life.

Actually, what he threw at you was a basic fried soft-shell crab, perhaps with a genuinely good light brown meunière sauce of the Arnaud's ilk. And they had them all the time. If they were out of season, they were frozen. Big deal; almost everybody used frozen crabs and fish back then.

None of that mattered. The food was good enough, if never brilliant. The prices were a shade above those of a neighborhood joint, but The Riverbend's kicky environment obviated that, too.

The place was a tremendous hit. As the Buck Forty-Nine had been, The Riverbend was open for breakfast, lunch, and dinner, seven days a week. It was always packed, not just with young people but people of all ages. It turned out there were a lot of middle-aged folks who also felt challenged by formal dining. The Riverbend suited them perfectly.

As time went on, many of them became regular customers to an absurd degree. Peter Uddo told me that he could count on seeing some people three times a day, seven days a week.

Over the years, a few specialties emerged. The pancakes and breakfasts were always terrific. The salads were big and lush and good. The fried seafood was beyond reproach. They made a fine crawfish bisque and a delicious skewer of charred filet mignon tips with a sweet-peppery sauce, steak Beaucage.

The Riverbend's fortunes declined in the mid-1980s. The Uptown bistros pulled away the best of its customers. The three-meals-a-day old-timers went the way of all flesh. And fern restaurants went out of vogue. The Riverbend was sold and operated as a restaurant only a little while longer before its place was taken by a drugstore.

Peter Uddo semiretired, even though he was still a relatively young man. Peter's younger brothers, Michael and Mark, opened a great restaurant in the French Quarter called the G&E Courtyard Grill; Peter turned up there now and then to help out. That was his last involvement with the restaurant business. He died when he was not quite fifty.

But his restaurant's memory is immortal. It was so popular that its name transferred to the neighborhood, which is universally called Riverbend now. (That's funny, because the river doesn't actually bend there.) It boasts one of the city's densest collections of small restaurants.

★★★★
Roussel's
Laplace: Airline Highway at US 51
1940s-84

The border between the lands of Creole cooking and Cajun cooking crosses the Mississippi River at the Bonnet Carre Spillway. The first significant town west of there, Laplace, the World Capital of Andouille, is clearly dominated by Cajun cooking.

The best evidence of that for decades was Roussel's, an old roadhouse so excellent that there was no argument as to whether it was worth the drive to dine there. The only question was whether you had the time. Because if you went to Roussel's, you had to take Airline Highway instead of the much faster interstate. You could, I suppose, route yourself up the relatively new I-10 instead of the old highway Huey Long built from Baton Rouge to New Orleans. But it just didn't seem right, somehow.

Roussel's was next door to another, flashier restaurant called Airline Motors. With its glass bricks, neon, and chrome, the Airline Motors restaurant got most of the attention from people looking for relics of an earlier time. Its food was similar to what they served at Roussel's but never as quite as good.

Roussel's was also a cool-looking place. Curved corners and round windows gave an Art Deco look. A big neon sign animated the image of a coffeepot pouring its electric brew over the door. The coffee was important. If you were traveling from New Orleans to Baton Rouge, Laplace was the first logical stop for a cuppa, snack, meal, or bathroom.

But the food was a better reason to stop, or to make a special trip in the first place.

Let's start with the gumbo (or gumbos—they had two). One was a fine seafood gumbo. But the other one was not only better but unique: oyster and andouille gumbo. It started with a dark roux but wound up as a lighter broth than today's vogue. The oysters went in right before the soup was served, nice and plump. The andouille was . . . well, it needs a paragraph of its own.

A BITE OF HISTORY

Rockery Inn
Corner of Robert E. Lee Boulevard and Canal Boulevard

The parking lot of the Rockery Inn (1930s-69) was a favorite among New Orleans teenagers. According to owner Vincent Signorelli, "The younger set would stay in the parking lot. You'd park, turn on the lights, the car hop would come to the car, take your order. Al Gaudet, who was a carhop at the Rockery a very long time, they called him the Whistler. So he'd whistle when he was coming with the order to warn the people smooching that he was coming to the car. He'd give them time to straighten up and roll down their window, since it's probably all fogged up, and then Al would hang their tray." (Courtesy of Vincent Signorelli)

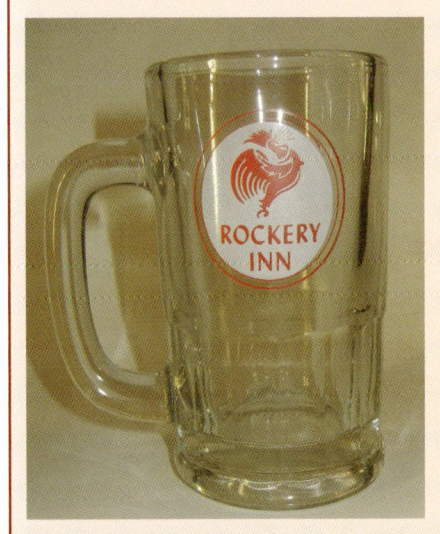

A beer mug from the Rockery Inn. (From the collection of Peggy Scott Laborde)

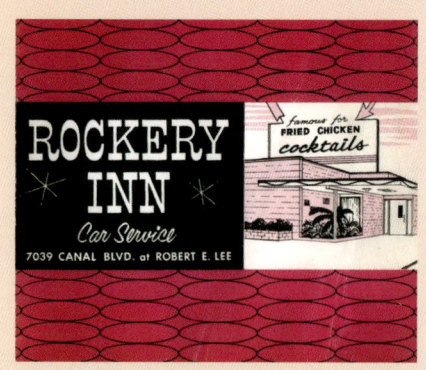

A menu from the Rockery Inn, located near Lake Pontchartrain. Among the restaurant's specialties were fried chicken, seafood, chicken-fried steaks, and club sandwiches. The restaurant's Rockery Bumstead, a variation on the Dagwood sandwich, was named after the popular cartoon character. (Courtesy of Vincent Signorelli)

Matches from the Rockery Inn. (From the collection of Edward Piglia)

—Peggy Scott Laborde

Roussel's was a popular stopping-off point on Airline Highway between New Orleans and Baton Rouge. (From the collection of Peggy Scott Laborde)

I'm not sure where Roussel's got its andouille sausage. It was probably Jacobs', but whatever the source, this andouille was definitive. It had a dark red-brown skin, thicker than on most sausages. Inside, the pork was in chunks, not all ground up. In between were just the right number and size of fat islands, and garlic and red pepper, too. It was just magnificent. The flavor was along the lines of a chicken gumbo, because of the smokiness of the sausage, and you added filé at the table. It remains in my mental bank of eating experiences among the finest of all my gumbos.

When crawfish were in season, Roussel's made much of them, but what you prayed for was that they'd made crawfish bisque. Those of us who live in New Orleans, where crawfish bisque is relatively rare (it's a Cajun thing, really), would shed tears if served Roussel's version. It was everything crawfish bisque should be: dark roux again, lots of bits of crawfish, thick, with stuffed crawfish heads. I am no fan of the process of either stuffing or unstuffing crawfish heads, but I love that flavor.

The rest of the menu was a curious mix of Cajun and Creole. They always had a roast duck on Sundays, with dirty rice and sweet potatoes. (My mother, who was such a great cook that she was difficult to impress, devoured this with great enthusiasm.) They had a roast chicken, too. (In a review I wrote in 1979, I see that the menu price for the half-chicken as a complete dinner was $3.50.)

Oysters en brochette and trout Marguery were there. No, not like Galatoire's, but they weren't bad. The big menu also offered fried chicken, fried catfish, hamburger steak, poor boys, and spaghetti and meatballs for the truck drivers.

You finished off with a good bread pudding with lots of raisins and a custard sauce. I wonder how there was any bread left over to make this. For some reason, the butter here was so good that you wound up eating an unbelievable amount of bread.

What killed Roussel's was the aging of its proprietors and the departure of the main stream of traffic from Airline Highway. Also, it was in the oldest part of Laplace, and development had moved west. But for as long as it lasted, this first outpost of Cajun cooking always beckoned devoted eaters to take the old highway and stop for a meal the likes of which could not be had just twenty miles east.

★★★★
The Royal Oak Restaurant and Pub
Gretna: Oakwood Mall
1971-83

What was the best Greek restaurant in New Orleans history doing in a large shopping mall on the West Bank?

If you stepped into the Royal Oak without knowing anything about it, you probably wouldn't guess that it was Greek. The dining room was handsome and comfortable, with no Greek décor to speak of. Its kitchen used the best raw materials for everything, at a time when the few other Greek places served canned stuffed grape leaves and the like.

The reason for the Royal Oak's improbable excellence was that its owners were avid gourmets. John "Chauncey" Newsham—a CPA by profession—and his wife, Julia Pappas Newsham, were members of all the wine-and-food societies we had in those days. They were also a pair of happy, unpretentious people. You took a liking to them the first moment you met them. John was always laughing about something or other—especially his own checkered fortunes in the restaurant business. He also owned the Seven Samurai, in the location where Mr. B's is now, when Japanese restaurants were not yet popular. "Of the three least popular kinds of restaurants in America," he told me once, "the only kind I don't own is a health-food restaurant!" Then he threw his head back and laughed.

Julia was the Greek connection, but John knew all about Greek cooking too. Royal Oak's menu included all the Greek classics. If you were there on a good day, the food was brilliant, served amply and even presented nicely, which is not a common appearance for Greek food.

You started well indeed if you had taramosalata. John made it personally, using carp roe, olive oil, lemon juice, and bread soaked in water and pureed. As unpromising as that may sound, the stuff was fantastic as an appetizer. Similar in appearance but totally different in flavor was the skordalia, a thick, smooth sauce of almonds and garlic that they served with two utterly different dishes: a cold beet salad and a fried seafood platter. The stuff was spectacular with both.

The Royal Oak was the first New Orleans Greek restaurant to serve saganaki, a slab of kasseri cheese coated with a light batter, broiled on a hot platter, then brought to the table and sizzled and flamed with ouzo and lemon juice.

The entrees included the most elegant gyro sandwich you ever saw, a marvelously light moussaka, and souvlaki of various kinds. They also had good lamb chops.

And they had one real oddity. The Royal Oak's chef had come from Pascal's Manale and knew the recipe for that restaurant's barbecue shrimp. The Royal Oak made them the same way, and they were terrific. Nobody ever questioned the obvious non-Hellenic aspect of that dish.

A case could be made that the best dish of all at the Royal Oak was a dessert called galaktoboureko. The lightest imaginable custard, flavored with honey and something like orange-flower water, was baked under a phyllo crust. It all but floated off the plate. Julia Newsham made that personally.

The Royal Oak had consistency problems. John and Julia had other irons in the fire and weren't there to watch the place all the time. Nor was the restaurant so busy that the kitchen kept a white heat going at all times. This became especially true in the last years of the restaurant, when the Newshams had given up on the idea of making a profit with the place. It folded when all the other good restaurants on the West Bank did, in the aftermath of the oil crash in the 1980s.

But to this day, even in Chicago and other centers of Greek citizenry, I have never found a better Greek restaurant than the Royal Oak was in its prime.

Royal Oak's Skordalia (Greek Garlic Sauce)

Skordalia is a thick, off-white garlic sauce fleshed out with either bread or mashed potatoes, plus olive oil and sometimes almonds. Hearing that description, you'd never believe how marvelous it is on fried seafood. Oddly enough, it's also delicious with salads, especially those made with root vegetables, most particularly beets.

4 slices white bread
5 cloves garlic, peeled
1 Tbs. vinegar
1 Tbs. lemon juice
¼ tsp. salt
3 drops Tabasco
¼ cup olive oil

1. Remove crusts from the bread. Soak the white part of the bread in water, and squeeze out the excess.

2. Place all the ingredients except the olive oil in the bowl of a food processor or blender. Process while adding the oil a very little at a time. Blend until the mixture is smooth. Serve cold with fried seafood or atop a beet-and-onion salad.

Makes about 1 cup.

★★
Ruggiero's
French Quarter: 911 Decatur Street
1960s-77

Ruggiero's was an Italian restaurant in the middle of a classic New Orleans Italian commercial neighborhood. It was between the Central Grocery and the Progress Grocery, the two most famous

Customers walked past a barbershop to get to Ruggiero's. (Photo © Mitchel Osborne MMX)

Chicken Livers a la Marsalla was a specialty at Ruggiero's. (Courtesy of The Historic New Orleans Collection)

The bar at Ruggiero's. (Photo © Mitchel Osborne MMX)

Ad for Ruggiero's. (From the collection of Peggy Scott Laborde)

vendors of muffulettas. Ruggiero's eats were decent, sometimes even delicious.

But what made it memorable was the presence of a full-fledged, working barbershop—rotating barber pole, antique Kochs chairs, shaving-cream machine and everything—right in the middle of the place. The tonsorial parlor was separated from the bar and the dining room (it was between them) by walls and windows. But if you wanted a haircut, you had to pass through the bar and expose yourself to the aromas of the red sauce and the rest of the food.

No explanation for this has ever been advanced, and I've never been able to find anyone who knew.

★★★
Sam's Place
Uptown: 3601 General Taylor Street
1938-78

The list of restaurants owned or founded in New Orleans by Croatian families is an honor roll. There was hardly a bad one among them. Drago's, Uglesich's, Ruth's Chris Steak House, Crescent City Steak House, Bozo's, and Gentilich's were the best-known names, but there were quite a few others, no less good.

By the time I got to Sam's, it was better known as Mrs. Sam's. Sam Batinich had passed away but his wife, Veronica, who pretty much ran the place anyway, kept it going—sometimes with the help of her dog.

Sam's was on the corner of three side streets in Broadmoor, in a narrow wedge of a block that gave the place windows on opposite walls. It's a neighborhood unknown to most New Orleanians; you practically had to live there to find your way into it. It wasn't as rough as the one where Uglesich's or the old Bozo's operated, but it was bad enough that they often kept the door locked, only admitting you after they got a good look.

The menu was simple, a lot like the one at Bozo's. Spectacular fried seafood dominated the list, with oysters at the top of it. Croatians had a lock on the oyster business, and fellow countrymen knew where the good ones came from. They had boiled seafood and an assortment of platters and sandwiches.

If I were to recall the finest fried seafood of my life, the lunches I had here would be on the list. Sam's frying was perfection: crisp, greaseless, ideally seasoned, and so hot you had to let it cool a minute or two before you could eat it.

Sam's Place was also a very adept purveyor of boiled shrimp, crawfish, and crabs. Some of the regulars included people who worked at Baptist and Touro hospitals (the former was just a few blocks away), who would come en masse and eat large piles of boiled shellfish.

Despite that excellence, the most memorable part of dining here was the way Veronica took and completed your order. There was no menu. Veronica more or less told you what you were going to be eating. You could influence the order but not dictate it.

Then, when you were finished, she would return to the table, run some arithmetical functions that only she understood through her head, and announce the total due. It was always a shade more than you expected, but not so much more that you'd be outraged—or declare that you'd never come back.

Veronica's calculus included such matters as how much she liked you. Once five coaches from a college football team came in and ate so well that they said they'd be back with the entire team the next day. Bring them in, said Veronica. The check for the team was less than it had been for the five coaches.

That story came from Klara Cvitanovich, whose family owns

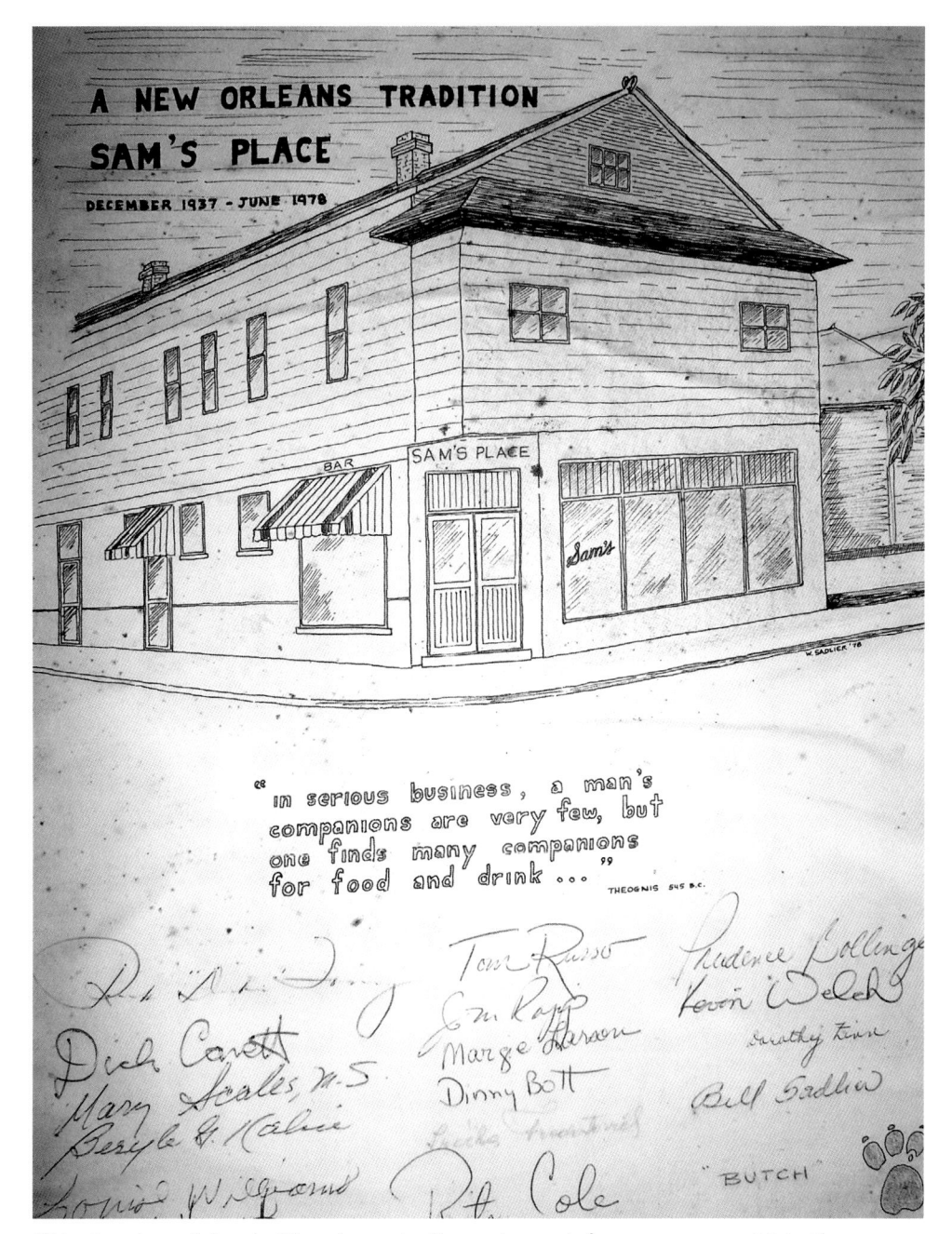

This drawing of Sam's Place hung in the restaurant for many years. Note the signatures from some of the customers, including talk-show host Dick Cavett and the restaurant's dog, Butch. (Courtesy of Betty Jean Hughes)

Drago's (she's Mrs. Drago). Sam and Veronica Batinich were such close friends with the Cvitanoviches that they were more like family. So was Sam's brother Drago Batinich. (Yes, there were two restaurateurs here named Drago.) The late Drago Batinich owned the Drago's that used to be on Harrison Avenue, which, to confuse things even more, was where Drago Cvitanovich worked before he opened his own restaurant in Metairie.

All that is as perfect a New Orleans story as that of Sam's Place, one of the two or three best fried-seafood joints that ever were.

★★★
Sclafani's
Metairie: 1315 North Causeway Boulevard
1945-87

Sclafani's was the first white-tablecloth restaurant in East Jefferson Parish. For a long time, it remained the only one.

Peter Sclafani didn't start his career as a chef, but one day he decided that he could become one by just saying so. His original restaurant was in Mid-City, on Palmyra Street between Carrollton and the cemeteries. It was a small place, always busy, serving the Sicilian dishes everybody in New Orleans considered real Italian food.

The restaurant succeeded because Sclafani had more of a gift for cooking than he realized. Even first-generation Italian mammas thought that he turned out creditable food—not as good as their own, of course, but good enough. That was high praise indeed, and Sclafani became as famous an Italian chef as anyone in town, with the possible exception of the Turci family.

In the late 1950s, Chef Pete moved his restaurant to Causeway Boulevard. That thoroughfare had just been built through the old Harlem neighborhood and was now the main north-south route through Metairie. Many of his customers came from the adjacent Old Metairie neighborhoods, but probably even more were people who had just built houses along the relatively new Veterans Memorial Boulevard corridor.

Singer Rudy Vallee—who liked Chef Pete's food—broke ground for the sprawling new restaurant. It was big enough not only to serve all those people but also to host meetings of every organization in the area. Rotary, Kiwanis, Sertoma, Knights of Columbus—every Metairie group had its meetings at Sclafani's.

The core of the menu was Italian food, but Chef Pete was equally as adept at Creole and seafood cookery. The menu was comically large, even by the standards of those big-menu days. It listed well over a hundred dishes in tiny type. When they ran out of room, they ran even more dishes up, down, and sideways along the margins and added typed pages of specials.

Sclafani's food was always good. They were famous for shrimp remoulade (enough so that they bottled the sauce and sold it in grocery stores). The red snapper soup was to Sclafani's what turtle soup is to Commander's: not to be missed. Great baked oysters with seafood dressing, and really good Rockefellers, too. Soft-shell crabs bordelaise, really garlicky but wonderful. (Speaking of garlic, the house salad gave you all you wanted of that.)

The most famous dish at Sclafani's, though, was its stuffed shrimp hollandaise. Everybody ordered it. By the time I got there, however, something funny had happened. They decided that they'd make large batches of hollandaise in advance, refrigerate it, and scoop a ball of it on top of the hot shrimp when served. It would then melt like butter over the shrimp, completely broken. I never once had a proper hollandaise on this dish. This would be considered an atrocity these days, but they got away with it in Metairie.

The Sclafani family had numerous restaurants, but the North Causeway dining establishment was one of their best known. (From the collection of Peggy Scott Laborde)

Chef Peter's sons Frank and Peter Jr. were heavily involved in operating the restaurant, but they parted ways in the late 1960s. Frank continued to run Sclafani's for a number of years after his father died. But times had changed, the Metairie restaurant scene was more competitive, and the old building needed major renovation. Ultimately it closed and was torn down.

Frank now runs a cooking school for professional chefs. Peter Jr. opened his own place in New Orleans East long enough that his own sons became chefs. Peter III ran a couple of good restaurants in New Orleans before relocating to Baton Rouge. He's now one of the owners of Ruffino's there. He keeps a few old Sclafani's dishes alive there.

★★

The Steak Pit
French Quarter: 609 Bourbon Street
1960s-90s

The Steak Pit never served what could be called great steaks. However, in its prime (and we are not talking about USDA Prime grade beef here), it filled a niche perfectly. And its customers were always raving about it.

In my pre-restaurant-critic days, I was one of those. Among college students in the 1960s and 1970s, the Steak Pit was legendary. I'll get to why this was in a moment.

The Steak Pit's famous offering was a three-quarter-pound chopped-steak dinner. Chopped steak—a.k.a. hamburger steak—has almost completely exited the restaurant scene. But it was still widely served and taken seriously back then. A thick oval of chopped sirloin came off the Steak Pit's superheated flattop grill with a thick, almost hard brown crust, while remaining juicy and medium rare in the center. A hamburger steak is a lowly thing, but the Steak Pit created the apotheosis of the genre and turned it out with almost perfect consistency.

That was the centerpiece. The dinner began with an extraordinarily tall glass of water with ice cubes frozen into it, such that they remained at the bottom. It was very welcome on a hot day. Then came a plate of sliced wheat bread and an ordinary salad with French dressing (the only kind they had), served in a bowl stamped out of sawdust and glue.

A second, empty bowl of the same kind came, too. You'd use that to help yourself to all the thin but acceptable French onion soup you wanted, from a big stainless-steel bucket that circulated from table to table. You added your own gratinee from a canister of low-level Parmesan cheese.

Next came the steak. Most people went for the chopped steak, but the Steak Pit also offered a full range of all the standard steak cuts, filets to strips to porterhouses. These, however, were never as outstanding as the chopped steak. Other options included pork chops and barbecue ribs. A foil-wrapped baked potato shared the plate with whatever was on it.

The meal came to a screaming halt at that point. There were no desserts of any kind. You might be able to hang on to your spot at the picnic-style table if you ordered a cup of the weak coffee, but it was hardly worth it. The waiters (the one I remember most gave forth with

---

A BITE OF HISTORY

Solari's
201 Royal Street

In addition to serving food, Solari's was known for gourmet grocery items, including olives in barrels. (Courtesy of The Historic New Orleans Collection)

Opened in 1868 as what we would today call a gourmet-goods grocery store by Angelo M. and Joseph Solari, its final location included a popular lunch counter. Solari's, which closed in 1965, sold meats, fish, cheeses, baked goods, and specialty food items. Upperline Restaurant owner JoAnn Clevenger recalls, "They would have showcases and you could see the candied oranges and marzipan and they were all glistening like jewels behind the windows of the candy cases. And at Christmas they would have all the dried fruits that you would use in a fruitcake." And then there was the lunch counter. According to attorney and bank executive Allain Andry, "They had wonderful New Orleans waitresses. Everybody was 'dawlin',' 'honey,' etc. And I survived, I guess for the first five or six years of my law practice, with

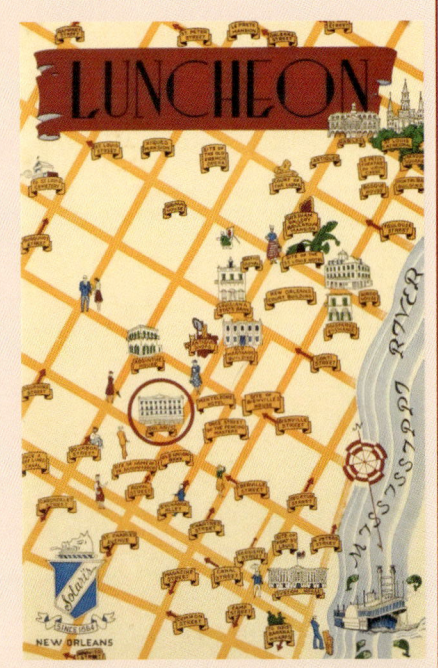

The cover of a luncheon menu from the much-missed Solari's in the French Quarter. (Courtesy of The Historic New Orleans Collection)

the vegetable plate at the counter at Solari's."

—Peggy Scott Laborde

more grunts than words) clearly wanted you to beat it so they could make up with volume what the checks lacked in dollars.

Okay, here's the punch line. The chopped steak, with the salad and onion soup and potato—plenty enough to stuff yourself uncomfortably—cost all of $1.35 in 1972. In 2011 dollars, the price would be $5.82. That was enough to make its customers ignore deficiencies that would be atrocities by today's standards.

The environment was memorable, too, more for its uniqueness than comfort. The placemats were made of those tiles that fake the look of a brick floor. A large backlit poster of a downtown, traffic-clogged scene full of 1950s cars captured your attention; one studied it to determine which year and in what city it had been taken. I never figured that out.

Otherwise, the Steak Pit was like a little bit of Texas in a dark French Quarter building. If you walked far enough into the rear, you'd discover that you had entered the rear of the Bastille Bar, around the corner on Toulouse Street. You would not be likely to stay there long, either.

Menu board at the Steak Pit. In addition to a well-priced steak, the onion soup was a favorite. (Menu collection gift of Richard and Rima Collin courtesy of The Historic New Orleans Collection)

★★★
Stonebreaker's
Metairie: 2700 Edenborn Avenue
1993-95

Steve Stonebreaker was one of the original New Orleans Saints. After he retired from football, he was in a succession of businesses, from a typesetting shop (trivia: his outfit set the type for Richard Collin's last restaurant guide) to opening restaurants—something quite a few Saints have tried over the years.

Stonebreaker's originally opened as a branch of TJ's Ribs, a popular LSU hangout in Baton Rouge. The specialty of the house was barbecue baby back pork ribs. At that time, barbecue of any distinction was rare around New Orleans. We had Harold's Texas Barbecue, and that was about it. Corky's wasn't here yet (indeed, I met Sam Chawkin, the man who ultimately brought Corky's to New Orleans, during lunch at Stonebreaker's).

Well-prepared baby back ribs are lusty eating. So are the larger St. Louis-style pork ribs and roast prime ribs of beef, both of which were specialties at Stonebreaker's. I even know some people who claim to like barbecue beef ribs, although that taste is beyond me.

Steve Stonebreaker was a hail-fellow-well-met salesman. He was always ready to tell you the details of where he got his ribs and how well selected they were. If you pressed him on matters such as why his ribs were baked and grilled instead of smoked, he told you that smoked ribs are not his style. The former linebacker was bigger and fitter than you are, so he persuaded you.

The menu was simple and rather similar to those of some chain restaurants. It began with spinach-artichoke-cheese dip, a big bowl of green stuff served with tortilla chips. My wife loved it enough to force me to try to duplicate it at home. The fried chicken tenders were well seasoned, light, completely ungreasy, and one of the best items on the entire menu.

The flagship entree was as good as the smokeless style gets. The main appeal of baby back ribs is that the ratio of meat to bone is a lot higher than on most other ribs. Stonebreaker's were trimmed better than most, resulting in very little in the way of globby fat. The vogue is for ribs that fall off the bone as you pick them up. Stonebreaker's ribs were tender but not that tender—which I liked.

Two cuts of prime rib were a second specialty. The "quarterback" cut was what would in other restaurants be called a "ladies' cut" (joke). The "linebacker" cut was for real eaters.

Stonebreaker could have become famous for crab cakes, which were not nearly as widespread on local menus then as now. The were made with pure jumbo lump crabmeat, barely held together by a breadcrumb crust. They were terrific, but when the price shot up in the colder months, Stonebreaker took them off the menu. I think he could have charged whatever he wanted for them and gotten away with it. They were really that good.

The premises were originally built for Frank Occhipinti's restaurant and were quite handsome. The chair backs were upholstered with custom slipcovers that showed the names of NFL teams. The walls were full of football memorabilia, as you might imagine. Stonebreaker was a highly motivated positive thinker, and he infused his staff with that great attitude.

But it didn't work. The restaurant had a big problem: it was off the main traffic stream, in a funny part of Metairie that's off most people's mental maps. You needed to know where it was to find it.

The restaurant—and Steve Stonebreaker himself—came to a sad end. He committed suicide, reportedly after learning that he had cancer. The restaurant was struggling at the time and closed shortly after his death. He was too nice a guy to have such a fate. And if he'd held on a bit longer, and put some smoke into those ribs, he could have caught a wave of interest in barbecue that soon passed through New Orleans. *Ave atque vale,* Steve.

★★

Tally-Ho

French Quarter: 400 Chartres Street

1960s-90s

The Tally-Ho was one of the quirkiest restaurants in the French Quarter, which is saying something. But that's what people liked about the Tally-Ho and its owners, Bert and Tillie.

Most of the Tally-Ho's customers were local. All of them said the same thing about the place: that it served the best breakfast in town. That was not really true. But the Tally-Ho did indeed serve an excellent breakfast—and not a bad lunch, either.

The place was the most ordinary of diners. Most of the service was at a lunch counter. Bert, the owner and cook, stood at a flattop grill and cranked out the bacon, sausage, eggs, hash browns, and sandwiches. His wife, Tillie, was the waitress. She'd get to you when she could. So would Bert. This was not a restaurant to come to when you were in a hurry.

In fact, it wasn't really the best restaurant to visit if it were essential that you ate there. They had a way of closing early, or not opening at all, unpredictably. The cause of this was that Bert and Tillie could work themselves up into quite a row. I don't know whether their fights were real or trumped up for dramatic effect, but they could be intense. If it were bad enough, they'd just close for the rest of the day.

Of course, this dynamic was an attraction to a lot of their customers. And there was another one: Bert's cheese omelette.

How good could a cheese omelette get? you might well ask. Well, these were in a class by themselves. They were big and moist and fluffy and unscorched—a rare enough thing right there. What made them great was an additive Bert had on the back of the stove. A juicy blend of finely chopped onions and bell peppers was spooned into the omelette before it was folded over. It made that omelette so good that even as you ate it you were thinking about the next one.

I don't know what happened to Bert and Tillie. The Tally-Ho closed for awhile and then reopened with new owners, a new menu, and a new style. It was much more ambitious than Bert and Tillie's Tally-Ho, with things like alligator sausage and pancakes so enormous that I can't imagine many people ever finished one.

What did not remain was the cheese omelette. Somehow, the recipe was lost. I've tried to recreate it at home dozens of times, and what I get is good but not what I remember. Bert's cheese omelette really was magical.

The building once occupied by the Tally-Ho has been restored and is now owned by The Historic New Orleans Collection, a research center/museum. All we can do is keep trying to reproduce that omelette.

★★★
Tchoupitoulas Plantation
Waggaman: 6535 River Road
1963-86

The word "plantation" conjures up a rich image in this part of the world. While many restaurants have used the word in their names, only two real plantation homes became major restaurants: Elmwood (see index) and Tchoupitoulas. They seemed to have a lot in common. Both boasted buildings dating back to the late 1700s. Both were on the Mississippi River—almost across the river from one another, in fact. Their heydays as restaurants were in the 1960s and 1970s. Each had a style all its own, grand grounds full of enormous live oak trees, and staffs dominated by old black waiters and cooks who worked as if their clocks had been turned back fifty years.

Although it was much loved and had many stories to tell, Tchoupitoulas Plantation always lived in the shadow of the Elmwood. Its building was much less grand. It was a raised Creole cottage that, twice in its life, had to be picked up and moved when the river levees were relocated. Comparing the food at the two restaurants was almost unfair, since Tchoupitoulas never intended to be the grand establishment that Elmwood was.

But it was still worth making the circuitous ride to go there for lunch or dinner. After threading your way through Avondale Shipyard and the Southern Pacific rail yard, you'd pull off River Road into the gigantic pecans and oaks. Peacocks walked around the yard of the restaurant, unafraid of the people who came and went. You sat down in surprisingly small rooms in which no two lines met at a right angle.

If you didn't already know the history, you'd learn that Tchoupitoulas (an Indian name that refers to the mighty river) first became a restaurant in 1963. It was already famous as the home base for Norma Wallace, for decades the most celebrated bordello madam in New Orleans. Anywhere else, this might have been a negative, but in New Orleans it was considered local color.

Norma sold the restaurant in 1968, but by then the style was set. The menu was handwritten (and copied, in later years). It was much smaller than those of the grand restaurants of the time, with only about a dozen each of appetizers and entrees. All of it was unmistakably

Creole, with an emphasis on seafood. Its kitchen was also good with duck and quail.

The best dish in the house was oysters Tchoupitoulas, the bivalves awash in a dark roux-based sauce with red wine and a lot of A-1 Steak Sauce. It vaguely resembled oysters Ellis at Antoine's but had a flavor all its own.

For an entree, the best bet was to go for one of the specials. The meal would always last longer than you figured it would. The service was intentionally leisurely.

While dining, you'd comment on the nude paintings left over from Norma Wallace's hegemony here. And you'd depart with a stronger connection with our city and its culture. It always felt good to eat at the Tchoupitoulas Plantation.

And you'd always feel it necessary to compare it to Elmwood. But Tchoupitoulas won a big contest. Elmwood long ago burned to the ground. Tchoupitoulas Plantation is still there, even though it hasn't served a la carte in a long time. It's a reception and party hall now, with the perfect atmosphere for weddings.

Tchoupitoulas Plantation's Oysters Tchoupitoulas

This was the signature dish of Tchoupitoulas Plantation. The recipe doesn't sound right, but I'm sure it is, having made it more than a few times. The strange part is all that steak sauce and roux, which makes the sauce almost thick enough to eat with a fork.

4 dozen freshly shucked oysters, with their liquor
2 cups chicken stock
1 stick butter
⅓ cup flour
4 green onions, tender green parts only, thinly sliced
¼ cup dry red wine (Chianti would be my choice)
2 Tbs. Worcestershire sauce
¼ cup Tabasco Caribbean-style steak sauce (or Pickapeppa sauce)
1 Tbs. lemon juice
½ tsp. salt
Black pepper
Chopped parsley

1. Drain the oysters in a sieve and collect all the oyster liquor. Pour the oyster liquor plus enough chicken stock to make 3 cups of liquid total into a saucepan. Bring it to a boil and lower to a simmer.

2. Combine the butter and flour in another, large saucepan and make a medium-dark roux, stirring constantly. When the roux is the right color, remove the pan from the heat and add the green onions, stirring until they become soft—about 1 minute.

3. Add about ½ cup oyster liquor-stock mixture to the roux and

stir lightly until just combined—about 5 seconds. Add the wine, Worcestershire, steak sauce, and lemon juice. Return to a simmer over low heat.

4. When you see the first bubbles return, add the remaining stock to the roux mixture and stir with a wire whisk until uniformly blended. Cook for about 10 minutes or until the sauce is thick enough to coat the back of a spoon. Add salt and pepper to taste. The sauce is now complete. You may do it ahead up until this point and hold it (refrigerated if it will be longer than 1 hour) until serving time.

5. When it's time to serve, bring the sauce to a simmer and add the oysters. With a big spoon, stir them into the sauce to avoid breaking them. Bring the sauce back to a simmer and cook until the oysters are curly at the edges. Serve the oysters over slices of toast or in a small ramekin, topped with chopped parsley.

Makes 8 appetizers or 4 entrees.

★★★
Toney's Pizza and Spaghetti House
French Quarter: 212 Bourbon Street (across from Galatoire's)
1936-90

No restaurant in New Orleans now is comparable to Toney's Pizza and Spaghetti House in its heyday. That heyday was from the late 1940s through the early 1970s, when Bourbon Street was in its prime. Most customers were still local people, out for an evening in the many restaurants and jazz clubs along the strip. If they were out late, Toney's might be the last stop, for a pizza or a plate of spaghetti (nobody called it "pasta" then).

Anthony Bonomolo founded Toney's during the depression, in a small space where most of the seating was at a counter. The restaurant tripled its size after World War II. That's also when it gained its distinctive look: brightly lit, utilitarian, the walls covered with photos of notables (and no small number of unknowns) who either visited or worked on Bourbon Street.

And the neon signs were all over the place, selling hard. One of those became its logo: a man seated at a table eating spaghetti.

Toney's Italian food was very simple. Here was the apotheosis of New Orleans "red gravy," not much more than tomato puree simmered for a long time. It was thick and good on the spaghetti, stuffed macaroni (sheets of pasta wrapped around a mixture of breadcrumbs, Parmesan cheese, and a little meat), meatballs, Italian sausage, or (Wednesdays only) lasagna. Toney's was the last place in New Orleans where you could walk in any day and order a plate of spaghetti with daube—sliced roast beef simmered in the red sauce for hours.

The upper limit of the menu was somewhere in the vicinity of

This neon sign of a man eating spaghetti was in the window at Toney's Pizza and Spaghetti House for many years. (Courtesy of Jay Bonomolo)

The walls of Toney's were lined with photos of celebrities who performed in New Orleans through the years. (Courtesy of Jay Bonomolo)

veal Parmigiana. They made Creole-Italian dishes: stuffed eggplant, oysters with spaghetti, fried seafood, and daily specials of the likes of red beans and rice. But mainly you came for a mountain of spaghetti with red gravy, served for an almost ridiculously low price.

Toney's went on with all this, always busy, till one in the morning. It reopened the next morning at six with an excellent breakfast. The highlight was the fantastically good, light biscuits, made from scratch and always served hot with lots of butter. They were worth getting up for.

Toney's was managed in its glory years by the founder's son, Joe Bonomolo, whose operating philosophy seemed to be that whatever it took to keep the dining room full for as many hours as possible was worth doing. The menu was enormous; if he couldn't get you with pasta, then how about a poor boy? The prices constituted a bargain not just for the French Quarter but anywhere else in town.

Jay Bonomolo, grandson of the founder, took over in the 1980s. By then, the French Quarter in general and Bourbon Street in particular had gone over to tourism. Far fewer locals shopped or even worked downtown. In an effort to grab their attention, Jay renovated the restaurant completely, finally getting rid of the old lunch counter and creating a much nicer-looking dining room. But nothing could have arrested the trends. In 1990, he decided to move Toney's to Metairie, saying that he was tired of full days when he didn't recognize a single customer.

Toney's seemed out of place in Metairie. The restaurant (it was on Hessmer Avenue, just off Veterans Boulevard, where Toys R Us is now) lasted just a few more years before it closed for good in 1993.

Toney's was popular with locals and tourists. (Courtesy of Jay Bonomolo)

Toney's Pizza and Spaghetti House Stuffed Macaroni

Stuffed macaroni was a major house specialty at Toney's on Bourbon Street and a dish I've never encountered anywhere else. It's essentially a very light, soft mixture of the same things you'd use to make meatballs but in different proportions. Many customers ordered it with meatballs, in fact. The macaroni part was the biggest tubular pasta available. You could also roll it up in sheets of pasta, like cannelloni but smaller, or in large pasta shells. Thanks to Jay Bonomolo, the final owner of Toney's, for the recipe.

Sauce:
2 28-oz. cans tomato puree
1 tsp. salt
¼ tsp. black pepper

Stuffing:
1 Tbs. olive oil
1½ lb. ground round
½ lb. ground pork
1-2 Tbs. water
1 medium onion, chopped
1 egg, beaten
½ cup grated Parmesan cheese
1 cup plain breadcrumbs
½ bunch flat-leaf parsley, leaves only, chopped
1 Tbs. chopped garlic
1 tsp. salt
¼ tsp. black pepper

2 8-oz. boxes pasta shells, manicotti sheets, or large pasta tubes
2 Tbs. olive oil
½ cup grated Parmesan cheese

Preheat the oven to 350 degrees.

1. Make the sauce first. (Or use your own recipe.) Pour the tomato puree into a large saucepan over medium-low heat. When it comes to a boil, lower to a simmer. Add the salt and pepper.

2. Simmer the sauce, covered, stirring every 20 minutes or so (and scraping the bottom as you do), for 6 hours. Adjust the salt and pepper to taste. (No kidding—this is how they made the basic sauce at Toney's.)

3. To make the stuffing, heat the olive oil in a large saucepan over medium heat, and add the ground round and ground pork. Add the water and cook, using a kitchen fork to stir the meat and keep it from clumping up.

4. When the ground meat is completely browned, drain any excess fat from the saucepan. Lower the heat to the lowest possible.

Stuffed macaroni was a specialty of Toney's. (From the collection of Peggy Scott Laborde)

A BITE OF HISTORY

Tortorici's Restaurant
441 Royal Street

(Courtesy of New Orleans Magazine)

If you knew about Tortorici's century-long history (1900-2005) and its prime location across from Antoine's, you'd likely have guessed that it was one of the city's better restaurants. If you spoke with someone who ate there in the 1960s or earlier, you'd certainly think so. In a time when few Italian restaurants were serving menus more ambitious than red sauce on top of some kind of meat on top of some kind of pasta, Tortorici's stood out with its scampi, veal dishes, and fish.

However, the place developed a reputation for thinking more highly of itself than perhaps was warranted. Over the years this was accompanied by a decline in the food. That, combined with the opening of other more ambitious Italian restaurants in the area, made Tortorici's less popular, even though to this day I'm asked about it often.

The Karno family—which

---

5. Add all the other stuffing ingredients. Stir to blend everything uniformly. Cook for 20 minutes, stirring now and then. Taste it and add salt and pepper to taste. Remove from heat and allow to cool. (You may do it up to this point and refrigerate.)

6. Cook the pasta until al dente (soft but still firm). Drain. In the same pot, cover the pasta with cold water and add 2 Tbs. olive oil. Set aside.

7. Ladle about ½ cup sauce in each of two 9" x 11" x 3" casserole dishes. With clean hands, scoop up enough of the stuffing to fill 1 piece of pasta, and roll it like a sausage (or push it into the pasta tube). If using shells, use a spoon for all this.

8. Lay the stuffed pasta in the casserole dishes, 1 layer deep. (You can stack a few on top if necessary.) Ladle enough sauce to cover the stuffed pasta. Cover with a generous sprinkling of Parmesan cheese.

9. Bake the stuffed pasta until the sauce is bubbling—about 20 minutes. Serve 2 per person for an entree.

Serves 8.

Toney's Oysters and Spaghetti Bordelaise

A delicious and very simple combination: spaghetti aglio olio (or "bordelaise," as we call it in New Orleans) with fresh Louisiana oysters. The crushed red pepper develops as it cooks, and spreads warmth.

¼ cup extra-virgin olive oil
24 fresh large oysters
4 Tbs. butter
2 Tbs. finely chopped fresh garlic
4 Tbs. finely chopped green onion tops
½ tsp. crushed red pepper
¼ tsp. salt
1 lb. vermicelli, cooked al dente
8 sprigs flat-leaf parsley, chopped

1. In a small skillet over medium-low flame, heat the olive oil and then add the oysters, cooking them by shaking the pan and making them roll around until they plump up.

2. Add the butter, garlic, green onions, crushed red pepper, and salt. Cook, agitating the pan all the while, until the green onions have wilted. Don't cook more than 1 minute, or the garlic and green onions will lose their flavor.

3. Remove from heat and add cooked, drained pasta to pan. Toss the pasta with the other ingredients to distribute the sauce evenly. Top with fresh chopped parsley. (Parmesan cheese should not be served with this.)

Serves 4.

★★★
T. Pittari's
Broadmoor: 4200 South Claiborne Avenue
1895-1980

Whenever a discussion of lost restaurants gets started, T. Pittari's inevitably comes up. Often, the people who ask about it or relate their memories of the place can't remember its name. But they very well remember the big restaurant with the mosaics of lobsters and beef cattle next to the doors, the neon signs, and the wild game—especially the wild game. They served hippopotamus, didn't they?

The main reason T. Pittari's is widely remembered decades after it closed is that Tom Pittari, Sr., was perhaps the most skillful and studied restaurant promoter in the history of the local business. In many ways, he was ahead of his time. He learned what pushed people's buttons and how to push them.

He also found out that if people get excited about a dish, they would pay prices way out of line with the intrinsic value of the food involved. That's why a lot of people who remember T. Pittari's never actually dined there.

However, the restaurant couldn't have become famous if it hadn't been good. Its best dishes really were as memorably good as Tom Pittari said they were—well, almost, anyway.

The funny thing was that the specialties for which T. Pittari's was known—wild game and lobster—were in fact the worst and most overpriced dishes in the house.

Pittari's was around a long time. Tom's uncle Anthony opened it on the downtown river corner of Washington and Magazine. It moved to South Claiborne in the late 1940s, taking up a whole block. Especially at night, you couldn't drive past without taking a long look. And Claiborne Avenue was the main route through town in those pre-interstate days.

Tom Pittari advertised his restaurant heavily in every way he could think of. Among his more innovative gambits was giving cabdrivers who brought visitors from the French Quarter an extra tip.

Tom had a good story to

Anthony Pittari opened a restaurant on the corner of Washington Avenue and Magazine Street in 1895. His nephew eventually purchased the business. The restaurant relocated to South Claiborne Avenue in 1948. (Courtesy of Tom Pittari, Jr.)

operated a few other restaurants in the French Quarter—took over in the late 1980s, and things improved, although not enough to bring many locals back. After Katrina hit, Tortorici's never really reopened. A few years later, the Royal House—a seafood restaurant—renovated the prime corner and moved in.

REMEMBERING T. PITTARI'S

Tom Pittari, Jr., shares a bit of history and stories of the restaurant in its heyday.

Q.: What's the origin of T. Pittari's?

A.: T. Pittari's was started in 1895 by my father's uncle, my great-uncle, Anthony Pittari. He was an immigrant from Ustica, Italy, an island right north of Palermo, Sicily. He and three brothers and a sister and their mother came over. Two of the brothers went into the restaurant and bar business and Anthony started his restaurant on Washington Avenue and Magazine Street, not far from the Irish Channel.

Q.: When did the restaurant move to South Claiborne Avenue?

A.: When I was very young, my father moved the restaurant, in 1948. He opened on South Claiborne at Milan Street. His uncle Tony passed away in 1936 and at that time my father took over the restaurant. He moved because the original restaurant was quite small and I guess my father was thinking big. He was quite innovative and always looking for ways to improve in any way he could, like bringing in Pecorino and Romano cheese from Italy.

Q.: Any particular reason for the location?

A.: You notice a lot of restaurants were across from funeral homes. When people would go to wakes, afterward there would a social gathering. The restaurant was right across the street from Sontheimer funeral home on South Claiborne

sell. His famous Maine lobsters were kept alive in a tank of chilled water right in the dining room. You could pick the lobster that would be cooked for you. He was the first in town to do that. Pittari's was the pioneer, and to this day the mere mention of lobster brings Pittari's to the mind of anyone who was around back then. As well it should. In its heyday, T. Pittari's sold 2,000 lobsters a month.

Lobster was boiled, or broiled with the head filled with seafood stuffing. (That was cheaper, because it didn't require live lobsters.) The signature lobster was a unique concoction called lobster Kadobster. I had the Kadobster often enough to remember (a) that it had a rich, yellow-tinged, somewhat spicy sauce and (b) that

T. Pittari's specialty was live Maine lobster. This restaurant was the first in town to have a lobster tank. Dining patrons could choose their own. (Courtesy of Tom Pittari, Jr.)

T. Pittari's dining room in the 1950s. (Courtesy of Tom Pittari, Jr.)

T. Pittari's had a distinctive Art Deco-style neon sign. (Courtesy of The Historic New Orleans Collection)

T. Pittari's was one of the first restaurants in New Orleans to have a revolving steak tray, considered quite the innovation in the 1950s. (Courtesy of Tom Pittari, Jr.)

it was unreasonably expensive. (I'm asked now and then for the recipe for Kadobster but have never been able to locate it.)

The other big-time nonconformity at T. Pittari's was wild game, including hippopotamus steaks and lion. When I got around to dining at Pittari's in the 1970s, endangered-species concerns whittled the list down to buffalo, venison, and bear. The buffalo was the best—like a lean beefsteak. The venison tasted like dark veal. The bear was nasty in both appearance and flavor. Prices for all this were into double digits, at a time when a steak at Ruth's Chris was $6.

The best strategy, though, was to forget about all of the above and pore over two other sections of the menu. The Italian food—and there was as much of that as on any straight Italian restaurant's entire menu—was terrific. The red sauces were irresistible, the portions enormous (I don't see how anyone ever finished their lasagna), and the prices within the range of normal.

The Creole dishes were better still. The dish I remember most fondly was crab bisque, made with a medium roux, a good bit of claw crabmeat, and two crab boulettes that the waiter would bring in a separate dish and plop into the soup right in front of you.

Tom Pittari no doubt saw the crowds waiting to eat barbecue shrimp at Pascal's Manale (a near neighbor). He developed his own excellent version. They baked very fine oysters Rockefeller and Bienville, broiled fish and meats with interesting sauces, and fried seafood well. Really, Pittari's was a respectable all-around Creole restaurant. But nobody seems to remember that.

Avenue. Also, at the time Highway 90 was the highway through New Orleans.

Q.: When did he start serving lobster?

A.: He brought in live Maine lobsters in 1952 and that was unheard of in the city of New Orleans. That's when the lobster tank came and that was quite exciting. People in New Orleans had never seen a big "crawfish" before. You could pick out your own lobster and then have it prepared and served to you within minutes. In New Orleans it was a first. My father fixed lobster broiled, lobster Thermidor, lobster Diablo, and lobster Kadobster and that was a very, very good recipe people really enjoyed. We actually had the name patented.

Q.: Who came up with the name lobster Kadobster?

A.: My father came up with it. It kind of rhymed.

Q.: What's in it?

A.: Actually it's a combination of six different seafoods: king Crabmeat, Louisiana crabmeat, shrimp, lobster, Louisiana oysters, and redfish. The lobster was boiled and cut down the back so the top of the lobster was removed. All of the ingredients were mixed. We had two different sauces we prepared and then it was combined, put back in the shell, basted with lemon butter, and baked. Really, really fine tasting. Served with Brabant potatoes, it was excellent.

Q.: How many lobsters did you serve a month?

A.: We would average somewhere between two thousand and

This advertisement shows how diverse the menu was at T. Pittari's. Proprietor Tom Pittari, Jr., can been seen behind the table. (Courtesy of New Orleans Magazine*)*

No matter what you ordered, you had to be careful. The table d'hôte lunches and dinners were good values, but if you deviated from the meals as listed, the a la carte prices kicked in, and the cost would double. (I'm not exaggerating.) If you had oysters on the half-shell at the bar, you had to note whether you wanted regular oysters

T. Pittari's bar. (Courtesy of Tom Pittari, Jr.)

or "special selects" (at a higher price). Anything that had a gourmet ring had a gourmet price. Flaming desserts were for those intent on blowing a wad of money.

I think it's that last matter that caused locals to fall out of love with T. Pittari's, especially in its later years. They overheated the concept and pushed too hard to maximize check averages. New Orleanians can spot that from a mile away and did.

T. Pittari's was ahead of its time in one other way. Flooding killed it a quarter-century before Katrina. The May 3, 1978, flood and the April 13, 1980, flood—caused not by hurricanes but extraordinary rainfalls and inadequate drainage systems—put two feet of water into Pittari's. The building was at ground level in one of the lowest parts in the city.

Tom Pittari, Jr., who was running the place by then, gave up, sold the property, and moved the restaurant to Mandeville. The North Shore in 1980 was not the place for a restaurant like this, and it closed in a year or so, never to return. The grand Claiborne restaurant was torn down, replaced by a Wendy's raised above flood level.

But the fame of T. Pittari's lobsters and wild game just kept on going.

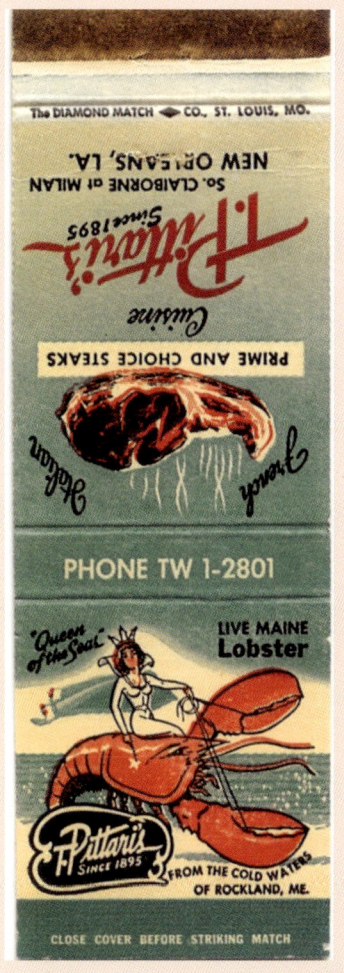

In addition to "surf and turf," T. Pittari's was famous for serving wild game, much of which would be on an endangered-species list today. (From the collection of Edward Piglia)

five thousand pounds of lobsters; that's gross live weight. Yeah, it was a lot of lobster.

Q.: Whose idea was it to serve wild game?

A.: It was my father's idea. He talked it over with my mother and me and we all thought it was good, and at the time there wasn't any endangered-species list. He'd always try to come up with new dishes and new items. When we first started the wild game we got it in from Chicago, a place called Zimmer's in Chicago, Illinois. This place was actually a broker for wild-game items. We brought in tiger and water buffalo, hippopotamus, elephant, and of course as we went on we evolved some of these items off the menu because they really weren't quite palatable; I mean they were chewy. The elephant and the hippopotamus, they were the first ones to slide off, but they were different and people wanted to try them. The wild game that's found in the United States, like bear, buffalo, elk, and venison, came out of the state of Montana. All of this was properly tagged, properly inspected, totally kosher.

Q.: Can you describe what elephant tasted like?

A.: Elephant is quite chewy. We got in one piece of elephant and that was the last piece of elephant. But I will say that buffalo, buffalo is really a fine-tasting piece of beef; I say beef because it's almost like beef but it's tangier. It's not as subtle as beef. A buffalo T-bone is really, really nice.

Q.: What about tiger?

A.: Tiger is a carnivorous animal, as you know, but it really tastes a lot like veal. It was quite palatable.

Q.: What other food was on the menu? Was this an Italian restaurant?

A.: You think of an Italian restaurant with the white-and-red-checkered tablecloths and the Chianti bottle and the candle, or you think of the French Quarter restaurants, or of a classier type. We just did it our way. It was more cosmopolitan. We didn't really have a style; we had our own style.

T. Pittari's Crab Bisque

For all its fame for wild game and lobster, the best food at the extinct T. Pittari's was its Creole cooking. Whenever I went there, I hoped the soup of the day would be their crab bisque. It wasn't the creamy concoction that goes under that name now but a brown-roux potage with claw crabmeat. The waiter brought the bowl to the table and dropped in two just-fried crabmeat croquettes. I have only rarely encountered anything that compared with this.

4 lb. crab claws
1 bay leaf
½ gal. cold water
1 cup flour
½ cup vegetable oil
1 cup chopped onion
½ ripe green bell pepper, seed and membranes removed, chopped
2 cloves garlic, chopped
6 sprigs flat-leaf parsley, chopped
½ cup tomato sauce (preference: a good prepared marinara sauce, your own or from a jar)
½ tsp. salt
⅛ tsp. cayenne

Crab boulettes:
6 Tbs. butter
1 cup chopped onions
1 rib celery, chopped
½ ripe green bell pepper, seed and membranes removed, chopped
2 cloves garlic, chopped
1 Tbs. Worcestershire sauce
1 tsp. black pepper
¼ tsp. cayenne
½ tsp. salt
¼ tsp. thyme
2 Tbs. lemon juice
6 inches stale poor-boy bread, cut into cubes, with all crumbs
2 green onions, thinly sliced
10 sprigs flat-leaf parsley, leaves only, chopped

1. Pick the meat off the crab claws, reserving the shells. Divide the crabmeat into 2 equal portions and set both aside.

2. Put the shells into a food processor and grind them for about 10 seconds. Scrape the processor contents and the bay leaf into a saucepan containing the water. Bring it to a light boil, then lower to a simmer. After 45 minutes, strain the stock into a clean large saucepan. Reserve ½ cup for the boulettes. Bring remaining stock to a simmer.

3. In a saucepan, make a roux, stirring constantly, with the flour and vegetable oil. When it reaches a medium-dark, old-penny color,

remove the pan from the heat and quickly add the onions, bell pepper, garlic, and parsley. Cook, stirring, until the vegetables are soft.

4. Stir in the tomato sauce, salt, cayenne, and about ½ cup crab stock. Stir until the stock disappears.

5. Add the roux mixture to the simmering crab stock and whisk until blended. Cover the pan and keep on the lowest heat setting.

6. Now, make the boulettes. In a large skillet over medium heat, heat 3 Tbs. butter until it bubbles. Add the onions, celery, bell pepper, and garlic, and cook until the vegetables are soft.

7. Stir in the Worcestershire, black pepper, cayenne, salt, thyme, and lemon juice. Cook while stirring until all the ingredients are combined.

8. Wet the bread cubes with the reserved crab stock. Add them and half of the reserved crabmeat to the pan contents. Stir until everything is well mixed and the mixture is starting to get noticeably drier. Lower the heat and allow to cool for 5 minutes.

9. Stir the green onions and parsley into the crabmeat mixture. With a round soup spoon, scoop up balls of the crabmeat mixture about 1 inch in diameter. Roll them gently with your hands to make them uniform.

10. Heat 3 Tbs. butter in a skillet over medium heat until it bubbles. Add the crab balls, a few at a time, and roll them around until browned all over. (You can also bake these for about 15 minutes in a 375-degree oven.)

11. Check the seasoning of the crab bisque and add salt, pepper, or Tabasco to taste. Add the remaining reserved crabmeat. Let it simmer 1 or 2 more minutes, then ladle the bisque into bowls or cups. Drop 1 or 2 crab boulettes into each bowl at the table.

Makes 6 to 8 first courses or 4 entrees.

★★★★
Turci's
French Quarter: 229 Bourbon Street
1917-43
CBD: 914 Poydras Street
1940s-74

No lost restaurant in New Orleans engenders the fervent yearning felt by anyone who ever ate in the original Turci's. Although it's been gone for decades, many people still harbor vivid memories of this great Italian restaurant. That's because they ate there regularly when

---

We had many people come in our restaurant and say, "Gee, this looks like the restaurants in California," but we were a New Orleans-based restaurant. That was just the way we did it. My father felt that the people in New Orleans, even though it was a seafood town, really like to eat beef. They were a lively group and he brought in the best beef that he could possibly find. And he called one of the rooms the Black Angus Room.

Q.: So who decorated?

A.: We did, my father, my mother and myself and we'd bring in some people to assist us, but there were certain colors that he noticed were stimulating. He used a lot of red. Red stimulates your appetite. There was a fair amount of red in the décor.

Q.: Any memories of stars or VIPs who dined at your restaurant?

A.: There were quite a few. Sonny and Cher came in, even before they had become nationally known. Fats Domino used to come in a lot. Charlton Heston, James Coburn, Muhammad Ali.

Q.: Any particular night stand out?

A.: You have your off nights and you have your real good nights. Well, this was a real good night and everybody was in sync and in harmony. We had flaming desserts and waiters were carving ducks at the table and deboning flounders and making Caesar salad, tossing Caesar salads and Italian salads, and there was a whole bunch of tableside service. And this lady, as she left, she told me she had a delightful experience and said, "I've been to a lot of restaurants, but I've never been to a restaurant where every time I turned around someone was flaming a dessert or carving a duck. It was like going to a theatre." That was a real compliment, very touching.

—Peggy Scott Laborde

Even though Turci's has been closed for many years, patrons still recall the creativity of Signora Turci in the kitchen. (From the collection of Peggy Scott Laborde)

they were small children. Turci's was decidedly a family place, where tables of six and eight and more outnumbered the deuces and fours.

Turci's history reads like the setup for a novel. Ettore Turci (native of Bologna) and his wife, Teresa (from Naples), were opera singers who came to America to perform in 1909. New Orleans had America's oldest opera house—and a lot of Italians by that time. The Turcis stayed. In 1917, they opened a restaurant called Turci's Italian Gardens in the French Quarter. It thrived, then it became famous. The Turcis retired in 1943 and sold the restaurant. (One of the new owners was the father of Joe Segreto, who now operates Eleven 79 in the Warehouse District.)

Turci's wasn't in limbo for long. It reopened after the war on Poydras Street, where the next generation of Turcis began carrying the load. The food remained the same, the old regular customers came back, and Turci's second life went on for nearly three decades.

It wasn't a fancy place. Not even as nice as the one on Bourbon Street, says one of my older correspondents. The big room was blocky and noisy. A lot of that came from the clatter of tables filled with too many plates and bowls, the latter holding the sauce for the restaurant's most famous dish: spaghetti alla Turci.

Spaghetti alla Turci was spaghetti and meatballs—sort of. It seemed simple, but its making was complex. It had a thick, ruddy-brown sauce riddled with chopped meat and accretions of meat that evolved into meatballs. Also in there were mushrooms and chicken. There was nothing else like it in any other restaurant. It wasn't until I traveled to Italy that I encountered a similar sauce. It was in Bologna, where they don't include one meat in a sauce if they can possibly include six meats. The recipe for spaghetti alla Turci is out there (and here), but not many people go to the not-inconsequential trouble of making it.

The menu was large, as was the style of the time. The spaghetti section of it (the word *pasta* was never seen on menus back then) included more varieties of serving it than you'd be able to think up now. Many dishes would be unfamiliar to today's diners. Even classics

AROUND THE CORNER—
TURCI'S RESTAURANT

914 POYDRAS   RAymond 2934

OPEN 11:30 A. M. TO 9:30 P. M. DAILY EXCEPT FRIDAYS

TRY SIGNORA TURCI'S HOME MADE RAVIOLI

WE HAVE YOUR FAVORITE ITALIAN DISHES
ALSO CHOICE STEAKS—FULL COURSE DINNERS
LIQUORS — WINES — LIQUEURS

Turci's was famous for its delicious and creative versions of traditional Italian dishes, including homemade ravioli. (From the collection of Peggy Scott Laborde)

such as veal Parmigiana were made differently from the current style. Many of Turci's dishes went extinct after the restaurant closed. One of them was the last truly exciting ravioli in town. Only lately have restaurants caught up with the goodness of that handmade, veal-stuffed, mushroom-and-butter-sauced wonder.

As I think back on the Turci's experience, a miracle that I didn't notice at the time is striking. At Turci's, New Orleans eaters—even first-generation Italians—put on hold their suspicion of spaghetti made any way other than the way their mothers made it. I have spoken to hundreds of people who remember Turci's; not one of them has ever told me he didn't like the food there.

The failed attempt to revive Turci's in 1976 is another story. Regular customers bemoaning the closing of the restaurant were ecstatic to hear that a consortium of local businessmen had put together a deal to reopen Turci's. The new place was at 3218 Magazine Street. (Byblos is there now; the entrance was around the corner on Pleasant Street.) Giving an air of authenticity was the presence of Rose Turci, the one-armed second-generation cook from the old place.

Rose wasn't really running the place, however. The new Turci's never came close to reviving the magic of the original. It only lasted a couple of years, ending ignominiously by evolving into a pop-Italian place called Spaghetti Eddie's.

Who was it who lamented that so many great institutions end up as parodies of themselves?

Spaghetti alla Turci

One of the most famous lost recipes in New Orleans, Turci's spaghetti showed the Bolognese origins of founder Ettore Turci. In Italy, people regard the food of Bologna in much the same way we do Cajun food here. I've heard more than one Italian say that in Bologna, they eat anything and usually cook it all in one pot. That's the essence of this dish, which includes far more meats than is normally found in a pasta sauce. It's an old-fashioned flavor and takes two days to make authentically. You must also suspend our modern disdain for tomato paste.

Stock:
1 small whole chicken (gizzards and heart reserved)
½ gal. water
1 bay leaf
½ onion, cut into chunks
1 bunch celery, leafy tops only
1 bunch parsley, stems only

Sauce:
⅓ cup olive oil
1 lb. ground veal
1 lb. ground pork
Gizzards and heart from the chicken above, chopped
½ cup chopped onion
½ cup chopped celery
2 cloves garlic, chopped
1 8-oz. can tomato paste
1 28-oz. can whole Italian tomatoes, pureed
1 lb. ham steak with fat, finely diced
1 qt. reserved chicken stock
¼ tsp. thyme
½ tsp. basil
1 tsp. oregano

Meatballs:
½ tsp. salt
¼ tsp. black pepper
½ cup freshly grated breadcrumbs
¼ cup finely grated Parmesan cheese
1 tsp. Italian seasoning
12 sprigs fresh parsley, leaves only, chopped
2 eggs, beaten into a froth
2 Tbs. olive oil
8 oz. white mushrooms, sliced

2 lb. spaghetti

1. Put all the stock ingredients into a saucepan. Bring to a light boil, then lower to a simmer. Simmer for 90 minutes, uncovered. Strain the stock and set aside. Put the chicken into a food-storage bag and into the refrigerator.

2. Heat 1 Tbs. olive oil in a heavy, large skillet over medium-high heat. Remove a fistful each of the ground veal and ground pork (put the rest into the refrigerator). Add the meats to the skillet, along with the chicken gizzards and heart. Let the meat brown well, then break it up with a kitchen fork. Remove from the pan with a slotted spoon and set aside.

3. In a large saucepan or Dutch oven over medium heat, heat the remaining olive oil until it shimmers. Add the onions, celery, and garlic and cook until they get soft.

4. Raise the heat to medium high. Add the tomato paste and pureed tomatoes. Cook for about 10 minutes, stirring constantly, until it gets thick and noticeably darker in color.

5. Add the chopped ham and the browned veal and pork. Continue to cook and stir for another 3 minutes.

6. Add 5 cups of the chicken broth and the thyme, basil, and oregano. Bring to a boil, then lower to a simmer. Cover the pot and let it simmer for 2 hours. Stir the pot, scraping the bottom well every 20 minutes or so.

7. After 2 hours, turn off the heat and let the pot cool for a half-hour. Spoon the contents into a large bowl or food-storage container. Put it into the refrigerator overnight to let the flavors come together.

8. The next day—about 2 hours before you're ready to serve—put the sauce back onto the stove on low heat. If it seems too thick after it warms up, stir in a little more chicken stock.

9. Pull about 2 cups of chicken meat—a blend of white and dark—from the chicken you used to make the stock. Slice it if necessary into pieces the size of the tip of your little finger.

10. Make the meatballs next. Combine the salt, pepper, breadcrumbs, Parmesan cheese, Italian seasoning, and parsley with a fork. Wet your hands with cold water, and combine the remaining ground pork and veal with sprinklings of the breadcrumb mixture and the beaten eggs. Handle all of this as gently as possible, rolling the meatballs into rough spheres about 1 ½ inches in diameter. Cracks should show around the outside. Be gentle!

11. Heat olive oil in a skillet until it shimmers. Drop a few of the meatballs in. Every few seconds, roll them around (gently!) until they're browned all over (not cooked all the way through). Remove and drain. Keep going until all the meatballs are browned.

12. Add the meatballs and the chicken to the sauce. Simmer for 1 hour, stirring only very lightly (to avoid breaking the meatballs). Add the mushrooms and salt and pepper to taste. Cook another 15 minutes.

13. Cook the spaghetti until still firm (6 minutes or so). Drain and put it into a big bowl. Ladle about 2 cups of the liquid part of the sauce over the spaghetti and toss to coat. Serve in big bowls with the remaining sauce on top.

Serves 8 to 12.

★★★
Uglesich's
Lee Circle Area: 1238 Baronne Street
1924-2005

Until around 1965, the image of New Orleans held by most Americans who might consider visiting here was that it was a genteel Southern city with a penchant for raffishness. You'd come here to dine in the likes of Antoine's or Commander's Palace or the Camellia Grill. One day you might get funky and go to Mother's for a poor boy and some gumbo.

In the sixties, that ideal had changed. From then on, most out-of-town fans of our city came to believe that you couldn't have an authentic New Orleans experience unless you fetched up in a shabby building on a hard-to-find corner with an impossibly cheap menu. There you would find the true New Orleans flavor. Any establishment that didn't have a proper measure of seediness could not possibly be "true" New Orleans.

That's absurd, of course. But one restaurant testified to the possibility that it might be true. Uglesich's had the most convincing third-world look in town. And it really did have great food.

Uglesich's opened in 1924, another of the many restaurants around town opened by first- and second-generation Croatian immigrants. The streets were lined with old, spacious Greek-revival houses of strong architectural merit, built in the years when this was as cultured a part of town as any other. Lots of churches, theatres, and restaurants filled the area, with classy St. Charles Avenue running through it.

By the time most people who might read these words got to Uglesich's, the neighborhood had declined quite a lot. A slow but seemingly unstoppable process of demolition put many holes in the formerly grand blocks. Many of the remaining mansions were now subdivided low-income housing.

The office of the *Figaro* weekly newspaper, where I worked throughout the 1970s, was walking distance from Uglesich's. The staff went there often, because it was cheap and it fit the newspaper's image of real New Orleans. (We were the vanguard of that point of view.) We called it "Ugly's," not only because the real pronunciation ("oogle-SICH-ehs") was hard to say.

Anthony Uglesich, the second-generation owner, felt no urgency to make changes in his dad's restaurant. He deferred painting the place for a span of years during which most people would have painted it four or five times. In this, Uglesich's matched the deteriorating neighborhood. The ventilation system was so ineffective that when you returned from lunch there, nobody had

Anthony and Gail Uglesich served some of the most creative dishes in New Orleans in this very unpretentious-looking building near Lee Circle. (Photo © Kevin R. Roberts)

to ask where you'd dined. You smelled as if you'd fried fish all day.

That figures, because Uglesich's was primarily a fish house. Its Croatian heritage connected it with the oyster industry, then and now dominated by their countrymen. Uglesich's had a great oyster bar, and it fried oysters and every other kind of local seafood very well. Most of the menu was taken up with poor-boy sandwiches, including a roast beef with a reddish gravy unlike anything I saw elsewhere.

Lunch business from the big Brown's Velvet Dairy across the street kept Uglesich's going for a long time, as the number of neighborhood people declined. A host of unique characters—some of whom appeared in various media as examples of local color—hung around the place all day long. The most famous of them was Ding Ding the Singing Bird, who delivered sandwiches on a bicycle to the area and sold peanuts at Tulane Stadium.

In the 1980s, it suddenly became impossible to get a table at Uglesich's. The dining room filled up at all hours, every day. Not only with local people but tourists. Tourists at Uglesich's! How did they find the place? The city's best chefs—the likes of Frank Brigtsen, Susan

Spicer, and Jamie Shannon—came in often. Celebrities visiting New Orleans began to show up. Some of those would buy out Uglesich's for an evening and hold big parties.

Longtime Uglesich's customers found this newfound currency hilarious. It was the same old place it always had been. The only new development was that Anthony and his wife, Gail, began cooking a few daily plate specials to add to the poor boys and seafood platters. Those were indeed good but not enough to explain the crowds.

For the next twenty years, Uglesich's became for many people the ultimate expression of what eating in New Orleans was about. Its fame spread throughout the country among fans of New Orleans food. Flush with this success, Anthony finally performed a light renovation in 1997. He replaced some of the old fixtures, built a new kitchen, fixed the exhaust system, and even painted the exterior. The customers were wary of all this gussying up but got used to it.

Anthony and Gail cooked their great specials starting early in the morning. They liked seafood mostly, especially when abetted by a lot of garlic and red pepper. The specials done (the kitchen staff would take care of all the frying and shucking), Anthony presided over the customers from behind the bar, keeping track of every table in his head.

There was no printed menu, just an assortment of signs posted behind the bar. Even though Uglesich's never stopped being a neighborhood joint, its prices entered the gourmet bistro range. I spent thirty to forty dollars every time I went there (cash only).

As we entered the 2000s, conversations about Uglesich's among its fans shifted from how terrific its food was to how much longer it would be around. Each year, Anthony and Gail took a longer and longer vacation—June to October in 2004.

This only added urgency to Uglesich's fame. Volume increased right up until the day after the Jazz Festival in May 2005, when Anthony and Gail retired and closed the restaurant. That was a few months before Hurricane Katrina, which the old joint survived without serious damage.

During the final weeks, the line extended out the door and far down the sidewalk. Ever since the restaurant closed, it's published two cookbooks of its recipes. Every few days, an excited correspondent asks me whether there's any truth to the ever-floating rumor that Uglesich's will reopen. The answer is maybe, but I wouldn't count on it.

★★★

Vaucresson Café Creole
French Quarter: 624 Bourbon Street
1967-76

In the 1960s and early 1970s, the first waves of the Baby Boom generation began exploring the French Quarter without their parents. These were also the years of the Summer of Love and an expansion of bohemianism among young adults who grew up in the suburbs. They found the French Quarter scene and its attendant funkiness a pleasing contrast to their parents' worlds.

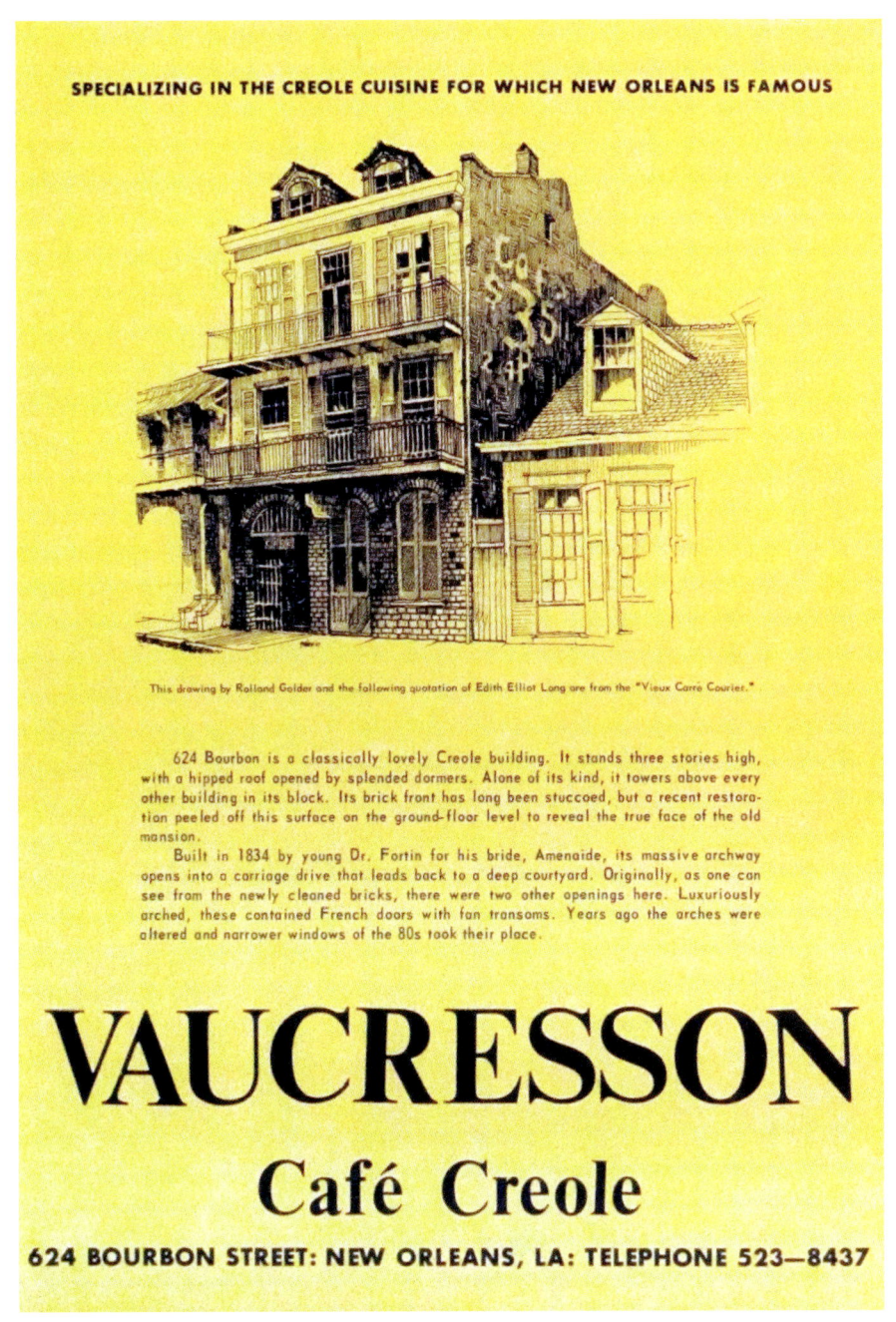

SPECIALIZING IN THE CREOLE CUISINE FOR WHICH NEW ORLEANS IS FAMOUS

This drawing by Rolland Golden and the following quotation of Edith Elliot Long are from the "Vieux Carré Courier."

624 Bourbon is a classically lovely Creole building. It stands three stories high, with a hipped roof opened by splended dormers. Alone of its kind, it towers above every other building in its block. Its brick front has long been stuccoed, but a recent restoration peeled off this surface on the ground-floor level to reveal the true face of the old mansion.

Built in 1834 by young Dr. Fortin for his bride, Amenaide, its massive archway opens into a carriage drive that leads back to a deep courtyard. Originally, as one can see from the newly cleaned bricks, there were two other openings here. Luxuriously arched, these contained French doors with fan transoms. Years ago the arches were altered and narrower windows of the 80s took their place.

VAUCRESSON
Café Creole
624 BOURBON STREET: NEW ORLEANS, LA: TELEPHONE 523—8437

In addition to owning the restaurant, Sonny Vaucresson and his family had their own sausage-making business. (Menu collection gift of Richard and Rima Collin courtesy of The Historic New Orleans Collection)

That new customer base would grow until the French Quarter began to tilt emphatically in the direction of tourist tastes. Until then, however, casual restaurants catering to locals visiting (or living in) the French Quarter found their fortunes swing upwards.

Vaucresson Café Creole was an exemplar of the genre. Owned by an African-Creole family with New Orleans roots going back generations, it served a menu of home-style Creole dishes that would not be adopted by mainstream restaurants for another decade or more. It seems hard to believe now, but in that era, panéed veal and jambalaya were rarely encountered in any kind of restaurant. That combination was the signature dish at Vaucresson's.

That was before the Cajun influence grew as strong as it is now. The jambalaya was red, not brown, with tomato and shrimp as its main flavors. The seafood-okra gumbo was light in texture but big in flavor.

The restaurant's environment was undiluted New Orleans. Its entrance was a carriageway on Bourbon Street. It was a couple of doors from the only intersection in town where live jazz clubs—usually with their doors open, to woo passersby—were on all four corners. The music quickened your step into the restaurant, where you could dine in a big, dark dining room with windows onto Bourbon Street or a courtyard at the end of the carriageway.

The most pleasant meal of all here was a late breakfast. It featured not only the standards of that meal but Creole classics such as calas (fried rice cakes) and grits and grillades. In the 1970s, both those dishes were threatened with distinction, with only Vaucresson's and its around-the-corner neighbor the Coffee Pot keeping them alive.

Finding its way into many of the Café Creole's dishes was a big homemade hot link sausage called chaurice. Red with pepper, its flavor was so intense that a bite would make you stop and pay attention. It was served with breakfasts, in omelettes, with red beans—all over the menu.

Although Vaucresson Café Creole has been gone for a decades now, its chaurice lives on. The Vaucresson family still makes the sausage and turns up at the Jazz Festival and the French Quarter Festival (to name two of many places) to serve it.

The Café Creole is now the dining room of Pat O'Brien's famous bar, whose main courtyard backs up to the one where we ate chaurice and jambalaya at Vaucresson's during a memorable era.

★★★★★
Versailles
Garden District: 2100 St. Charles Avenue
1972-85

The Carol is an upscale condominium tower whose occupants have tended towards the well-to-do, prominent side of the spectrum. As such, the building's managers wanted to have an excellent restaurant on the ground floor. The first two attempts—The Emerald Door and Lotar's—both had lofty goals but never attracted enough business from the outside world to keep them viable.

The third restaurant was the charm. The Versailles was created by Gunter Preuss, a classically trained chef in the European tradition. He had made a local reputation as executive chef at the Roosevelt Hotel in the mid-1960s. A major renovation of the hotel gave birth to the Sazerac restaurant—the new grand gourmet room, built next to the long-running Sazerac Bar. Its menu and style were the creation of Gunter Preuss.

Gunter and Evelyn Preuss outside Versailles in the 1970s. (Courtesy of Gunter and Evelyn Preuss)

A matchbook from Versailles. In 1985, the Preusses moved on to own and operate Broussard's in the French Quarter. (From the collection of Peggy Scott Laborde)

Chef Gunter was born in Berlin in the 1930s. He was a boy in World War II. He entered the European hotel apprentice system and its rigorous training of chefs. After moving from one deluxe hotel to another, he and his wife, Evelyn (also a Berliner), came to America and ultimately to New Orleans.

The 1960s and 1970s were a good time to be a European chef in New Orleans. For one thing, there were very few other chefs in town. Most restaurants—even the big ones—didn't have chefs but brigades of cooks. The few real chefs were almost all European, articulate, and well presented. They got on television a lot more than the homegrown guys.

People in The Carol and elsewhere Uptown took a liking to the Versailles. The room was modern, with low lighting, big windows giving onto the passing streetcars, and a comfortable bar (the Sun King Lounge, to continue the Louis XIV theme). The food was beautiful and delicious. Chef Gunter specialized in a few classic dishes not

Gunter and Evelyn Preuss's Versailles was a grand Continental dining establishment on St. Charles Avenue. One of their specialties was bouillabaisse. (Photo by George Long)

often served elsewhere, notably bouillabaisse. "With real saffron, the world's most expensive food ingredient," the chef liked to point out.

Things were going well enough that Gunter decided to open for lunch. He bought colorful plastic tablecloths to give a casual air to the place at midday. One day his wife—who as a mother of two boys had kept her nose out of the restaurant's operation—happened to pass the restaurant at noon. She saw the red and green and yellow tablecloths. What is that? she thought and pulled into the Versailles' driveway. "Gunter!" she called as soon as she got a closer look. She started pulling the tablecloths off. "You can't have this in a fine restaurant."

That was the beginning of Evelyn's involvement in the restaurant. Always beautifully dressed and groomed, she became as much a part of the place as her husband had been.

The Versailles was a study in consistency for a decade. Then, in 1983, Gunter and his fellow German restaurateur George Huber partnered to buy Broussard's from the Marcello family. Gunter ran both restaurants for a time and a few years later bought out Huber.

In the meantime, the shift in dining vogues Uptown to the bistro style softened business at the Versailles. The Preusses sold the place and moved their well-polished act to Broussard's—sort of. The day of the grand Continental restaurant, with elaborate plate presentations and formal service, was clearly ending. Instead of turning Broussard's into Versailles II, they allowed it to become more Creole, casual, and easygoing. They are still at that task.

★★★★★
Willy Coln's Chalet
Gretna: 2505 Whitney Avenue
1976-90

In the early 1970s, many of the European chefs whom big New Orleans hotels liked to hire to run their kitchens began to behave strangely. The typical career path for such chefs was to move from hotel to hotel every few years, often as part of the opening team for new hotels wherever in the world they were opening.

But a lot of those chefs got hooked by the uniquely funky appeal of New Orleans and its familiar European look. And instead of leaving for another assignment, they stayed and opened their own little restaurants.

Willy Coln was the executive chef for the Royal Sonesta Hotel in the early 1970s. He built New Orleans' first Sunday brunch buffet at Begue's, the hotel's Continental-plush gourmet room (where it still goes on). He had very good help—his chef de cuisine was Gerard Crozier.

Willy and Gerard left the Sonesta in the summer of 1976, with separate but similar goals. By the fall, they were both operating new bistros of their own in the New Orleans suburbs.

A native of Cologne (Koln, in German), Willy thought New Orleans needed a first-class German restaurant. He didn't consider Kolb's as filling that need. By that time, the big old Downtown restaurant was declining badly and serving cartoon German food. And there was nothing else.

Nobody told Willy that German food was a hard sell in New Orleans, because it is perceived as heavy and not suited to the climate. So he went ahead and assembled a brilliant menu of marvelously delicate dishes that nevertheless had the stamp of authenticity. His pre-New Orleans career had taken him to enough other places that he had a few non-German dishes in his repertoire, too.

It was good enough for Willy Coln's to become instantly popular.

Chef Willy Coln served German dishes with a lighter touch at his Willy Coln's Chalet. (Photo by George Long)

The West Bank, at that time, was home to quite a few gourmet places, so it wasn't perceived as an expedition to go there.

And the premises were pleasant. It was a renovated house with a cathedral ceiling, big openings in the wall separating the vestibule from the dining room, and other devices that made the small space seem expansive. (Footnote: the building was owned by another famous Gretna restaurateur, Warren Leruth.)

Willy cooked up some great food. Not all of it was German. His longtime Sonesta sous-chef, Cecil Palmer (who, many years later, would open a Jamaican restaurant here), worked with him to cook Caribbean dishes. The Bahamian seafood chowder, spicy and light, was a must-order. Willy Coln's was, strangely, the first New Orleans restaurant to my knowledge that ever served ceviche, the Latin-American cold, marinated fish. He made good baked oysters in a little casserole, topped with gruyere cheese and onions.

The menu had relatively few German clichés. He had wiener schnitzel, beef rouladen, and a sausage and sauerkraut platter—all excellent, fresh, and light. But from there he went Continental (which is what we called generic French-inspired food back then). The steak au poivre, made with red pepper instead of peppercorns, was as good as it was different. Willy also knew that New Orleans people would lose control at the prospect of having fish topped with shrimp, crawfish, and shrimp. So that was available.

Of all the dishes I remember from the early days at Willy Coln's, the one that stands out most in my mind was beef Stroganoff. Not German, not even what most people would consider a gourmet dish, but it was here. The sauce had, in addition to sour cream, little matchsticks of pickles. It soon fell off the menu, but I still remember that idea and use it now and then at home.

As time went on, new dishes appeared. The jaeger (hunter's) schnitzel was a particularly good one. It started with sautéed veal medallions, covered with a light sauce with five different wild mushrooms. In the 1970s, that was quite an achievement; exotic mushrooms were very hard to come by.

The dish that made Willy Coln's famous was the veal shank. This was the same cut of meat used for osso buco, but it was the whole shank, not cross-cut. It was enough for two people (at least) and came out with the meat falling off the bone in absurdly lip-smacking goodness and tenderness. The sauce, if you could call it that, was not much more than some of the natural outflowings from the thing, and it soaked the assortment of vegetables that surrounded the shank on its plate. It was wonderful.

It also taught a lesson to the chef. For a long time, he ran the veal shank as an off-the-menu special. Then, since he had it every night, he added it to the menu on its next printing. Sales of the thing plummeted. Apparently it was better to be described verbally than to be written about. So he reprinted the menu without it.

The restaurant was successful enough that Willy added on to the building in 1981 and gave it a more distinctly German look and name: Willy Coln's Chalet, it was now. He'd already added an Oktoberfest celebration, featuring the wild music of Helmut Fricker, heavy decorations, and a special menu that filled the place even more than usual. After Willy closed the restaurant and became executive chef of the Inter-Continental Hotel, he took his whole Oktoberfest act with him and kept it going for over a decade.

He tried to keep from closing Willy Coln's Chalet, but the forces were against him. Like many fine-dining establishments on the West Bank, when the oil bust of the early 1980s hit, Willy Coln's saw a great drop-off in business. The appearance of dozens of hip bistros in the Uptown section—from which many of his customers came—also hit him hard. The food was as good as ever, and he tried all sorts of promotions, but nothing worked. He sold out and went to work for the Inter-Continental Hotel, staying until early 2005, when he retired completely.

The chalet Willy Coln built is now Clementine's Belgian Bistro and looks much the same as it did when Willy and his then-wife Erna filled it with *Gemütlichkeit*.

Crawfish Willy Coln

Chef Willy Coln came to town to run the kitchens of the Royal Sonesta, then opened his own terrific German restaurant on the West Bank. He worked for over a decade afterwards as executive chef of the Inter-Continental Hotel. Here is one of the dishes he developed for the hotel's Veranda Restaurant, where it was served as an appetizer.

2 Tbs. butter
1 Tbs. chopped French shallots
1 tsp. chopped garlic
1 Tbs. chopped green onions
1 lb. crawfish tails
1 oz. brandy
2 Tbs. peeled, seeded, and chopped fresh tomato
½ cup crawfish stock
⅔ cup whipping cream
¼ tsp. salt
⅛ tsp. cayenne
4 sheets puff pastry dough, 3-inch square (available at better grocery stores)
1 egg yolk, beaten

Preheat the oven to 400 degrees.

1. Melt the butter over medium heat in a medium skillet until it bubbles. Sauté the shallots, garlic, and green onions until limp.

2. Add the crawfish tails and sauté until heated through. Carefully pour the brandy over the skillet contents and touch a flame to it (if you're comfortable with flaming things and have firefighting resources). When the flames die down (or all the alcohol boils away), stir in the tomato and the crawfish stock and bring to a boil.

3. Stir in the whipping cream, salt, and cayenne and heat through (but do not boil). Adjust seasonings and remove from the heat. Spoon into small ramekins.

4. Top each ramekin with a piece of the puff pastry. Push it down around the sides to form a cap. Brush the pastry with egg and bake until the top browns lightly. When your guests cut into the pastry cap, the wonderful aroma will hit them in the face.

Serves 4.

Milton Wise was the owner of Wise Cafeteria. (Courtesy of Milton Wise)

"Where Quality Prevails" was Wise Cafeteria's motto, and customers certainly agreed. Among its many highlights was the stuffed eggplant. (From the collection of Edward Piglia)

★★★
Wise Cafeteria
Mid-City: 909 South Jefferson Davis Parkway
1933-88

Two things come to mind when I think of eating sliced roast turkey and gravy with mashed potatoes and cornbread dressing.

The other one is Wise Cafeteria.

Like all cafeterias, Wise had turkey and dressing on the hot line every day, all day, with cranberry sauce, just as if it were Thanksgiving.

Unlike all other cafeterias in my experience, Wise also served good food—very good food, in fact.

Like most people of my generation, I ate in cafeterias a lot when I was young, mainly because my parents took us to them on the rare occasions when we dined out. We kids were used to them, because we ate in cafeterias in our schools every day of our lives. They weren't like real restaurants. You didn't have to abide by any unknown rules of

Customers in line at Wise Cafeteria. Among the restaurant's specialties were stuffed crabs, fried chicken, and seafood gumbo. (Courtesy of Milton Wise)

etiquette. You only paid for exactly what you asked for. For example, cafeterias sold butter and margarine by the pat, in the most extreme form of a la carte pricing in the history of food service. And unless you had a waiter carry your tray to the table (and who did that but the infirm?), there was no tipping.

Then, one day, I learned about Wise. A co-worker of mine at the Time Saver—another young guy paying his way through college (he became a pianist)—was as enthusiastic about Wise Cafeteria as any person I've spoken to since about any other restaurant. "It's the best!" he claimed, shooting down my own cafeteria experiences at Morrison's and A & G as impossibly inferior to the wonders to be found on the line at Wise.

So I went. The year was 1969. I had turkey and dressing, a salad with blue-cheese dressing, and bread pudding. I thought it was good but not to the degree claimed by my buddy. It was the first example I can remember of a restaurant's disappointing me because of inflated expectations. "You got the wrong thing!" he claimed. (It was the first time I'd heard that line, too.) "The turkey is okay, but what you want is the shrimp remoulade, the boiled brisket with vegetables, or the corned beef, or even the red beans!"

It took me awhile to return—Wise closed at a quarter to eight and all day Saturday, which made it tough for me to get there. But finally I did, and I had the vegetable soup, the brisket, the vegetables, and the custard.

And every bit of that was great. And from then on my love of Wise's food matched that of my friend, even after I discovered many other kinds of restaurants and dishes on a much higher culinary plane.

Even when I found it, Wise's was one of the last of its breed. It opened near the Board of Trade in the Central Business District in 1933, using a line of steam tables and booth tables that founder Harold Wise bought used—ten years used. When Esso built a skyscraper (relatively speaking) on Jefferson Davis Parkway at the foot of the overpass over the former New Basin Canal (now the I-10), Harold moved into its first floor. His son Milton moved into the business, and the legend of Wise Cafeteria and its one and only location (every other cafeteria had multiple venues) began. It was close enough to Uptown to get many of its denizens, plus everybody in Mid-City and Broadmoor.

Wise was the only cafeteria I ever went to that seemed to understand that it was in a town where good food is a major part of the local culture. Its prices were higher than those of other cafeterias, but the food was far better. Milton Wise did all the buying, butchering, and recipe development himself. He used salt, pepper, herbs, garlic, bits of smoked pork, and other Creole seasonings to create dishes that lacked nothing for flavor.

At peak hours, the line of people waiting to fill a tray with food pushed to the front door, where it doubled and tripled on itself. At the head of the line was a letter board outlining some of the recommended items, with the advisory at the bottom that the average time of employment for Wise's staff was over ten years.

Just past the pile of beat-up trays and paper-napkin-wrapped silverware were salads, ranging from cafeteria mysteries such as shredded carrots with raisins and Jell-O with fruit (people expected these things from a cafeteria) to a really fine shrimp remoulade, a stack of ripe tomatoes with a homemade blue-cheese dressing, and some very well composed green salads.

Next—strictly for marketing reasons—was dessert. The great ones came from pans behind the pies and cakes: a wonderful old-fashioned egg custard, mellowed with cinnamon and nutmeg, tasting almost like eggnog; light bread pudding and rice pudding with a custard sauce; delicious homemade cobblers.

Then the soups, also made on site—a great vegetable soup, as I noted, but also a fine seafood gumbo. Next on the line were a couple of carved-to-order roasts—brisket or corned beef. Roast beef and ham were always up there and often a nice pork loin, each with a homemade gravy.

No rhyme or reason revealed itself from then on. The entrees were just there, unadorned, no fake parsley or decorations, steaming in their sauces. Plump stuffed crabs, nicely seasoned, were among the most popular dishes. Fish—either fresh or bearing a sign telling you it was frozen—broiled or fried with a good cornmeal crunch. Beef stew. Tender, buttery quarters of baked chicken. Fried chicken—better than most fast-food joints, and cheaper. Consistently great red beans and rice. They'd grill a steak to order and bring it out with a tasty natural gravy. And, occasionally, cafeteria atrocities such as cheese-stuffed, bacon-trussed weenies.

Finally came the side dishes. Fresh spinach, corn on the cob, baked potatoes, great baked macaroni, the famous eggplant casserole, peas, turnip greens, Brussels sprouts, and other stuff. Breads, including excellent fresh bran muffins (sweet enough to work as dessert), garlic bread, cornbread, and those inevitable parkerhouse rolls.

The biggest danger in eating at Wise's was in getting too much food. It wasn't expensive—it was hard to run up a $10 total—but so many dishes looked good enough that you'd overload. And if you did, you wound up eating too fast, because your whole meal was before you, getting cold. In the later years, Milton Wise attempted to solve this problem by installing microwave ovens in the dining room. Most customers, however, just did it the time-honored way: they inhaled their meals. Some people would pack it all away in ten minutes, which might be half the time they spent in the line.

In its last decade, Wise's went on momentum through some dire business conditions. The worst of those began when its office building was deserted by Exxon in the late 1970s. It filled up with other concerns but emptied out yet again in the mid-1980s. Meanwhile, the cafeteria format was so out of vogue that the average age of the customers appeared to be "deceased." I took my mother there once when she was in her seventies, and she complained that she didn't like eating with so many old people. It didn't help that the premises were becoming very, very worn.

Through all that, the food remained good. And then, one day in 1988, Milton Wise told his staff not to come in the next day; he was closing the place down. I never spoke to him about the suddenness of it all, which perplexed his regular customers and distressed his employees. But that was that.

The Restaurants of West End Park (1859-2005)

West End Park is a manmade rectangle of land at the western end of the Lake Pontchartrain waterfront in New Orleans. Actually, part of West End is in Jefferson Parish. From the 1830s on, it was the most popular getaway for people living in and around New Orleans.

Most would arrive by boat. The docks at West End were the busiest anywhere along the lakeshore. Later, people would come by rail and, much later, by automobile—once the wetlands separating the city from West End had roads built through them (with great difficulty) in the 1920s.

They came for a variety of pleasures, beginning with the most innocuous ones of swimming, fishing, and lying around on the beach. The restaurants were good, specializing in the tremendous supply of unusually delicious seafood from the lake. As the clock ticked later, the nightclubs got rolling with their bands. Bawdier activities were available for those looking to enjoy misbehaviors of the flesh, to whatever degree they wished.

West End became as much a part of New Orleans culture as any part of the city, with the possible exception of the French Quarter. For example, it was a prime incubator of jazz. Louis Armstrong and Earl "Fatha" Hines

West End, on Lake Pontchartrain, was the place to go for restaurants that specialized in seafood. (Photo © Mitchel Osborne MMX)

recognized that when they recorded the King Oliver tune "West End Blues" in 1928—it became a major jazz hit.

The longest-running restaurant at West End Park was Bruning's. It opened in 1859 and persisted under the same family's ownership all the way to August 29, 2005—the day Hurricane Katrina hit. That day put an end to all the restaurants at West End Park. Because the park is outside levee protection—open to the lake and its potentially towering waves—it's unlikely that any restaurant will ever open there again.

If one does, it won't be much like the restaurants for which West End was known. All were very casual, inexpensive places serving big platters of boiled, fried, broiled, and stuffed seafood. The kind of building that could survive a major hurricane—and the cost of the insurance it would require—would result in prices that would make everyone who remembered the old days scream with pain.

When I started writing about restaurants in 1972, the West End Park's eateries were near their peak. Ten of them lined up along the waterfront. Their menus were practically interchangeable. You could get a fried seafood platter, boiled shrimp, gumbo, stuffed crabs, and soft-shell crabs anywhere. The very best places featured the signature dish of West End: a fried whole flounder stuffed with crabmeat dressing. When Katrina hit, that dish almost became extinct.

The most desirable property a West End restaurant could have offered a view of the lake—preferably derived by building on stilts over the water. But that introduced a few problems. If a restaurant were over the lake, it existed in a legal limbo called "squatter's rights," with no title to the area beneath the building. What's more, the Jefferson-Orleans parish line ran along the waterfront. West End Park—with its roads and parking lot—was entirely in Orleans Parish. But most of the restaurants were actually in Jefferson Parish and paid their taxes to that entity.

This gave little incentive to the City of New Orleans to keep up the roads. It wasn't a problem until it was decided in 1976 that the old parking lot—built with clamshells dredged from the lake, and full of big holes—needed to be rebuilt. The city paved it and put a toll on it. It was only a dollar, but this infuriated just about everybody, who always parked there for free. Making matters worse still was that the city charged tax on the dollar—so you had to find another six cents to exit the lot. That one little thing was enough to keep a lot of potential diners from going to West End Park.

I wrote a survey of the West End Park dining scene for the *Vieux Carre Courier* in 1973. I returned there every four or five years after that. The trend was obvious and discouraging. With each new survey, the restaurants were fewer. The food remained good, although even that took a hit now and then. Limitations on seafood catch forced change in the fried seafood platter. First, soft-shell crabs became an option instead of a standard. Speckled trout gave way to catfish for the fried-fish component.

West End took a particularly bad hit in 1998. Hurricane Georges ended the lives of a few restaurants, bringing the population of eateries to just four and ruining Bruning's old building. The area never recovered from that blow. Katrina's quietus left nothing standing anywhere in West End.

Many restaurants have come and gone in West End Park. We chose the middle 1970s as our snapshot moment. I wrote that first complete survey in 1973, and with only a couple of exceptions the restaurants there then are remembered by many lovers of seafood.

We begin with the most famous of them all—Fitzgerald's. Looking north from the parking lot, it was at high noon. From there, we'll go around the parking lot counterclockwise.

★★
Fitzgerald's
West End Park
1940s-98

Richard Collin, the Underground Gourmet, once wrote: "For many people Fitzgerald's is the only restaurant in town." That was an accurate statement. Even people who thought that Fitzgerald's wasn't as good as it once was would always bring it up in any conversation about dining out, as if it were as essential to the local dining scene as Antoine's. Fitzgerald's must have been a fine place indeed at some time. Just not in my time.

Or the explanation could be that it was as perfect a slice of New Orleans local color as could be imagined. A tin-roofed building on stilts over Lake Pontchartrain, it was set out farther from the shore than any other West End restaurant. It had lake views in three directions; most other places had only one. You reached it by walking up a wooden pier, above which was an animated neon sign of a smiling fish flapping its tail.

Then you'd wait for a table. Sometimes for a long time. For most of its history, Fitzgerald's was a packed house, and its supplicants would put up with almost anything to get in there.

The menu was bigger than most others in West End, although in essence it was the same. Boiled and fried seafood accounted for most

Fitzgerald's had an enviable view of Lake Pontchartrain. (Photo © Mitchel Osborne MMX)

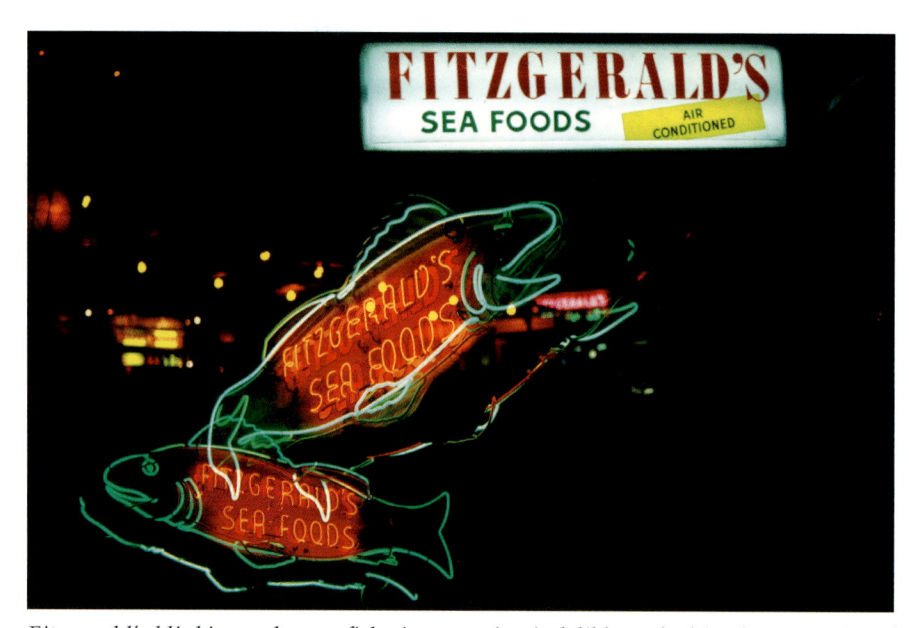

Fitzgerald's blinking red neon fish sign remains indelibly etched in the memories of locals who would line up to get in to this West End restaurant on Fridays, especially during Lent. (Photo © Mitchel Osborne MMX)

of the orders. The boiled crabs, shrimp, and crawfish were served ice cold. The fried seafood came out in huge platters that held a great deal of seafood on them. By today's standards of overfeeding—Deanie's, for example—it would not be considered supersized. But if you ordered soft-shell crabs, you always got at least two of them. Three full slices of buttered (was that butter, or oil from the seafood?) bread underlined all of these plates—for what purpose, no one has ever divined.

Fitzgerald's was highly regarded by its fans for its lobsters. These folks would repeat what the menu said, about how Caribbean lobsters were better than Maine lobsters because they weren't tough. (They were also half the price of Maine lobsters, but never mind.)

Like most West End restaurants, Fitzgerald's stuffed a lot of fish and shellfish with crabmeat stuffing. The making of crabmeat stuffing was an art at West End. It was two arts, in fact. One was to make it taste good. The other—more of interest to the owner than to the customer—was how to use the maximum amount of breadcrumbs without making people ask, "Where's the crabmeat in this?" Fitzgerald's was a master of the latter skill.

Fitzgerald's, like all other restaurants at West End, suffered when the new pay parking lot came in the early 1980s. With each passing year, the crowd at Fitzgerald's got smaller and older. The big parties of a dozen people with lots of kids were much rarer.

Ownership changed at least twice. One of the latter proprietors was Andrew Jaeger, whose family had run seafood restaurants for decades—although never before at West End. He kicked some life back into the restaurant, but its reputation among younger diners was hopeless, and the older customers complained about every change. And the place was in pretty bad shape. Hurricane Georges hit the restaurant so hard that it had to be torn down.

★★
Pier Orleans
West End Park
1975-80

Pier Orleans was one of several attempts by West End restaurateurs to rise above the seafood-platter level and serve a more ambitious menu in nicer surroundings. It was a brand-new restaurant over the water at the end of a long wooden ramp. The ramp was a nice place to hang with a glass of wine in the middle of a meal. The dining room had a great view of the lake, but the décor didn't stop there.

The food was reasonably good, but it had a marketing problem. Although the basic platters were well prepared, the pile on the plate was lower than at the old places. The fancier dishes sported what was probably the best crabmeat stuffing at West End, full of lump meat (claw meat was the West End standard). All of the prices were higher than one was accustomed to seeing at West End. Some people liked the step up, but not enough to keep the place going more than five years.

I've always thought that if this place had come around in the mid-1980s, with food like what was being served at Mr. B's or Clancy's, it would have been a hit. And it would have encouraged the West End restaurants to diversify and innovate.

★★★
The Bounty
West End Park
1975-95

There was a spate of new restaurant construction along the west side of West End Park in the mid-1970s. The Bounty was the longest-lived of those. It was managed in its first eight years by John Fury, a longtime operator of neighborhood-style New Orleans restaurants. The menu he assembled at the Bounty included all the fried and broiled fish you could get everywhere in West End. But it went on to include a few Italian dishes of surprising goodness, excellent fried chicken, barbecue shrimp, and a full line of steaks.

The Bounty was a shade upscale of most of the restaurants at West End. There was no boiled seafood and all the mess that entails. It was the first restaurant at West End Park to pass the $10 barrier for a seafood platter, in 1982. It attracted a reasonably loyal clientele. But West End regulars who wanted a little variety probably thought the place overpriced. And the style of frying—a coating of seasoned flour was used on almost everything—struck some people as lacking excitement.

The food outlived the restaurant. John Fury left the Bounty to open Fury's in Metairie in 1983. He's still cooking most of what he did at the Bounty there, including stuffed whole flounders.

★★
Maggie & Smitty's Crabnett
West End Park
1963-2003

Most people who dined at Maggie & Smitty's recall the cats before the food or surroundings. Two or three felines were always on the premises, walking around through the open-air part of the dining room. If one of them thought he had a good shot, he'd jump on one of the picnic-style tables in search of fishy orts. But they usually didn't have to put that much effort into their quest for food. Lots of the diners would throw the cats a piece of catfish.

Maggie & Smitty's was the most informal and cheapest of all the restaurants at West End. Although some of this can be discounted because of the low prices, a sizeable number of customers were of the opinion that Maggie & Smitty's had some of the best fried seafood and certainly the best boiled. They usually served boiled seafood hot—not a common practice in West End or anywhere else in town.

It was not the cleanest place in the world. The indoor dining room was more presentable for those with an aversion to flies and cats. But hardly anybody ever ate in there. The regulars thought of the alfresco aspect of Maggie & Smitty's as the main draw.

It never seemed to change until it finally closed, more a victim of the decline of West End than anything else.

At one point, Maggie & Smitty's had curb service. (Courtesy of Maggie Hemard)

Maggie & Smitty's was famous for its boiled crabs. (Courtesy of Maggie Hemard)

Maggie & Smitty's casual setting was much loved in the West End. (Courtesy of Maggie Hemard)

★★
Pique's Wharf
West End Park
1975-77
★★★
Willie G's
West End Park
1977-79

The handsomest of all the new restaurants along the west side of West End Park, Pique's Wharf tried to go full-tilt gourmet, but with a style that reminded one more of places like Houlihan's. The hand-drawn menu was on an enormous card that cut off communications among the diners at a table while they read the thing. Which took awhile. Not only were many dishes on it, but a majority were things that required explanations. How else to find out what "oysters Smokey Mary" were like? The menu also sported a byzantine set of symbols that told which dishes were spicy, which were gourmet, and which were house specialties. And, as if that weren't enough, advertising for outside businesses ran along the perimeter.

It was all a bit too much to take in. If the food had been good, it might have been worth it. But it always seemed to me to have been conceived by someone who had read about fine dining but not actually experienced it—let alone cooked it. A little too creative.

After Pique's closed, the good-looking space with its lake view became Willie G's. The seafood platters were as generous as those at Bruning's and Fitzgerald's but better. Nothing was ever overcooked or tepid; it all seemed to be fried to order. I was so impressed that I talked about it a lot on my new radio talk show. The business didn't boom, but Willie G's seemed to be doing pretty well.

Then one of the owners had what he thought was a brilliant idea. Unlike most other seafood-loving cities, New Orleans had never had a steamed-seafood restaurant. Willie G's rebuilt its kitchen to that end and one day swapped out the fried for the steamed.

It was a disaster. You have to grow up with steamed seafood to like it. Nobody around here had. You also need to like seafood that tends to the mild side of the flavor spectrum. (Some of it can be spicy, but not much.) And you have to get over the idea that food is best served piping hot—which steamed seafood often is not. It would not be the last time a seafood steamery opened with a bang and died with a whimper. (Visko's, which also tried steaming seafood, was brought down by it.)

They put the fried stuff back, but the momentum was lost. I don't think Willie G's lasted out the year. It closed, and the building sat unused for awhile. One night, it had a big fire, leaving only the stilts poking out of the water.

★★★★
Bruning's
West End Park
1859-2005

Bruning's saw the whole history of West End Park from the big windows of its big house over the lake. It seemed timeless. It may have even been definitive. The menu at Bruning's contained everything that a meal in West End Park would be expected to include, and almost nothing else. Boiled and fried seafood, stuffed everything, gumbo, whole fried or broiled flounder, and fried chicken—that about covered it.

Bruning's style of cooking was from another time. The gumbo recipe, for example, had no evidence of the trend towards a very thick broth. It was light but very flavorful. One of its most distinctive entrees was called a crab chop. This was crabmeat dressing made into

Bruning's bar was originally from the West End Hotel and was a fixture in the restaurant until it closed in 2005. The bar has been refurbished and is on view at the Southern Food and Beverage Museum. (Courtesy of Sam Urrate)

Bruning's was known for its flounder dishes. Until Hurricane Katrina, it had been in operation for almost 146 years. (Photo © Mitchel Osborne MMX)

the shape (roughly) of a pork chop and fried. An oddly shaped crab cake is what it was.

You entered through a room that could have been used to shoot a movie set in the Old West, with an enormous old bar in the darkest wood imaginable. A few antique arcade machines stood here and there. You couldn't figure out whether they worked or not.

That led into the dining room, whose many large windows left no doubt that you were over Lake Pontchartrain at the extremity of New Orleans. There was the outflowing end of the 17th Street Canal, at the other end of which the world's largest drainage pumping station sucked most of New Orleans dry (most of the time, anyway). A footbridge crossed the canal for those wanting to take a walk to Bucktown after dinner. On a sort of peninsula was a Victorian house that looked out of place until you found out that it was where the third-generation owner of Bruning's lived. Her grandson, Sam Urrate, managed the restaurant.

Usually, restaurants this old take on airs about themselves, become crotchety, and raise their prices. None of that was ever true of Bruning's, which remained easygoing and inexpensive.

The dining room—always full—had a West End oddity. Hanging on an interior wall was an old washbasin, with a towel rack above it. It looked as if it had been placed on the wrong side of a bathroom wall. It was there for you to wash up before and after you plowed through a pile of boiled crabs, shrimp, or crawfish.

Bruning's was a happy family place for a lot of people. How many became known after Hurricane Georges in 1998. Although Bruning's had survived many hurricanes, this one seemed to have it in for the old place. It filled Lake Pontchartrain with water eight to ten feet

Established 1859

ORIGINAL Bruning's SEA FOOD RESTAURANT

featuring

- OYSTERS
- FISH
- CRABS
- SHRIMP
- STEAKS
- CHICKEN
- COCKTAILS
- LOBSTERS

Phone 282-9395

CLOSED WEDNESDAY

Sam Urrate, Mgr.

OUT CANAL OR PONTCHARTRAIN TO YACHT BASIN & WEST END PARK

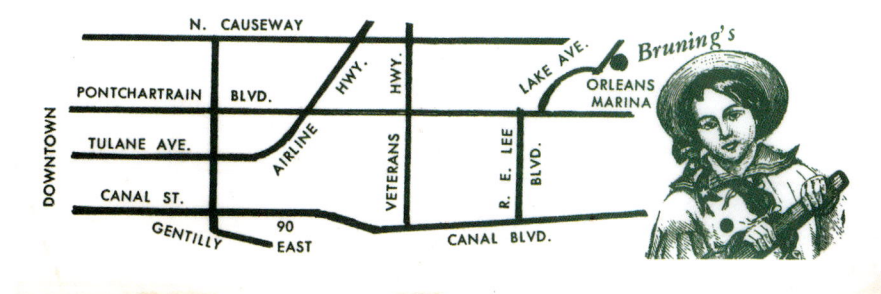

Menu from Bruning's. (Courtesy of Sam Urrate)

higher than normal. The winds blew waves high enough to wash up with great force beneath anything they could reach. They reached the underside of Bruning's and did terrible damage.

Sam Urrate moved the restaurant to a building he owned on the land in front of Bruning's and set about fixing the old place. But the insurance industry said that this was flood damage, not wind damage. How does a building that's always standing in water get flood insurance? Answer: It can't. The money never came. Bruning's original building would never be repaired. The best they could do was to remove the historic bar, the arcade machines, and some other things. The bar is now on view at the Southern Food and Beverage Museum.

Seven years later, Katrina's waves were twice as high as Georges'. They washed over West End Park and left no building standing. Not even the pilings that once supported all these restaurants remained. And Sam Urrate's grandmother's Victorian house was gone.

A couple of months after Katrina, Sam told me that he wanted to reopen Bruning's, either at West End or elsewhere. That was the last I heard from him. We can't blame him. But we can hope, can't we?

Bruning's Whole Flounder Stuffed with Crabmeat

Bruning's great specialty was stuffed whole flounder. The restaurant may be gone (although maybe not forever), but the dish lives on. Use the biggest flounders you can find. (Fishermen refer to those as "doormats.") I use claw crabmeat for the stuffing, because it has a more pronounced taste.

Stuffing:
½ stick butter
¼ cup flour
3 green onions, chopped
3 cups shrimp stock
1 Tbs. Worcestershire sauce
1 lb. claw crabmeat (or crawfish in season)
¼ tsp. salt
Pinch cayenne

4 large whole flounders
1 Tbs. salt-free Creole seasoning
1 tsp. salt
1 cup flour
2 eggs
1 cup milk
½ cup clarified butter
1 lemon, sliced
Chopped fresh parsley

Preheat the oven to 400 degrees.

1. Make the stuffing first. Melt the butter and stir in the flour to make a blond roux. Stir in the green onions and cook until limp. Whisk in the shrimp stock and Worcestershire and bring to a boil, then add the crabmeat, salt, and cayenne. Gently toss the crabmeat in the sauce to avoid breaking the lumps.

2. Wash the flounders and pat dry. Mix the Creole seasoning and salt into the flour and coat the outside of the flounders with it. Mix the eggs and milk together in a wide bowl and pass the fish through it, then dredge in the seasoned flour again.

3. Heat the clarified butter in a skillet and sauté the fish, 1 at a time,

about 4 minutes on each side, turning once. Remove and keep warm.

4. Cut a slit from head to tail across the top of the flounders. Divide stuffing among the fish, spooning inside the slit and piling it on top. Place the flounders on a baking pan and put into the oven for 6 minutes.

5. Place the flounders on hot plates. Garnish with lemon slices and fresh chopped parsley.

Serves 4 to 8.

★★★
Papa Rosselli's
West End Park
1960s-2005

Papa Rosselli's was the most nonconforming restaurant in West End Park. It stood in front of Bruning's on dry land. The few windows only gave views of other restaurants. And although you could get a good fried seafood platter there, it was more likely that you'd eat Italian. Not because the Italian food was so much better than the seafood—it wasn't. But . . . well, what's this place doing here if not to serve spaghetti and meatballs?

Joe David III—publisher of *New Orleans Magazine* during my tenure as editor—described the interior of Papa Rosselli's perfectly as "Early Christmas Tree." Big Christmas-tree lights were strung up on the walls all around, all year long. This was the first sign of many that this was a place that didn't take itself too seriously.

So you felt no hesitation about starting with a dozen raw oysters, then following with lasagna and Chianti. (Between the Christmas-tree lights were more than a few wicker-covered Chianti fiascos.) What you didn't do at Papa Rosselli's was go in a hurry. I sometimes got the feeling that only one person was in the kitchen and one in the front of the house. This had an advantage, though. If you were on a date, there were few interruptions. This slightly goofy place may have been the most romantic restaurant at West End.

★★★
Swanson's
West End Park
1940s-2005

Swanson's was, with Fontana's and Fitzgerald's, a member of the post-World War II expansion of the restaurant community on West End Park. It came along at a propitious time for restaurants. Not only were there lots of new customers as the economy expanded, but Jefferson Parish had legalized gambling. Swanson's sat athwart the parish line, which was clearly marked on the floor. On one side of the line, you ate and drank. On the other, you played slot machines.

Swanson's had at least three lives, opening and closing with different owners (although usually with some connection to the original Swanson family). When I first dined there in the mid-1970s, it served a mix of seafood and Italian food, and I got the impression that the management wasn't at the top of its game.

A few years later, it was taken over by a young guy named Danny Meyer (not the New York restaurateur). He made Swanson's into the best seafood house at West End. There was a fine edge on everything they did, but he introduced a great new idea: he served boiled seafood steaming hot. That's still not often seen. Boiled seafood needs to be chilled for food-safety reasons, but there's nothing that says you couldn't give it a quick dip in the boiling pot before serving it. Danny did that, and everybody went wild over it.

But then, still in his thirties, Danny died. Swanson's kept going, but it wasn't the same, and it closed. It would open and close once more before Katrina came to take it away.

★★★
Fontana's
West End Park
1940s-80s

Fontana's was on dry land in a Spartan building. That fact could be used to separate the people who were more interested in food than environment. Those who insisted that no other West End restaurant could match Fontana's seafood were difficult to talk into going to Fitzgerald's or even Bruning's, no matter how much nicer the views were.

The people at Fontana's seemed to be into seafood more than their competitors. They also ran a retail seafood operation and were intimately connected with the markets every day. This worked wonders on their food. You never got secondary cuts of fish here. I remember in particular a fried trout fillet so large that if I had not been in my twenties and hungry, I wouldn't have been able to finish it. It wasn't just big, though, but well seasoned, hot, crisp, and meaty.

This resonated with the guys going out to dinner. All you had to do was talk the girls into it. One meal was usually all it would take to convert them. Fontana's was always a favorite place to start the evening if you were on a date and were thinking about driving out to the Point (one of the great necking venues in the 1970s and before, at the end of the West End breakwater).

A link to Fontana's is still in the restaurant business. Rick Gratia, whose family owned the place, is the managing partner of Muriel's on Jackson Square. He put in his share of youthful time at Fontana's.

★★
Seymour's
West End Park
1975-81

Seymour's distinction among its fellow West End Park restaurants had nothing to do with food, but it brought a certain number of customers anyway. It was the only eatery out there with its own parking lot. On the other hand, it didn't feel a lot like West End. The building was modern and surrounded by windows. But there was nothing much to look at except the big oak trees outside. It was farther from the water than any other West End place.

Seymour's added to its appeal by letting its menu extend beyond fried platters. They got a little bit into saucing. But mainly the menu was like the one you'd find at Mandina's today, including the daily specials: red beans, a few Italian dishes, and steaks. Not many people remember Seymour's, but I always found it better than I expected it to be.

West End's Seymour's was the second restaurant under that name. For a time in the late 1960s, Seymour's was a neighborhood cafe on North Carrollton Avenue near Canal. The next generation of the family now has another Seymour's on Sauve Road at Hickory at the northern tip of Harahan. The menu there is reminiscent of the one at West End but not the same.

West End Oyster Stew

This is the oyster stew that was once common in the casual seafood restaurants, especially around West End. Like West End itself—which was totally destroyed by Hurricane Katrina—this dish is little more than a memory. But it's a very good memory, and one we can revive in our own kitchens. The element that makes the difference is the oyster water, which you can get from your oyster dealer if you give a little advance notice.

1 stick butter
1 Tbs. chopped onion
1 Tbs. chopped celery
1 qt. oyster water, strained well
1 pt. half-and-half
¼ tsp. black peppercorns
1 sprig fresh thyme or ¼ tsp. dried
3 dozen oysters
4 green onions, chopped
Salt to taste

1. In a saucepan, heat the butter and sauté the onions and celery until tender.

2. Add oyster water, half-and-half, peppercorns, and thyme. Bring to a very light simmer and cook slowly for 15 minutes.

3. Add oysters and green onions, and cook for another 3 to 5 minutes, until the oysters are plumped up and the edges are curly. Add salt to taste (you may not need any, depending on the saltiness of the oysters and oyster water).

Serves 4.

Some Drugstore Soda Fountains

★★
Katz & Besthoff Drug Stores
(Around town)
★★
Bradley's Pharmacy
South Carrollton Avenue at South Claiborne Avenue
1962-70

From the earliest days of the modern pharmacy, beverages of various kinds were dispensed in drugstores at least as often as drugs were. The first makers of cocktails were pharmacists. So were the guys who invented Coca-Cola, made ice-cream sundaes, and created the likes of nectar soda.

In the beginning of the era covered by this book, all the drugstores of New Orleans had soda fountains. It was like that everywhere in America. Few people in 1970 would have guessed that by 1980, the percentage of drugstores with soda fountains would go from almost 100 percent to zero.

The dominant drugstore chain in New Orleans during the twentieth century was Katz & Besthoff. Its big stores were all over town, full of signs, bags, and product labels in their trademark purple livery. And they all had soda fountains—good ones, too, with a signature soda found nowhere else in America.

The nectar soda was created in New Orleans in the late 1800s. The flavor was a blend of almond and vanilla. What made it distinctive was its unique color: a brilliant pink, originally that of cochineal, an extract from a beetle. It's unclear why nectar had that name or whose idea it was. There is no doubt that, by the turn of the nineteenth century, nectar sodas were so popular that K&B engaged the I. L. Lyons Company, a manufacturer of drugstore products, to make the flavoring for them.

The K&B soda fountains prepared much more than sodas, though. Their menus were as extensive as those of a full-fledged restaurant. They began the day with chicory coffee, made-in-house biscuits, bacon, and eggs. Around lunchtime, the K&B grill got to work on its long list of sandwiches, from soda-fountain standards such as grilled cheese to K&B's signature hamburger: the King Burger. (The KB—get it?) They cooked daily specials like red beans and rice and gumbo, too.

In the early 1970s, K&B decided to modernize and streamline its stores. Over the course of that decade, each of their stores was renovated to remove the soda fountain and replace it with more retail goods—much of it like what you'd find in a convenience store. The locals bemoaned the change. But K&B found that what it lost in fountain sales was less than half what it made back from the new merchandising scheme.

It took years for all the K&B fountains to disappear. The last of them was in the store in Harahan. By that time, almost all independent drugstores had followed suit. The last holdout was Schweickhardt's in Carrollton. Finally its famously good fountain closed, too.

We came to love the last of the old fountains. The one that engaged me was Bradley's. It was on the downtown river corner of Carrollton and Claiborne, a highly visible location, and a strategic one for those who took the bus or streetcar to school or work. Bunny Matthews noted in one of his cartoons that the intersection was the center of the known universe.

Bradley's took over an old K&B store, rendered surplus when K&B built a much larger new store diagonally across the intersection. The old place was very similar to the still-operating former K&B (now Rite-Aid) at the corner of St. Charles and Broadway.

It seems odd now that K&B would turn its old place over to a competing drugstore, but apparently Mr. Bradley (I don't remember his first name, if I ever knew it) thought it was a good opportunity. If he made any renovations before he moved in, they were not apparent.

The soda fountain looked the same as soda fountains had looked for decades. You could slake your thirst with anything from a Coke to a nectar soda. From a small grill came hamburgers, hot dogs, grilled cheese, and a few other sandwiches.

It was the crinkle-cut French fries, however, that made me a regular customer. They were fried to order in a vat of oil that, for some reason, foamed up as they fried. They had a unique flavor that I've never been able to put my finger on—or find again.

No fewer than nine bus and streetcar lines converged in front of Bradley's. The drivers popped into Bradley's for coffee, of which both pure and chicory were on tap from the big urns. Bradley's was at my transfer point from the electric Tulane buses to the Huey P. Long line, en route from home to Jesuit High School. Every afternoon between buses, I was in Bradley's for a cherry Coke and an order of fries, along with a lot of other high-school kids. It was also my source for the latest Spider-Man, Fantastic Four, and other Marvel comic books.

I continued my afternoon snack stop at Bradley's for years after I stopped taking the bus. That didn't end until Mr. Bradley retired after the building was bought out from under him. The old drugstore fell to the wrecker's ball in 1971, to be replaced by a bank.

Bradley's was my Schweickhardt's, my "Happy Days"-style hangout. It lingers in my memory still. I'd love to taste fries like those again.

Some Pizza Places

★★★
Domino's Pizza
Uptown: 701 St. Charles Avenue
Late 1940s-late 1970s
★★★
Artista Pizza
Gentilly: 2941 Franklin Avenue
Late 1960s-late 1970s
★★★
Sandy's Pizza Place
Chalmette: 2023 Paris Road
Late 1960s-mid-1970s
★★
Tower of Pizza
New Orleans East: 4428 Downman Road
Late 1960s-80s (Metairie location still open)
★★
Mr. Pizza
Around town
1965-80s

With a large population of immigrants from Southern Italy since the late 1800s, somewhere in town pizza must have been baked and served before World War II. But it wasn't until the late 1940s, when the pizza trend swept across America, that New Orleans had anything like a pizza parlor.

The first restaurant to make a specialty of pizza was Domino's, on the corner of St. Charles Avenue and Girod—where the tony French bistro Herbsaint is now. The national takeout pizza chain has no connection with the original Domino's in New Orleans, nor, as it has been suggested, was it named for Fats Domino, who was becoming famous at the time.

Domino's "pizza pie" (which is what the menu and neon signs called it) was clearly based on the New York model, and it was well executed. Its thin crust held a restrained layer of sauce and cheese, plus everything else that you ordered on it. Perhaps their most distinctive pie was a garlic pizza: a cheese job sprinkled with a great deal of garlic. It was delicious, and as long as your date also ate it you wouldn't regret ordering it. Domino's set an atmospheric standard, too: a dark space only lightly renovated from some past use, with a jukebox with a mix of hits from two highly disparate eras of popular music (Elvis *and* Frankie Laine).

Some of the new pizza parlors that opened across New Orleans in the 1960s were locations of chains. Others were existing Italian restaurants that decided to add pizza to their menus, whether they knew how to make pizza or not. The good ones were far outnumbered by the bad. The best pizzas of that generation were at Toney's Pizza and Spaghetti House (see index), Venezia (still in business), and the Tower of Pizza.

The Tower of Pizza was one of three similar and excellent pizzerias that opened in the late 1960s. In his *New Orleans Underground Gourmet*, Richard Collin notes that the link uniting the three was a woman named Sandy, who he says taught the employees of the three parlors. It was a great pie in the New York style, perhaps not quite as crisp at the bottom. You can get an idea of what they were like at the second location of the Tower of Pizza, still open in Metairie decades after the original closed.

The most memorable of this trio of pizzerias was Artista. A lot of this has to do with its location. It was in the lakeside corner of the Tiger Theater, a big old neighborhood movie house. In its final years in the late 1970s, the Tiger kept changing its name by rearranging the letters in its sign. It was the Riget (pronounced in the French way, it showed art films), then the Grit (X-rated movies).

Artista was a terrific pizzeria, held in particular esteem by the student body of the University of New Orleans. They had a reason: Luigi's Pizza, across the street from the campus, was so terrible that UNO people would gladly make the run for Artista's much better pie.

Still, Artista had a battle on its hands. After the I-610 expressway cut through the neighborhood, Artista and the big empty theatre were isolated and spooky. As if to confirm this, the owner of Artista in its last years had a revolver stuck into the waist of his apron, intentionally very visible. Somehow, his pizza remained great.

Meanwhile, a local chain called Mr. Pizza suddenly appeared. It was in almost every neighborhood: Metairie, Gretna, the Eighth Ward, River Ridge, you name it. It was heavily advertised on television with a memorable slogan: "World's Worst Pizza." It wasn't the worst, really. They threw their own crusts and baked their pizzas in the classic Blodgett stone-floored ovens. But it wasn't the best, either.

One of the most memorable innovations from Mr. Pizza—now widely practiced in places such as the Italian Pie—was its use of pizza dough to make poor-boy sandwiches. They'd partly bake it, make up the sandwich, and then finish baking the bread in the oven, so the whole thing came out hot and crisp. The chain fell apart in the 1970s, but some of the restaurants kept going for years. VIP Pizza in River Ridge started as a Mr. Pizza and has never closed, although it's not much like Mr. Pizza anymore.

The Uptown Bistro Boom—The Revolution of 1983

The shift in local dining habits that went ballistic in 1983 had a lot in common with what happened to popular music in 1955—1954: Doris Day, the Ames Brothers, and Perry Como; 1956: Elvis, Little Richard, and Fats Domino.

The hot restaurants of 1979 were the reborn Arnaud's, Jonathan, and Christian's. The hot restaurants of 1985 were Gautreau's, Clancy's, and the Upperline. Before: big, formal, dressy, expensive. After: small, casual, easygoing, moderate price. The coming of the nouvelle-Creole gourmet bistros transformed the dining scene more than any other development in the city's history.

The tidal force behind this sea change was the coming of age of the Baby Boom generation. We were very excited by all these new places and kept them busy, most of them, for awhile. Some members of that generation of eateries didn't make it. These were the best of the fallen.

★★★
Stephen & Martin
Uptown: 4141 St. Charles Avenue
1943-98

Stephen & Martin had two lives. The first was as a neighborhood cafe in the same category as Mandina's or Pascal's Manale. It was in an old building that seemed not to have been designed as a restaurant. It was a maze, and rare among New Orleans casual eateries in having both upstairs and downstairs dining rooms. Its kitchen could send you anything from oysters Rockefeller to a poor-boy sandwich to fried chicken. The prices were low, and the place was busy all the time, well into the wee hours of the morning. Stephen & Martin's slogan was "The Next Best to Eating in Your Home," which always sounded like faint praise.

Then, in 1976, the place was sold to the owners of Forty-One Forty-One, a sleek, chic new bar on the corner in front of Stephen & Martin. (It replaced a popular Uptown boite called Ched's.) The new owners decided to chuck the whole Stephen & Martin concept. A deep renovation was designed by Charles Gresham (previous work: Brennan's, Broussard's, and Commander's Palace). It created a lofty entrance atrium, flanked by a wine rack so tall the waiters had to climb to reach some of the bottles. The design was contemporary, with a suggestion of Art Deco.

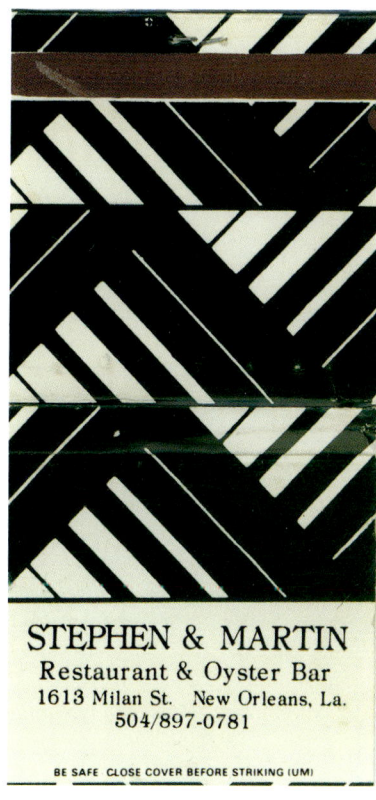

Stephen & Martin evolved into one of Uptown's early bistros in the 1970s. (From the collection of Richard Morelock)

Everything else about the restaurant was rejiggered too. Manager Tim Gannon hired younger, more casual waitresses, put in a real wine list, raised prices, and created a much more engaging, hip scene.

The chef was Ron Sciortino. He had worked at LeRuth's and for his mother's catering company. He had a free hand and took advantage of it. The result was the forerunner of the gourmet Creole bistro, which would shortly become the most pervasive kind of restaurant in town, as it still is.

Chef Ronnie's dishes weren't wildly innovative by today's standards. But he brushed up everything, gave it a new edge. I remember that the gumbo, barbecue shrimp, baked oysters, and fish were more along the lines of what we would later eat at places such as Mr. B's (still three years from opening) than what we were being served in other restaurants.

It was a tremendous success, and for a few years it was tough to get a table. Then Sciortino left (he ultimately took over his family's Sno-Wizard business, which he still runs). Gannon departed to open Bouligny. (In ten years, he would cofound the Outback Steakhouse.)

A contingent of Manale's expatriates came in and turned Stephen & Martin into a slightly polished version of that restaurant. When the bistros started popping up all over Uptown in the early 1980s, it was nearly forgotten that Stephen & Martin had been the prototype of the genre.

Stephen & Martin settled into a desultory groove. After a few changes of ownership, it became the very dull Cannon's, which itself sold out to New Orleans Hamburger and Seafood Company. The end.

★★★★

Indulgence
Warehouse District: 1539 Religious Street
Garden District: 2727 Prytania Street
1981-86

Frank Bailey was a different sort of restaurateur. He came to New Orleans from Texas, where he worked as a food writer and caterer, after spending enough time in France to know his way around a dining room. He is the brother of Texas politician Kay Bailey Hutchison, with whom he has worked off and on since leaving town, between further extended stints in France.

Not long after he fetched up in New Orleans, he began writing a food column for the *Dixie Roto* magazine in the *Times-Picayune* and later for the newspaper's food section. While doing that, he started a catering operation in a unique building on the edge of a large, desolate railroad yard, on the corner of Religious and Orange streets. The structure—built by the Jesuits in the early 1800s—was old even by New Orleans standards, and looked it, with extra-thick walls and small windows.

Bailey built a dining room in there and began serving lunch. Indulgence became a word-of-mouth phenomenon, requiring reservations

Indulgence was initially located in a cottage from the late 1700s. Today it's the home of Le Citron Bistro. (Photo by Jackson Hill)

days in advance. It soon surpassed the catering business, opening a few nights for dinner. In that neighborhood, however, armed guards were a necessity.

A better location turned up. A little French place called the Garden Café gave up the ghost in The Rink, a new boutique mall on Prytania Street at Washington Avenue. Bailey and his partner, Liz Page, moved Indulgence's a la carte dining room there in 1982. The timing was perfect: the Uptown gourmet bistros were just beginning to appear across Uptown, and each new venue brought more attention to all of them.

Indulgence was always different from the other bistros, however. It was more French than anything else, and not very Creole. Still, French and Creole dish names have enough similarity that nobody was scared off. And when they realized that what they were being served was different from what they were used to, the goodness of the food was enough to leave a favorable impression.

So you got goujonettes (fingers to you and me) of chicken or fish. Instead of shrimp remoulade, you got fried oysters remoulade, with celery root—because celery root was what was most often paired with remoulade in France. Frank liked organ meats; sweetbreads, liver, and even kidneys turned up frequently. No matter what, the food here was quite different from anything else hereabouts in those days. It was the Lilette of its time.

The menu was not entirely beholden to French food. Fritto misto (Italian for a plate of fried this and that) was a common appetizer. There was a Basque salad. They made great omelettes at lunch, filled with the likes of feta cheese, fresh basil, and fresh tomatoes. Lightness was a hallmark of the entire menu.

Frank had strong feelings about what was good, and this led

Indulgence into some quirks. Instead of serving the standard New Orleans French bread, they had a big loaf of rustic French bread on a sideboard and cut off a hunk for each new table. There were no peppermills (which had just caught on big in New Orleans restaurants), but Frank ground a pile of peppercorns every day and served the coarse result out of little jars with littler spoons. There were no envelopes of artificial sweetener. "I hate the whap-whap-whap sound it makes when people open them," he said.

Ultimately, Indulgence was a little too cool for New Orleans. And Bailey cooled on New Orleans. After five or six years, he shut Indulgence down and made himself scarce—although he kept writing his newspaper column for a long time. He and I and Dick Brennan, Sr., had lunch together once a month for a few years. I learned quite a few things from Frank. He was the best combination food writer-restaurateur in the annals of the New Orleans food scene—one of the only ones, really.

★★★
Bouligny
Uptown: 4100 Magazine Street
1982-91

Bouligny was the restaurant that made everybody hip to the news that eating Uptown had changed. In a renovated firehouse on Magazine at Marengo—with a substantial parking lot, yet—it was a place you liked from the moment you set foot in the place: lots of big windows, lots of greenery, and lots of Baby Boomers in their thirties and starting to making money.

Manager Tim Gannon had worked out his new restaurant concept at Stephen & Martin, and he rolled out Creole Bistro 2.0 at Bouligny. The chef was Sebastian "Buster" Ambrosia, who after a few years at Commander's Palace was the first chef of Mr. B's Bistro, the archetype of the new casual gourmet places. His menu was decidedly Creole but a little more Cajun than usual (darker roux, andouille in new places, more cayenne). The fish was more likely to be grilled than fried—a hallmark of the bistros.

I remember that Bouligny changed my own dining schedule. I'd wind up in there two or three times a week, eating the oysters bonne femme, veal with Choron sauce and fried crawfish, or grilled duck breast with a nest of vegetables. A lot of this was influenced by Chef Paul Prudhomme, who'd started cooking like this at Commander's five years earlier. But here it was in a moderate-price, dress-down restaurant with a very cool look.

By all rights Bouligny should still be around. What happened was that the owners weren't particularly into food. One of them—a nice guy in the wrong business, who was happy to get out of it—had no sense of smell.

Bouligny's last years were exciting, though. In 1989, Michael Uddo took over the kitchen and started cooking the best food in

Bouligny was located in a former fire station. (From the collection of Richard Morelock)

Bouligny's history. But by that time the Uptown restaurant scene was overpopulated, and the owners threw in the towel. Uddo would shortly open up his own place, the G&E Courtyard Grill, discussed elsewhere.

The name (it was that of the plantation and then the faubourg in which the place was located) lives on. John Harris of Lilette calls his bar Bouligny.

★★★★
Flagons
Uptown: 3222 Magazine Street
1983-92

Flagons opened during the great blossoming of Uptown Creole bistros. It became much like those restaurants. But it started out with humbler—if no less innovative—aims. Flagons was the city's first wine bar. In the early 1980s, many restaurants had good collections of wine by the bottle. But almost none of them had more than a handful of wines served by the glass. And most of those were cheap house wines of little interest.

Flagons opened with forty wines by the glass. The selection changed constantly. Even the best-versed wine buffs found it interesting to pore over the list and have a taste or two of many different wines.

The system Flagons used to serve so many wines without their going bad was high tech and fascinating. The bottles were held inside handsome wood-and-glass cabinets at ideal serving temperatures. Tubes supplying nitrogen under pressure not only forced the wine out through a tap into the glass but prevented the wine from deteriorating after the bottle was open.

Flagons was owned by Eugenie Vasser and Tim Garrard, who were married to each other (but not for much longer, as it turned out), plus wine merchant Mark Hightower. All were knowledgeable wine buffs and had worked in the wine business somewhere along the line. Their wine selection was always intriguing, because they served the wines they were interested in. Nothing was off limits—not even old Bordeaux, not even if half-glasses had to be sold in double digits. (That was something else nobody had done here before.)

Flagons fooled everybody in the wine business, who wanted to see it take off but didn't give it much of a chance. Largely because of Eugenie Vasser's sense of style (she was from Natchez and very charming), Flagons became a popular upscale hangout.

They opened with a minimal menu of food—boards of cheeses and cured meats and patés, soups, a few sandwiches. It wasn't long before the kitchen expanded to serve a short bistro menu. That was well received, so a door was knocked through the wall into another, larger dining room.

Parker Murphy was the first in a series of brilliant young chefs brought in to run all this. They would stay just long enough to become well known, then move on to open their own places. Among Parker's best successors was Michel Fouqueteau, a French chef who later turned up at Christian's and La Provence. Each new chef left a great dish or two behind. Regular customers almost looked forward to the next turn of this revolving door.

In short, Flagons in the mid-1980s was enormous fun for food and wine aficionados. I dined there far too often—enough so that I sometimes was pressed into service as an unpaid bartender.

Flagons expanded again, extending the dining room all the way to Pleasant Street, buying the building, and building a major new kitchen. That came, unfortunately, just as the local restaurant economy—which was overbuilt—took a downturn. Then some bookkeeping problems appeared. Back taxes nearly bankrupted Flagons. Eugenie split with Tim (who had already left town). She continued to develop innovative ideas to jump-start the place. But the hole was too deep, and the restaurant closed right before wine really started going crazy in the mid-1990s.

It would be a decade before anything like Flagons came along again. Or needed to. Most restaurants began offering full pages of wines by the glass. And the ever-changing menu that made Flagons' food interesting is common now. But it sure was fun while it lasted!

Flagons' Oysters Sazerac

This recipe was created at Flagons by chef Kevin Curran, who noticed how well the flavor of anise and oysters go together (in oysters Rockefeller, for example). He flamed the cocktail over some double-battered fried oysters and napped them with a little butter sauce, and it turned out to be wonderful.

1 cup flour
1 tsp. salt
½ tsp. white pepper
Pinch cayenne
2 egg yolks
¼ cup milk
3 oz. 86-proof whiskey
2 Tbs. Herbsaint
1 tsp. Peychaud's bitters
1 tsp. Angostura bitters
3 Tbs. butter
24 large, fresh oysters
Seasoned breadcrumbs
3 Tbs. chopped green onion tops

Beurre blanc:
1 Tbs. whipping cream
2 sticks butter
1 Tbs. lemon juice
¼ tsp. white pepper

1. Sift together the flour, salt, pepper, and cayenne into a broad bowl.

2. Combine the egg yolks and milk in a small bowl.

3. Mix the whiskey, Herbsaint, and both bitters in a glass to make a Sazerac in the rough (the finished cocktail would be sweetened with simple syrup and shaken with ice).

4. Heat the butter in a skillet.

5. Coat the oysters with the seasoned flour mixture, then dip them into the egg wash. Coat them again with the breadcrumbs.

6. Sauté the oysters in the butter until lightly browned. Then pour the Sazerac into the skillet and carefully touch flame to it. Let the flames die out and most of the liquid evaporate.

7. Serve the oysters topped with the green onions and moistened with beurre blanc.

8. To make the beurre blanc, heat the cream over low heat in a saucepan until it comes to a boil. Cut in, bit by bit, all of the butter, whisking all the while. Remove from heat and whisk in lemon juice and pepper.

Serves 6.

World's Fair Fare

A German oompah band performed nightly at the Miller Beer Garden at the 1984 World's Fair. The Chicken Dance was popular with patrons. (Photo © Mitchel Osborne MMX)

Many locals were introduced to Japanese cuisine at the restaurant within the Fair's Japanese Pavilion. (Photo © Mitchel Osborne MMX)

While the Gondola, Wonder Wall, and Vatican Pavilion are still pretty vivid in the memory of visitors to the 1984 New Orleans World's Fair, there are also some dining experiences connected to those six months (May 12-November 11).

Alas, the history of the Fair included bankruptcy, but some of the food concessionaires did make money. And it's common knowledge that what is today called the Warehouse or Arts District (the Ernest N. Morial Convention Center and Riverwalk, to name a couple of landmarks) got a kick start from the Louisiana World Exposition, the Fair's official name. For many locals, it became an elegant playground that included food, music, cultural attractions, amusement rides, and, at evening's end, a fireworks show over the Mississippi River.

There were food booths. The Gumbo Shop, a French Quarter mainstay, had an outlet that turned a profit, as did Dr. Bananas, which sold frozen chocolate-covered bananas, fresh fruit juices, and pineapple spears and frozen strawberries on a stick. Tropical Paradise sold daiquiris that were made of freshly squeezed fruit juices and did so well that the French Quarter's Tropical Isle bar and Orleans Grapevine Wine Bar & Bistro are outgrowths of that success.

New Orleans and Louisiana cuisine were plentiful: Popeyes Fried Chicken and Biscuits; red beans and rice at Pete Fountain's Reunion Hall; meat pies made by Mrs. Wheat's, originally from Natchitoches, Louisiana, boudin from Creole Country sausage makers; and Cajun-flavored fish dishes at Patout's Acadian Seafoods.

Of course, a "world's fair" implies the presence of other countries. Perhaps most famous for raucous crowds doing the Chicken Dance, the Miller Beer Garden in the Federal Fibre Mills served sauerbraten and pig's knuckle. It's no surprise that desserts included apple strudel and Black Forest chocolate cake. While beer was consumed in vast quantities, the choice of a nightcap could have included Schnapps or a liqueur relatively new to New Orleanians—the potent herb-based and bitter Jägermeister.

While we are now accustomed to sushi and can even pick up a tray in many area grocery stores, at that time an Orleanian's exposure to Japanese dishes was minimal at best. For many locals, their maiden voyage to the Land of the Setting Sun and its culinary treasures was a trip to the Japanese Pavilion and a restaurant included within.

A replica of the Piazza San Filippo di Giacomo in Venice, the Italian Village included such dining spots as Pasta di Vincenzo, Pizza del

Dr. Bananas (on the right) sold frozen bananas covered in chocolate on a stick. Food booths were incorporated into the Fair's Wonder Wall, an almost mile-long structure along what is today Convention Center Boulevard. It cleverly disguised unsightly power lines. (Photo © Mitchel Osborne MMX)

Paese, and Trattoria Pastore. Italian puppet shows, jugglers, and musicians, many of them imported from the mother country, enhanced an already talented group of local entertainers who made the Italian Village one of the Fair's most popular attractions. Brocato's sold gelato and cookies, and the Roman Chewing Candy man provided taffy from his mule-drawn cart.

The Belgian waffles booth was actually considered a bit of a novelty. By far the strangest concoction (that doesn't mean it didn't taste good) was Petro's Chili & Chips. This multi-layered dish topped with sour cream included green onions, tomatoes, grated cheese, and chili, on a bed of corn chips. Today the Tennessee-based company has franchises in Alabama, Arkansas, and Georgia and includes a few other dishes such as hot dogs on the menu.

Fulton Street was billed as a new entertainment/dining section that seemed primed for takeoff after the Fair. It took awhile for that to happen, but during the Fair, a welcome respite for the wine-and-cheese crowd was the Winery, on a lakeside corner of Julia and Fulton (today occupied by Feast restaurant). New Orleans guitarist John Rankin set a calm, easygoing mood there that was counterpoint to more of a midway pace along the Wonder Wall.

The menu cover from the Miller Beer Garden. (From the collection of Peggy Scott Laborde)

The Miller Beer Garden was located in today's Federal Fibre Mills apartment building. The commercial structure was renovated for the Fair and converted to residential use afterwards. (Photo © Mitchel Osborne MMX)

Most fairgoers did a double take when they saw a sign for The Nuthouse. Purveyor of "pecandy" (chocolate-covered pecan candy), pecan pies, and pralines, its charming Acadian cottage-style storefront added to the Fair's pastel "party mints" palette.

Local music legend "Deacon John" Moore had his first Belgian waffle at the Fair. Mardi Gras float builder Blaine Kern experienced a hangover from his encounter with Jägermeister at the Miller Beer Garden. *New Orleans Magazine* editor Errol Laborde learned how to use chopsticks at the Japanese Pavilion's restaurant. Rest assured they are part of a long list of folks who tasted something for the first time at the Fair.

—Peggy Scott Laborde

It was pretty easy to figure out what Snow Spree sold. Snoballs were among the more popular frozen desserts during the summer months of the Fair. (Photo © Mitchel Osborne MMX)

The World's Fair's Flurry of Fine Dining

The Louisiana World Exposition in 1984 created a mixed bag of effects on New Orleans, but one superb development was the opening of the grandest restaurants in the history of the city. Large new hotels, looking forward to World's Fair crowds, went up throughout the CBD.

Many of them felt it important to include a world-class gourmet dining room among their offerings. These were without exception stunning, spacious restaurants with the most exacting service imaginable, adventuresome and dramatically presented cooking, and record-breaking prices. The $20 entree barrier was broken for the first time, and the $30 threshold was crossed soon after (big bucks in those days).

Only one of these impressive hotel restaurants survived: the Windsor Court Grill Room. Most considered it the best of its class, and it attracted a strong local clientele that the others didn't. Here are the ones that didn't make it. They were great pleasures while they lasted—although, to quote a friend who'd dined in one of them the night before, "When it gets to $100 for two, it stops being fun."

I'm listing them in order of excellence. And they were all pretty good in their short peaks.

★★★★★

Henri
CBD: 611 Common Street
1983-90

Henri was the flagship restaurant of Le Meridien, a major new hotel owned indirectly (through Air France) by the French government. In Le Mcridien's top hotels, the gourmet restaurant was partnered with a highly rated restaurant in France. The New Orleans hotel hit the jackpot. Its patron was Auberge de l'Ill, one of the few restaurants rated three stars by the almighty *Guide Michelin*. Auberge de l'Ill was in Illhauersen, a small town with a German heritage south of Strasbourg, in Alsace. At the time Henri opened, Auberge de l'Ill was on a hot streak. Mimi Sheraton, writing in Travel & Leisure, declared it the best restaurant in the world.

Marc Haeberlin—whose father and uncle ran the restaurant in Alsace—visited New Orleans twice a year to install new dishes on the menu and make sure everything at Henri was up to snuff. The idea sounds iffy now; we've seen too many ordinary restaurants with famous names attached. But it worked brilliantly at Henri. The food was—to the extent possible, given the difficulty of getting exactly the same ingredients used in Alsace—very much like that of Auberge de l'Ill. I know, because I went to Alsace in 1988 and dined at the Haeberlins' masterpiece.

Henri was always good, but especially during Marc Haeberlin's visits to New Orleans. The hotel would make a big fuss over that and run special menus with the new dishes.

Three signature dishes were particularly memorable. The first was salmon soufflé, a cloud of fish essence wrapped in paper-thin salmon, with a wonderful velouté. The second was a filet mignon, served variously with sweetbreads, marrow, or oxtails. The third was a gratin of red fruits, made with strawberries and whatever else was around of that color, glazed over the top in the broiler to make a thin crust. All of these were memorable, and they were just the beginning of the chef's repertoire of magnificent dishes. The best dish of all was the venison with wild mushrooms, the likes of which could not be found in any other New Orleans restaurant in those days.

The maitre d'—whose name I've forgotten—was not only very French but a singer who would give artful readings of French songs with a rapid vibrato, accompanied by the pianist, who was always in a tuxedo.

The dining rooms were intimate feasts for the eyes, with hand-painted walls depicting an imaginary but very appealing garden from another, more delightful era. Although Henri has been closed for decades, the dining rooms still retain their original look. They're used for private dining for the Marriott, which took over Le Meridien in the 1990s.

What happened to Henri can be explained with the same two words that apply to the other three lost restaurants in this category: nobody came. It didn't matter how good the food was. This wasn't New Orleans food, and that made it a hard sell to visitors and locals alike. What person sophisticated enough to stay in a hotel like this would not cross Canal Street in search of New Orleans's famous restaurants?

Henri's Salmon Soufflé "Auberge de l'Ill"

This is one of the most delicate dishes I've ever eaten. The flavor of the fish is refined and carried on a cloudlike texture. It was created by and is the famous dish of L'Auberge de l'Ill, a three-star restaurant in Alsace, France. We had it in New Orleans through the grand hotel restaurant Henri.

Fish stock:
1 small whole rainbow trout, filleted
Bones of the fish (if available), rinsed
½ bottle white wine
¼ cup coarsely chopped onion
2 sprigs fresh thyme
5 fresh basil leaves
1 qt. water

Stuffing:
3 eggs
8 oz. of the fish (from the stock above)
Pinch salt
Pinch black pepper
Pinch nutmeg
8 oz. whipping cream

1 lb. cold-smoked salmon, unsliced
2 shallots, minced
Salt and black pepper to taste
½ bottle dry Riesling (Alsace preferred)
12 oz. fish stock
4 oz. whipping cream
2 Tbs. butter
Juice of ½ lemon

Preheat the oven to 375 degrees.

1. Make the fish stock first. Add all the stock ingredients to a large stainless-steel skillet. Bring to a light boil and cook 10 minutes. Remove fish fillets. Strain stock and discard solids. Set aside.

2. To make the stuffing, separate the eggs and, in a food processor, combine all ingredients except cream and the whites of 2 of the eggs. Process into a puree while adding cream gradually.

3. In a separate bowl, beat the egg whites until peaks form. Carefully fold egg whites into stuffing mixture. Refrigerate.

4. Slice salmon into long, thin fillets on a slight diagonal (about 4 ounces each). Place fillets in a buttered baking pan and sprinkle with chopped shallots. Pile stuffing atop each fillet. Sprinkle lightly with salt and

pepper. Add wine and fish stock to pan and bake for 15 to 20 minutes or until tops of stuffing are golden brown. Remove and keep warm.

5. Pour the liquids from the pan into a skillet and add cream. Reduce over medium-low heat by one-half. Chip in butter and whisk into sauce. Add lemon juice and salt and pepper to taste.
To serve, arrange salmon on plates and pour sauce all around (not on top). Garnish with very light vegetables.

Serves 4.

★★★★
Les Continents
CBD: 444 St. Charles Avenue
1984-87

The main restaurant of the Hotel Inter-Continental when it first opened was built to resemble the dining room of a ship at sea. It was so much longer than it was wide that trying to fix one's focus on the rear wall was like trompe l'oeil in reverse.

My favorite indicator of the opulence of Les Continents was that it threw away about a hundred 1980s dollars' worth of cheese every day to maintain its cheese cart. Cheese carts have never had much luck in New Orleans restaurants, but this one may never be equaled for its variety. Covered with cheesecloth, the cart had dozens of cheeses held at room temperature, ripening away, most of them never to be eaten, save by the chef and other Frenchmen in the dining room.

While Les Continents was not quite as stridently French as Henri was, its menu was very much tilted in that direction. The service style was showy. In vogue in those days was the practice of having as many waiters as there were diners at a table set down the entrees, then simultaneously whisk the silver plate covers away. It was impressive for a few weeks, then we all got tired of it.

The high point of the career of Les Continents came when the hotel struck up a friendship with Jean-Pierre Chavant, a chef whose family's restaurant in Grenoble dates back to 1852. Chavant came to New Orleans a few times, gilding the menu at Les Continents with his cuisine. He made a particularly brilliant dish involving veal kidneys and sweetbreads. Many of his dishes involved Chartreuse, the potent liqueur made in Grenoble. It was all really amazing. But nobody came, and the restaurant closed before many people knew it was there. The Inter-Continental shifted its food service to the much more impressive and informal Veranda, where it is today.

★★★★
Saffron
CBD: Canal Street at Common Street
1983-87

Saffron, in the Sheraton Hotel, was the first of the glitzy dining rooms to open in the big new hotels downtown. It was a suave, modern, angular place, quiet and gently lighted, with a man in a tuxedo playing light jazz and standards on a grand piano with a candelabra. Unlike Henri and Les Continents, Saffron wasn't especially French. In fact, its key staff were familiar to customers of fine-dining restaurants here. Chef Tom Kovacs had spent some time at Commander's Palace. Here, his menu was largely New American, with a few subtle Spanish touches (in order to work the saffron theme in). Australian-born maitre d' Keith Nelson had developed a following at Versailles and Broussard's, among other places.

The food at Saffron was marked by the use of a lot of foodstuffs not familiar to many New Orleans eaters. I think it was the first place I ever ate foie gras. Venison was almost always on the menu and excellent. The fish were often offbeat: John Dory fish, about which Keith Nelson went into raptures, was a standard, as were turbot and Dover sole. Getting these took some doing. This was before fish flew all over the world routinely.

Saffron will be remembered by the few people who dined there more than a few times as the place where baby vegetables made their first New Orleans appearances. Every plate came out with teeny carrots, turnips, squashes, and zucchini. We were all charmed by these, until someone noticed that baby vegetables don't have very much flavor.

Nobody went to Saffron, and the hotel turned the space into a showroom in which a Las Vegas-style troupe of singers and dancers put on the corniest imaginable tribute to New Orleans, its food, and its music. That didn't last long either.

★★★★
Le Jardin
CBD: Canal Place
1984-2002

Le Jardin was the last to open of the big-deal new hotel dining rooms. It saw the greatest number of ups and downs and changed its menus more times than I could keep track of. Even the hotel's name kept changing: first the Trust House Forte, Iberville, then the Westin, the Wyndham, and the Westin again. Despite all that, it lasted longer than any of the other restaurants in this chapter. And, under a new name, it's still there.

Le Jardin boasted an asset few other New Orleans restaurants have ever had: a view. The restaurant and the hotel's lobby were on the eleventh floor of the Canal Place complex. The windows were as large as they could be made and gave on to a magnificent vista of the curve of the Mississippi River, as well as most of the French Quarter. On a clear day, you could see the North Shore and far down the river.

If the windows had been covered with black paint, Le Jardin would still have been an arresting space. Tall and wide, the end closest to the river held terraces of greenery that lived up to the restaurant's French name ("the garden"). The wood that paneled everything had natural stripes in two perpendicular directions.

Like its competitors, Le Jardin started out with an unreservedly gourmet menu. That did not last long, because nobody came. Besides, the hotel had another, much less expensive, casual restaurant that got most of the hotel guests who were too unmotivated to hit the streets. (Having two restaurants was common for hotels then.)

One meal on Le Jardin's schedule was a resounding success. The Sunday brunch drew hundreds of people with the rare and irresistible duo of view and buffet. The food was very good and served grandly, too. In the long run, however, nobody came.

Le Jardin's All-White Scallops and Grouper with Champagne Sauce

Back around 1992, I casually tossed an idea to Felix Sturmer, the chef of the Westin Canal Place Hotel and its stunning restaurant, Le Jardin. Could he do an all-white dinner? Where all the food was white, I mean. He jumped at the challenge and gave a precursor of what became the Eat Club dinners. It was a fantastic evening of brilliant food. Its most memorable moment came when the first guests to arrive introduced themselves. They were an African-American couple who said they had to be there. Their name was White.

2 Tbs. chopped French shallots
1½ sticks butter
1 cup Champagne
12 oz. fresh grouper fillet (or redfish or black drum)
12 fresh dry-pack (dayboat) sea scallops
⅓ tsp. salt
⅛ tsp. white pepper
2 cups whipping cream
½ cup julienned fresh fennel
½ cup julienned leeks (well washed and white parts only)
Salt and black pepper
18 fresh white asparagus
1 tsp. black caviar

1. Sauté shallots in ½ stick butter for about 2 minutes.

2. Add the Champagne and bring it to a boil. Lower the heat to a simmer and add the grouper and scallops. Season with salt and pepper. Poach the fish and scallops in the Champagne for about 8 minutes, covered. Remove seafood and keep warm.

3. Raise the heat to medium and reduce the liquid in the pan by half, uncovered. Add the cream and reduce by half again.

4. While that's going on, in a separate skillet sauté the fennel and leeks in ½ stick butter. Season with salt and pepper.

5. Steam or poach the asparagus till crisp-tender. Rinse in cold water to stop cooking.

6. After the second reduction of the sauce, remove from heat and whisk in the last of the butter.

7. To serve, place the sautéed fennel and leeks in the center of a large plate. Pour some sauce around the plate, covering the entire bottom. Separate grouper into flakes about ¼ inch thick. Slice scallops to the same thickness. Alternate grouper and scallops around plate. Top each with a little caviar. Place asparagus tips on top of the leeks and fennel, with the tips meeting in the center. Or, if all this is a little too Martha for you, just throw everything on the plate and nap it with the sauce.

Serves 4.

Richard Collin, the Underground Gourmet

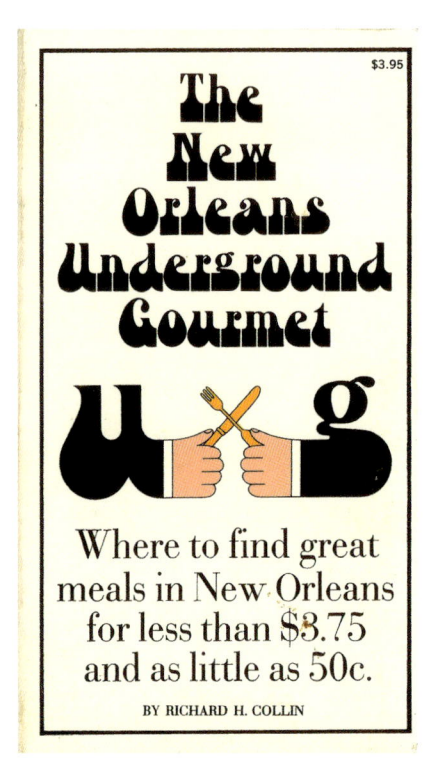

It's impossible to overstate the influence that Richard Collin had on dining out in New Orleans in the 1970s and early 1980s. His three dining guides were not only the first of their kind hereabouts but so exhaustive in their coverage that they're indispensable in researching the history of New Orleans dining.

Others before Collin wrote about New Orleans restaurants. But his books were the first to take a critical stance. He was the first person ever to give ratings to the city's eateries.

That alone would have brought a lot of attention to *The New Orleans Underground Gourmet,* his groundbreaking 1970 book. But his blunt, sarcastic, entertaining writing style elicited the strongest reactions from readers. He was even more carefully read by owners of restaurants, who had never been subjected to this kind of scrutiny before.

His negative reviews caused the greatest stirs. They were also his funniest writing—so entertaining that his readers also got into the spirit and began taking shots at underperforming restaurants that had, to that time, gotten away with everything.

Collin's kind of commentary was becoming more common elsewhere in the country in those days, when the consumer movement was on the rise and castigating businesses of all sorts was in vogue. But it's not what made Collin's work important. The reviews of restaurants he liked made a much bigger difference. It was impossible to read one of those pieces without wanting to drop everything and head over to the restaurant.

Collin motivated people to explore the full, rich panoply of eating possibilities in New Orleans. Perhaps the most telling measure of his persuasiveness is that, after reading Collin's glowing reports, white people started going to backstreet cafes in primarily black neighborhoods. Chez Helene and Buster Holmes were the most prominent of these, but he wrote about many more.

Shortly after he published his book, Collin began a weekly column in the *States-Item,* the now-extinct afternoon paper of the *New Orleans Times-Picayune.* His column was so widely read that it singlehandedly saved the *States-Item*'s floundering Saturday edition.

Collin's books came out in 1970, 1972, and 1976. There were minor updates to the 1976 edition in 1979 and 1983. Then he quit reviewing restaurants and continued writing and teaching history at the University of New Orleans until he retired. He died in 2010.

Richard Collin's The New Orleans Underground Gourmet, *first published in 1970, covered more than 250 local restaurants. This was the first extensive appraisal of the local dining scene. (From the collection of Peggy Scott Laborde)*

During the 1970s, Richard Collin, the Underground Gourmet, made many locals aware of some of the lesser-known restaurants around town that served good food. He collaborated with his wife, Rima, on two cookbooks. (Courtesy of Phyllis Mayronne)

Third Annual New Orleans States-Item — Underground Gourmet Ten Best Restaurant Awards 1976-1977

10 Best Grand Restaurants

1. LE RUTH'S
French Creole
636 Franklin Ave., Gretna

2. MOSCA'S
Italian Creole
Hwy. 90, Waggaman, La.

3. BRENNAN'S
French Creole
417 Royal St.

4. DRAGON'S GARDEN
Chinese Mandarin & Szechuan
3100 17th St., Metairie (new address)

5. LA PROVENCE
French
Highway 190, Lacombe, La.

6. ELMWOOD PLANTATION
Creole-Italian
5400 River Road

7. PASCAL'S MANALE
Italian Creole
1838 Napoleon Ave.

8. BROUSSARD'S
French Creole
819 Conti St.

9. GALATOIRE'S
French Creole
209 Bourbon St.

10. ANTOINE'S
French Creole
713 St. Louis St.

Candidates for the List
(in alphabetical order)

QUARTERDECK
Continental
Aurora Village Shopping Center, Algiers

ROMANOFF'S
Continental
3322 Turnbull Drive, Metairie

VERSAILLES
Continental
2100 St. Charles Ave.

In addition to his States-Item *column, Collin published a dining newsletter. (From the collection of Peggy Scott Laborde)*

The last time I saw Richard Collin was about a year before he passed on. He was dining at Galatoire's with the mother of pianist Harry Mayronne, Jr., who had also lost her spouse. Harry tells me Collin and his mother were the perfect couple, and they certainly looked the part. I asked him what he was up to. "I continue the quest for hedonism!" he said. He meant that in all seriousness.

Even with thousands of my own reviews since 1972 at my fingertips, researching this book would have been much more difficult without Collin's three books on my shelf. He rarely left any stone unturned.

The authors would like to acknowledge the generous assistance of The Historic New Orleans Collection in providing many of the images contained in this book.

THE COLLECTION
THE HISTORIC NEW ORLEANS COLLECTION
533 Royal Street • 70130-2179 • www.hnoc.org • (504) 523-4662

The Historic New Orleans Collection is a museum, research center, and publisher located in the heart of the French Quarter. It was established in 1966 by Gen. and Mrs. L. Kemper Williams, avid collectors of materials related to Louisiana history and culture.

Located inside a complex of historic buildings at 533 Royal Street are the Williams Gallery, where changing exhibitions are available to the public at no charge; ten permanent exhibition galleries devoted to illustrating the history of the city, state, and Gulf South, where docent-guided tours are available at a modest fee; the historic residence of the institution's founders, where guided tours are also available; and a museum shop. One of the most significant groups of buildings in New Orleans, the Royal Street complex centers on the house built by Jean François Merieult in 1792. The Merieult House survived the great fire of 1794, making it one of the oldest structures in New Orleans. Other buildings on the property date from the nineteenth century, including the Williams residence, built in 1889.

The Williams Research Center, at 410 Chartres Street, is located in a former police station and jail built in 1915. Following an extensive renovation by The Collection, it was opened to the public in 1996. The Collection's research facilities originally were located in three separate reading rooms at the Royal Street complex, serving the library, manuscripts, and pictorial divisions. The Williams Research Center allowed the reading rooms to merge as one beautifully designed facility, thus providing greater availability of materials and convenience to both patrons and staff. The Williams Research Center is open free of charge to anyone interested in studying the region's history—and while shelves are closed to browsers, staff is able to assist with The Collection's extensive holdings of manuscripts, books, and images.

A more recent addition to The Historic New Orleans Collection is a new building adjoining the Williams Research Center. Opened in 2007, it is designed with a public meeting space on the ground floor and three floors of state-of-the-art vaults above. The façade of the new building, which fronts on Conti Street, replicates the appearance of a nineteenth-century hotel that once stood on the site. Additional office and gallery space opened in 2011 at the corner of Conti and Chartres streets. The Collection has also acquired several neighboring French Quarter buildings, including the famed Brulatour Courtyard across Royal Street from The Collection's original Royal Street complex.

Index

A & G Cafeterias, 19-21
A & G Restaurants, 19
Acy's Pool Hall, 19
Alciatore, Antoine, 132
Alonso, Al, 20-21
Alonso & Son, 20-21
Ambrosia, Sebastian, 248
Andrea's, 106, 110
Andrew Jackson Restaurant, The, 21-23
Angello, Tony, 128
Ansel, Christian, 69
Antoine's, 21, 55, 105, 127, 160, 212, 229
Anything Goes, 24-25, 119
Arnaud's, 42, 45, 86, 105-6, 132, 166, 182, 245
arroz con calamares, 103
arroz con pollo, 103
Artista Pizza, 243-44
Arts District, 115-16, 252
Aschaffenburg, Lyle, 59
Auberge de l'Ill, 255-57

bacalao, 104
Bailey, Frank, 246
Bali Ha'i at the Beach, 25
Baquet, Eddie, 94
barbecue shrimp, 97, 124, 203, 231
Barrow, Billy, 29-30
Barrow, William, 29
Barrow's Shady Inn, 29
Bart's Lighthouse Inn, 30
Batinich, Sam and Veronica, 188-89
Bean Pot, The, 31-33
Beard, James, 120
Bechac's, 34-35
Beef Baron Steak House, 35-36
beef brisket, 166-67
Begue's, 219
Belgian waffles, 253
Bella Luna, 169, 171
Berdou, George, 37-38
Berdou, Ida, 37
Berdou's, 37-38

Bergeron, Henry, 70, 72
Bergeron, Vic, 26
Bertucci's Restaurant, 39-40
Beverly Dinner Playhouse, 40
Beverly nightclub and casino, The, 29
Bistro bread, 41-42
Bistro's eggs Bitoun, 43
Bistro Steak Room, 41, 43
Bitoun, Andre, 42-43
Bitoun, Jacques, 42
Bitoun, Maurice, 42-43
Bitoun, Simon, 42
B. Montalbano Italian Delicatessen, 44
Bonnot, Daniel, 176, 178
Bonomolo, Anthony, 197
Bonomolo, Jay, 198
Bon Ton Café, 84
Boot Lounge, The, 57
bouillabaisse, 132
Bouligny, 110, 246, 248-49
Boulion, Lete, 126
Bounty, The, 231
Bourgeois, Alma, 73
Bozo's, 188
Bradley's Pharmacy, 241
bread pudding, 45, 94, 117, 121, 124, 146, 167, 184
Brennan, Dick, Sr., 126
Brennan family, 24, 167
Brigtsen, Frank, 53, 145
Brigtsen, Marna, 53
Broadmoor, 46, 188, 201
Brocato, Jimmy, 133
Brocato's, 253
Broussard's, 135, 174, 219, 259
Brown, Angie, 87-88
Bruce, Robert, 167
Bruning's, 228, 233-38
Buck Forty-Nine Pancake and Steak House, 44-46
Buck Forty-Nine Steak Houses, 182
Bucktown, 48, 234
Bud's Broiler, 47, 56

bulgogi, 112
Bull's Corner, The, 46-48
Burton, Nathaniel, 59
Buster Holmes, 48, 51-52, 66, 262
butterbeans, 51
Bywater, 179

cabrito (barbecued baby goat), 32
Café Anglais, 23
Café Atchafalaya, 52-54
Café Degas, 176
Café Hope, 102
Café Pontchartrain, 54-55
Café Reconcile, 102
Cafe Sbisa, 23, 55-58
Cajun, 35, 84, 105, 126, 145, 183-84, 216, 252
caldo xochil, 64
Canard Ferme Frères LeRuth, 145
Cannon's, 246
Cantonese, 27, 92, 113
cap bread, 45
Caribbean Room, 54-55, 58-61
Carrollton Avenue, 44-46, 53, 75, 79, 82, 93, 112, 114, 117, 181-82, 190, 239
Casbarian, Archie, 86
Castillo, Carlos, 64-65
Castillo's, 64-66
Catalanotto, Vincent, 76
Central Business District (CBD), 67, 122, 126, 163, 207, 255, 258-59
Chalmette, 31-32, 243
Charlie's Steak House, 32
Chavant, Jean-Pierre, 258
cheese, 22-23, 33, 36, 41, 65, 84-85, 101, 104, 108, 110, 129, 136, 151, 185, 191, 193-95, 197, 202, 220, 243, 253, 258
Chefs' Charity for Children, 137
Chehardy, Jim, 135
Chez Daniel, 178
Chez Helene, 66-68, 262
chicken, 27, 32-33, 51-52, 64-65, 68, 84, 87, 92, 98-101, 103, 105, 108, 113, 118, 124
Chicken Grandee, 99
chilmole de puerco, 65
Chinatown, 92
Chinese, 26-27, 92-93, 102, 111, 113, 153
chongol hot pot, 112
Chris Steak House, 36, 188
Christian's, 68-72, 162, 172, 245, 250
Clancy's, 231, 245
Clarence and Lefty's, 73-74
Clevenger, Jason, 56
Clevenger, JoAnn, 56, 121-22
codfish, 104

Coffee Pot, 120
Collin, Richard, 66-67, 78, 92, 94, 130, 143-44, 147, 193, 229, 244, 262, 264
Coln, Willy, 80, 219, 221-22
Commander, Anthony, 86
Commander's Palace, 73, 86, 212, 245, 248, 259
Compagno, Maria, 76
Compagno, Sal, 75
Compagno's, 75-76
Corinne Dunbar's, 76-78, 108
Cosmopolitan, The, 79
Cosner, Jack, 119
Court of Two Sisters, 142
Cowman, Tom, 120-22, 142
crab bisque, 206
crabmeat Berdou, 37-38
crabmeat ravioli, 136
crabmeat Remick, 59
crabmeat St. Francis, 143
crabmeat West Indies, 54
crawfish, 84-85, 105, 222
crawfish topas, 85
crawfish Willy Coln, 222
Creole, 21, 23, 34-35, 37, 45, 48, 50, 52-53, 56-57, 59, 64, 67, 77, 79, 81, 84-85, 87-88, 94-95, 97, 102, 104, 106, 110, 124, 127, 135, 158-59, 166-67, 171-72, 174, 182-84, 190, 198, 203, 206, 216, 219, 225, 236, 245-49, 252
Creole eggplant gratin Delmonico, 88
crepes suzette, 106
Crescent City Steak House, 36, 188
Crozier, Gerard, 79, 219
Crozier's, 79-82
Curran, Kevin, 250
Cvitanovich, Klara, 188

Dante by the River, 52-53
Darling, Gary, 102
De Angelis, Agnello, 106
Deanie's, 230
DeFelice, Etienne, 105
Delerno, J.B., 84
Delerno's, 84-85
Del Frisco's, 36
Delmonico, 86-88
D. H. Holmes department store, 67-68
Diamond Jim, 133
Dietrich, Rose, 87-88
DiPiazza's, 89-90
Doll, Paul, 107-8
Domino's Pizza, 243
Dooky Chase, 66, 69
Downtown, 66, 87, 100
Dragon's Garden, 92-93

Drago's, 188-89
Dr. Bananas, 252
duck pate, 81
Dunbar, Corinne, 77

Eddie's, 94
Eighth Ward, 73, 244
Eleven 79, 172
Eli's, 69
Elmwood Plantation, 34, 95, 97-99, 135, 142, 172
El Ranchito, 100-101
enchiladas de res, 65
enchiladas Texanas, 65
Enraged Chicken, The, 102
Escoffier style, 138
España, 103-4
Etienne's Cuisine Francais, 104
Evans, Louis, 59-60
Eva's Spot, 89-90

Fein, Joe, Sr., 142
fettuccine, 133, 169, 171
filet mignon, 27, 37, 81, 98, 177, 182, 256
Finley, Robert, 158
Fitzgerald's, 229-30, 233, 237-38
Flagons, 249-50
Flagons' oysters Sazerac, 250
Flamingos, 107-8
Fontana's, 237-38
Fontenot, Homer, 146
Forty-One Forty-One, 245
Fouqueteau, Michel, 250
Fraccaro, Goffredo, 136
French cooking, 21, 41, 50, 56, 58-59, 67-68, 72, 75, 79, 81, 95, 105, 126-28, 132-33, 136-38, 142, 145-46, 150-51, 158, 167, 169, 172, 176-77, 191, 220, 222, 243-44, 247-48, 250, 255-56, 258-60
French Market, 55
French Provincial style, 105
French Quarter, 21, 24, 44, 48, 50, 53, 55, 57, 64, 66-67, 89, 109, 113, 119, 121, 124, 132, 136, 150, 152-53, 155, 169, 186, 191, 194, 197, 201, 206-7, 214-15, 227, 252
fried catfish, 29
fried chicken, 41, 67-69, 94, 117-18, 231-33
fried parsley, 41
fritto misto, 247
Fury, John, 231

galaktoboureko, 186
Galatoire's, 21, 37, 55, 68, 70-72, 86, 93, 105, 127, 143, 146, 184, 197, 264
Galvez, 171

G&E Courtyard Grill, 109-10
Gannon, Tim, 246, 248
Garden District, 19, 54, 59, 102, 176, 216, 246
Garrard, Tim, 249
Gatipon family, 114
Gautreau's, 245
Genghis Khan, 111-12
Gentilich's, 188
Gentilly, 68, 94, 243
German, 122, 124, 219-22, 255
Gin's Mee Hong, 113
Gluck's Restaurant, 113-14
gratin of red fruits, 256
Greek, 79, 108, 185-86
green enchiladas with crabmeat, 33
Green Goddess dressing, 144
Gresham, Charles, 245
Gretna, 37, 44, 46, 137, 142-43, 148, 153, 185, 219-20, 244
Gumbo Shop, 252

Haeberlin, Marc, 255-56
Harvey, 39
Hayes Chicken Shack, 69
Henri, 255-59
Henri's salmon soufflé "Auberge de l'Ill," 257
Herbsaint, 243
Hernandez, Rosa "Mamita," 101
Hightower, Mark, 249
Hill, Larry, 23, 55
Hollygrove, 29-30
Home Plate Inn, 114
Hotel Inter-Continental, 258
Houlihan's Old Place, 115
House of Lee, 116, 172
Howard's Eatery, 67
Huet, Roland, 70
huevos rancheros, 65
Hughes, Richard, 53
Hummingbird Grill, 115-17
Hurricane Georges, 228, 230, 234
Hurricane Katrina, 20, 30-32, 55, 57, 67-68, 72, 82, 93, 100, 112, 114, 137, 139, 167, 171, 205, 214, 228, 236, 238

Il Ristorante Tre Fontane, 136
Indulgence, 246-48
Italian, 39, 55, 58, 75, 97, 99, 102, 104, 106, 109-10, 121, 127, 129, 133, 136-37, 147, 153, 169, 173-74, 186, 190, 197-98, 203, 206-7, 231, 237-39, 244, 252

Jaeger, Andrew, 230
Jim's Fried Chicken, 117
Joe's Crab Shack, 31
Johnson, Phil, 114, 136

Jonathan, 119-22, 142, 245
Jonathan's red pepper vichyssoise, 122

Katz & Besthoff, 241
Kerageorgiou, Chris, 137
kimchee, 111
Kolb, Conrad, 122
Kolb's, 122, 124, 126, 219
Korean, 111-12
kosher eggs Benedict, 42
Kovacs, Tom, 259
Krauss Department Store, 95

La Charcuterie, 172
La Crepe Nanou, 176
La Cuisine Restaurant, 126-27, 129
La Cuisine's Joe's hot shrimp, 128
La Cuisine's oysters Deanna, 129
LaFleur, Gilbert, 146
LaFranca, Anthony, 87
Lagasse, Emeril, 86
Lakefront, 30
Lake Pontchartrain, 20, 30-31, 97, 130, 227, 229, 234
Lakeview, 126, 138
Lakeview Seafood, 130
Lakeview Seafood's oyster boat, 131
La Louisiane, 132-33, 135, 169
La Louisiane's trout LaFreniere, 135
Landry's, 31
Laplace, 46-48, 183-84
La Provence, 137, 250
La Riviera, 136-37, 172
Le Chateau, 137-38
Lee, Henry, 111-12
Lee Circle area, 76, 86, 107, 212
Lehrmann family, 114
Le Jardin, 259-60
Le Jardin's all-white scallops and grouper with Champagne sauce, 260
Leman, Douglas, 60
Le Meridien, 255-56
Lenfant, Louis, 138, 142
Lenfant's, 121, 138-40, 142
Leruth, Warren, 126, 137, 148, 220
LeRuth's, 21, 137, 142-49, 246
LeRuth's crabmeat St. Francis, 149
L'Escale, 150-51
Les Continents, 258-59
Leslie, Austin, 66-68
Les Symphonies Brettone, 151
Les Voyages Nordiques, 151
Levata's, 69
Li'l Dizzy's, 95
Little Jane, 69
Liver à l'Orange, 122
lobster Kadobster, 202, 204

Lopez, Antonio, 103
Louis XVI Restaurant, 135, 150-51, 176-77

Maggie & Smitty's Crabnett, 232
Magic Time Machine, 24
Maison Pierre, 152
Mandarin, 92-93
Mandeville, 34, 205
Mandina's, 84, 182, 239
Marcello, Carlos, 135
Marcello, Joe, 135, 142
Marco Polo, 153
Marigny, 153
Martin, Joe, 127
Martin Brothers Restaurant, 153
Martin's Poor Boy Restaurant, 153
Marti's, 55, 155
Masson's almond torte, 162
Masson's Beach House, 158
Masson's Restaurant Français, 158
Masson's shrimp Robert, 161
Maxcy, Jim, 119
Maylie, Willie, 167
Maylie's, 34, 163, 165-67
Maylie's turtle soup, 168
Meal-A-Minit, 168
meatballs, 39, 133, 136, 237
Metairie, 44, 79, 82, 84-85, 92, 104-6, 127, 135-36, 172, 174, 178, 189-91, 193-94, 198, 231, 244
Mexican food, 31-33, 64-66, 79, 100-102
Meyer, Danny, 238
Michael's Mid-City Grill, 169-71
Mid-City, 35, 79, 111, 114, 169, 172, 190, 223, 225
Middendorf's, 171
mile-high ice cream pie, 60, 62
Miller Beer Garden, 252, 254
mole poblano, 65
Montestrucq, Jean Louis, 150
Moore, "Deacon John," 254
Moran, Jim, 133
Moran, Jimmy, 133, 169
Moran's Riverside, 133, 169
Morrison's Cafeterias, 172
Mosca, Nick, 97, 99, 135
Mosca's, 97
Mr. B's, 42, 132, 231, 248
Mr. Pizza, 243-44
Mrs. Wheat's, 252
Murphy, Parker, 249
Muse's eggplant with seafood (eggplant Vatican), 175

Napoli, Charles, 57
Napoli, Craig, 57
nectar soda, 241-42

New Orleans East, 79-81, 93, 130, 153, 191, 243
New Orleans Hamburger and Seafood Company, 246
Newsham, John, 185
Norton, Mike, 47-48

Occhipinti, Frank, 172, 193
Old Absinthe House, 113
Old Jefferson, 20, 29, 31, 40, 95, 103
omelettes, 81, 108, 216, 247
Onorio, John, 176
Orleans Grapevine Wine Bar & Bistro, 252
Outback Steakhouse, 246
oyster-artichoke soup, 143
oysters Dunbar, 78
oysters Roland, 72

Palace Cafe, 167
Papa Rosselli's, 237
Pascal's Manale, 185, 203
Pasta di Vincenzo, 252
Pasta puttanesca, 110
Pat O'Brien's, 66, 216
Patout's, 252
Paul Gross' Chicken Coop, 69
Peck's, 69
Pelican Club, 53, 136
Peppermill, 44-46
Pete Fountain's Reunion Hall, 252
Petro's Chili & Chips, 253
Petrossi's Seafood Restaurant, 53
Pfeifer, Horst, 169
Pier Orleans, 231
Pique's Wharf, 232
Pittari, Anthony, 202
Pittari, Tom, 201, 203
Pittari, Tom, Jr., 202, 205
pizza, 41, 197, 243-44
Pizza del Paese, 253
Plauche, Jimmy, 77
Pollock, Helen, 66-67
pollo pibil, 65
Pontchartrain Beach, 25-26, 28, 138
Pontchartrain Hotel, 54, 58-59, 61, 176
poor-boy sandwiches, 19, 45, 244
Pope, Iler, 52
Portia's, 68-69
potage LeRuth, 143
Preuss, Gunter, 216
Progresso Foods, 110, 182

quiches, 108

red beans and rice, 20, 39, 52, 69, 94, 116, 252

Red Onion, The, 172-74
Restaurant de la Tour Eiffel, 176
Restaurant Mandich, 179
Rety, Annick, 137-38
Rety, Denis, 137
Riccobono, Joe, 44-46, 182
Riccobono, Josie, 44
rice, 27, 51, 65, 81, 84, 87, 92, 98, 103, 111
Riverbend, 31, 45, 53, 75, 183
Riverbend, The, 46, 181-82
Riverside, 169
roast-beef poor boy, 19, 73-74, 114
roast-beef sandwich, 70
Rockery Inn, 183-84
Roosevelt Hotel, 22, 216
Roussel's, 183-84
Rovere, Valentino, 137
Royal Oak Restaurant and Pub, The, 185
Royal Oak's skordalia (Greek garlic sauce), 186
Royal Sonesta Hotel, 80, 219, 222
Ruggiero's, 186
Ruth's Chris, 203

Saffron, 259
saganaki, 185
salads, 108, 151
salad with avocado dressing, 144
salmon soufflé, 256
Sal & Sam's, 172
Sam's, 69
Sam's Place, 188-89
Sandy's Pizza Place, 243
Sazerac restaurant, 216
Schaeffer brothers, 102
Schweickhardt's, 242
Sciortino, Ron, 146, 246
Sclafani, Peter, 190
Sclafani's, 172, 190-91
seafood, 20, 30-31, 34, 42, 45, 64, 75, 84, 87, 94, 104-5, 112, 127, 130, 159, 166-67, 171, 174, 182-83, 185, 188-90, 198, 202-3, 207, 213-14, 216, 220, 225, 227-33, 237-38
Segreto, Joe, 172
Seymour's, 239
Sheraton Hotel, 259
shrimp remoulade, 37, 45, 97, 105-6
shrimp Saki, 61
shrimp toast, 93
Sicilian, 39, 169
Silver Whistle, The, 54-55
Simon, Neil, 40
Smith and Wollensky, 167
Smith, Charlie, 130
Smith, Mark, 135, 150-51
Solari's, 191-92

soufflés, 177-79
soup and salad bars, 24
soups, 108, 121, 249
spaghetti alla Turci, 210
Spanish, 50, 102-4, 171
squid, 103
steak, 35-36, 42, 44-48, 81, 98, 105, 127, 145, 151, 167, 174, 177, 182, 184, 191-92, 203, 220, 231, 239
Steak Pit, The, 191-92
Stephen & Martin, 245-46, 248
Stonebreaker, Steve, 193-94
Stonebreaker's, 193
strawberry soufflé, 178
Struve, Tom, 107-8
stuffed crab, 45
stuffed shrimp hollandaise, 190
Sunset Grill, 69
Swanson's, 237-38

Tally-Ho, 194-95
Tardo, David, 23
Tchoupitoulas Plantation, 195
Tchoupitoulas Plantation's oysters Tchoupitoulas, 196
Tea 'n' Tiques, 52-53
Toney's oysters and spaghetti bordelaise, 200
Toney's Pizza and Spaghetti House, 197, 244
Toney's Pizza and Spaghetti House stuffed macaroni, 199
Torkanowsky, Teresa, 103
Tortorici's Restaurant, 200-201
Tower of Pizza, 243-44
T. Pittari's, 201-3, 205-6
Trattoria Pastore, 253
Tropical Isle bar, 252
Tropical Paradise, 252
trout Eugene, 58
trout Veronique, 59
Trust House Forte, Iberville, 259
Tsai, Andy, 92-93
Tujague's, 45, 163, 167
Turci's, 207
turkey poulette, 23
Tuscan, 110

Uddo, Elaynora, 110
Uddo, Giuseppe, 110
Uddo, Michael, 110
Uddo, Peter, 182-83
Uddo & Taormina, 182
Uglesich's, 32, 73, 130, 188, 212-14
Underground Gourmet, The, 48, 262-63
Upperline, 57, 121, 245
Uptown, 42, 52-53, 57, 75-76, 81, 87, 104-5, 148, 174, 182, 188, 217, 219, 221, 225, 243, 245-49
Urrate, Sam, 234-36

Vasser, Eugenie, 249
Vaucresson Café Creole, 214-16
Vazquez, Ignacio, 31
veal Oscar, 159
Venezia, 244
Veranda, 222, 258
Versailles, 216-19, 259
Vincent's, 75
Virginia Kitchen, 70

Waggaman, 195
Wamstad, Dale, 36
Warehouse District, 246
West End, 34, 42, 158-59, 162, 227-34, 236-39
West End oyster stew, 239
West End Park, 30-31
Westin, 259
Westwego, 41
whole flounder stuffed with crabmeat, 236
wild game, 201, 203, 205-6
Willie G's, 232-33
Willy Coln's Chalet, 219-21
wine, 43, 52, 58, 81, 85, 93, 106, 110, 138, 146-48, 151, 171, 185, 231, 249-50, 253, 257-58
wine bar, 249
Wise Cafeteria, 223-25
World's Fair, 252
Wyndham, 259

Zachary's, 94-95
Zea, 102

Buck's

PANCAKE AND

From Our Lounge

Cocktails
Highballs
Beer
Wines
Mixed Drinks

Air Line Highway

Deliciously exciting Pancakes from around the World — Seven varieties of Pure Fruit Syrups

In Downt

JIM'S PLACE
3100 S. CARROLLTON • PHONE AU 0226 • NEW ORLEANS, LA

CASTILLO'S MEXICAN RESTAURANT

When it's Mexican food...
Castillo's has the real thing.

Popular dishes are offered—
but the unusual is there also
and at reasonable prices.

Open every day from 11:30 A.M. til
midnight and on Fridays
and Saturdays til 1:00 A.M.

620 Conti St. • 581-9602